Once There Was a City Named Dilli

Once There Was a City Named Dilli

INTIZAR HUSAIN

Translated by

GHAZALA JAMIL AND FAIZ ULLAH

SIMON & SCHUSTER

London · New York · Sydney · Toronto · New Delhi

First published in India by Yoda Press 2016

[English Translation by Ghazala Jamil and Faiz Ullah 2024, published by Simon and Schuster India and Yoda Press]

1 3 5 7 9 10 8 6 4 2

Simon & Schuster India
818, Indraprakash Building,
21, Barakhamba Road,
New Delhi 110001.

www.simonandschuster.co.in

Yoda Press LLP
C-28 Basement
Mayfair Gardens
New Delhi - 110016

www.yodapress.co.in

Simon & Schuster: Celebrating 100 Years of Publishing in 2024

Paperback ISBN: 9788198128546
eBook: 9788198128539

Printed and bound in India by Replika Press Pvt. Ltd.

Intizar Husain was born in the United Provinces, India, in 1922 or, as he is known to have remarked in a newspaper interview, '1923 or perhaps 1925'. A prominent name in South Asian Literature, Husain wrote several novels and collections of short stories in Urdu, including the widely acclaimed *Naya Ghar, Aagey Samundar Hai, Basti, Aakhri Aadmi* and *Kachhwe.* As a storyteller he actively engaged with contemporary concerns while drawing eclectically from the subcontinent's syncretic cultural heritage. He carved out a unique place for himself among his progressive, religious nationalist, and traditionalist peers by refusing to put his work in the service of narrow ideological projects. His nonfiction writings constitute a veritable archive of critical reflections on the history, contemporary culture and politics of the region. Intizar Husain died in 2016 in Lahore, Pakistan.

Brimming with sights, sounds, fragrances and flavours, *Once There Was a City Named Dilli* is a portrait of Intizar Husain's beloved Delhi. Presented as a series of richly textured tableaus, the book reflects the pasts and presents of the city which has been built and destroyed several times.

Ghazala Jamil teaches at the Centre for the Study of Law and Governance, Jawaharlal Nehru University, New Delhi.

Faiz Ullah teaches at the School of Media and Cultural Studies, Tata Institute of Social Sciences, Mumbai.

Siblings, Faiz and Ghazala share a common love for social theory and popular culture.

For dearest Paromita...

...another bit of Delhi

—Ghazala and Faiz

Contents

Translators' Note

Location is crucial to creating a world of imagination in fiction. Not only fiction but memories of pasts too are 'imaginations' contingent upon location. Once they came into being, post-colonial South Asian States found that their projects in 'imagination' were far from over. Nation-building essentially required them to get their histories wrong. As the French political thinker Ernest Renan had pointed out, 'Forgetfulness, and I would even say historical error, are essential in creation of a nation.' The nationalist imagination is a creation of interplay of remembrance and forgetfulness in just the right amounts. Languages are needed to mobilise these imaginations but any language will not do. Languages too, like memory, carry nationalistic burdens. Many South Asian languages have been at the heart of nationalistic constructions, and yet, paradoxically, they also transcend national territories. Intizar Husain's *Dilli Tha Jiska Naam* is of immense value because it does not suffer from the nationalist burden. Often accused of nostalgia, Intizar Husain's narrative of Delhi's past is an articulation of a memory that has lingered on, despite its uselessness in the nationalist discourses of both Pakistan and India because of the vagaries of location and national identity of the author. Perhaps, the Partition of India lends a certain quality to Urdu that makes it an apt language for expressing loss and nostalgia. It may even be argued that a peculiar expression of the North Indian syncretic Ganga-Jamuni culture can only be made through Urdu. It is this peculiarity of Urdu that we have tried hard to retain in this translation.

Dilli Tha Jiska Naam shines forth as a counterdiscourse in precisely these terms and therein lies our motivation to read this text and make it accessible to a wider readership. Strangely enough, English—despite its colonial legacy and hegemonic present or perhaps because of it—comes to the rescue.

Neither Urdu-daan nor English-wallas, and as learners of both the languages, we feel that translation of such texts should not wait for specialists or cultural elites but should be undertaken by everyone as a means of participation in the realm of culture and politics. It remains, however, that both English and Urdu have been languages of the elite classes or, like us, the members of the aspirational classes.

It is remarkable how many Urdu-daan can understand the language well due to the shared vocabulary and grammatical structure of Hindi and Urdu, but remain strangers to the Persian script in which Urdu is written because it is notorious for being difficult.

Urdu is strikingly different from English for ascribing less importance to vowels. In fact, vowels are indicated more often by signs (rather than letters of alphabet)—zabar, zer, pesh, madd, ulta pesh. Elementary learners of the script are the only ones expected to use these signs. Advanced users usually drop these while writing and proficient readers know by experience which signs have to be read where. Some consonant letters (alif, badi yay, chhoti yay and vao) can produce different vowel sounds but need to be supplemented by the vowel signs. This can be understood as Urdu having 'invisible' signs that are not written but have to be read, just as English has 'silent' letters that are written but not read. While silent letters are present only in a few English words, the invisible vowel signage in Urdu can make reading the script a daunting task for novice readers. As non-expert translators this proved challenging for us when confronted with Persian words that are not prevalent in spoken Hindustani. We found translation not only an interesting way of deepening and diversifying one's interest, but also a great way of gaining proficiency in reading the script.

Reading Urdu is challenging also because it is a highly stylised language with little punctuation in writing. Other than an occasional comma and a full stop marked by a baseline dash, very few punctuation marks are used. In addition, several words are meant to be read as connected words but the connectives are not always marked in the script. Also, an extremely formal register is often used to produce a satirical or jocular effect. Since we decided to stick close to our reading of Intizar Sahab's intent in the text in our translation, the stylistic issues posed an additional challenge. We have also tried earnestly to present to the reader an opportunity to savour the charm of Urdu—preserving the Urdu idiom so that the reader not only gets the meaning but also the flavour. As far as possible, we have tried to do this by translating literally, abandoning this effort only in places where the literal translation sounded too strange in English.

Towards this aim we have also retained many Urdu words which were either not translatable due to cultural specificities of the subject or because the context behind the use of the original word was so interesting that translating it to a fairly adequate English equivalent would rob the reader of an interesting vignette of history. In both cases, we have added a footnote. Yet other footnotes are very brief introductions to the authors and chroniclers referred to in the text by Intizar Sahab. All the research that this required has left us richer for our acquaintance with Urdu literary culture.

We would like to thank Qamar Fuzail Sahab whose love for Shahjanabad and rich knowledge of its literary culture helped us immensely by cracking open mysteries of many quaint words and making them translatable. We also thank Prof. Sayeda Bilqis

Fatema Husaini, retired professor of Persian from University of Delhi for her invaluable help with perfecting the translation of the Persian text in the book. We thank our family for all their support, especially our niece Sidra Fariah who is a student of both History and Urdu. Ghazala would also like to thank the Council for Social Development, New Delhi, where, working as Associate Fellow, she undertook a part of this translation.

Many thanks are due to our editor, Arpita Das. Her edits have elevated the translation by several degrees. We thank Shubham Mishra who met Intizar Sahab and got his permission for us to do this translation. Most of all we thank Intizar Sahab for granting us this permission. It is our deepest regret that we could not show it to him and will never know what he would have thought of it.

I

Apologia

Publishers generally request their novelists to write commercial novels for them; both parties benefit from this practice. When Niaz Sahab made a demand on me, and I am not exactly a top-seller, he had something else in mind. Actually, he had read 'Ajmal Aazam' while publishing it. He probably read it in such a moment that he was fated to be smitten by the description of Dilli in the book. So he said, 'Let's have a full account of Dilli. We'll publish a book.' I considered the request only fleetingly and did not think it was necessary to reply in the affirmative or negative. But he was serious about his request. So serious that he immediately announced the forthcoming book. He even suggested a name.

So I got caught like this. While the spell of this lost city has its own place, and so does the wish to understand and describe the magic, a person should be mindful of their own place too. Among the loose cobblestones[1] of Dilli born in the last century there have

[1] The author here uses the word 'roda' which means a loose piece of rock bigger than a pebble which gets rounded by kicks of the pedestrians when it gets in their way. '*Rah me rodey atkana*' is an idiom that means 'to obstruct'. We have translated 'roda' as 'loose cobblestone' because in the present usage the author means a city dweller who moves about aimlessly but *belongs*, unlike a rolling stone who may move anywhere. One can understand this person to be a little similar to the European flaneur.

been luminaries who have left incredible narratives of the city. For one, I am not a Dilli cobblestone. I am only a *qasbah*[2] pebble. They lived and consumed this city that is Jahanabad. Those who came later used it by the grace of these ancestors and imbibed the city in their person. I, a qasbah pebble, stand a considerable distance apart—both in the temporal and the spatial perspectives. Moreover, where shall I get a pen like theirs? Nasir Nazir Firaaq, Munshi Faizuddin, Mirza Farhat Ullah Beig, Ashraf Subuhi, Shahid Ahmed Dehlavi—have all left enchanted descriptions and visual marvels in the name of this city. I feel silly for insisting that I too will describe Dilli. But what could I do? On the one hand, there was the magic of this vanished city, and on the other were the images drawn by the elders. Topping it all was a very persuasive request. I got greedy. The pen was in the hand, it wrote.

So this urban lore was written like this. I am deeply indebted to all those Dilliwallahs and the loose cobblestones of the city from whose writing I benefited and which adorned my own writing.

14 January 2003 — Intizar Husain
Lahore

[2] *Qasbah* is a small market town.

2

Indraprasth to Dilli

No settlement shows its 'self' easily; and Dilli is the one about which Mir warned us. It is not just any settlement, it is Dilli! How much of its real face has Dilli shown even to those loose cobblestones who ambled about in its dusty streets? It hid more than it revealed. So, feel free to consider this attempt of mine a futile, leisurely pursuit. If you ask me for the truth, I have been obsessing about just one evening of Dilli. That sad evening in *Bhadon*[1] appeared for just a few moments and then vanished. To try to describe it again is not my intention. I was unable to describe it in an earlier attempt too. I am merely making a gesture at it.

It was one evening two and a half or three years after the Partition. I had arrived in Dilli after much planning and devising. When we set foot in the blessed neighbourhood called Dargah Hazrat Nizamuddin, it was dusk. But the usual hustle-bustle and throng of people rubbing shoulders[2] with each other were missing.

---

[1] *Bhadon* or *Bhadra* is the sixth month in various Indian solar and lunar calendars. It is the last month of the rainy season consisting of Ashadh, Saawan and Bhadon. It falls in August-September.

[2] In the original the author uses the idiom '*Khawe se khawa chhilta*'. *Khawa* means 'shoulders'. *Chhilna* implies peeling or being grazed. The author uses the idiom to describe a thick but fast-moving crowd such that shoulders rub against each other and are grazed.

The many shoppers at the shops selling roses, incense sticks and candle-sticks were also nowhere in sight. Silence had made a camp inside the *dargah*[3] too.

Suddenly, as if from nowhere, three *qawwals*[4] with harmoniums hanging from their necks appeared. They sat down, arranged the harmoniums before them, and immediately began,

Ghar-ghar mein udaasi chhai hai Shabbir Madina chhor chaley

(Sadness has filled all homes as Shabbir prepares to leave Madina[5])

We listened to them for a while and then walked out. 'We' means I and my old friends Revti and Singh, who were my hosts. Revti said, 'You know, Ghalib's *mazar*[6] is also here. Let's visit it too.' So we left the path and began walking in the tall grass. *Janamashtmi*[7] had just passed. The grass had grown really tall and green after the showers of *Saawan-Bhadon*.[8] Amidst the grass was a derelict plinth surrounded by a boundary wall in ruins. Inside the compound were three graves in a bad shape. One of these was Ghalib's. I recited the *fatiha*.[9] We came out and started walking in

---

[3] *Dargah* is a tomb of a saint. The word connotes an element of veneration and worship.

[4] *Qawwals* are singers who perform *Qawwali*—a form of devotional, meditative music performed often at the *dargah* of sufi saints. *Qawwali* is typically performed with a chorus of singers repeating verses and clapping rhythmically.

[5] A reference to Prophet Muhammad's grandson Hussain (also called Shabbir) leaving the city of Medina. This was the beginning of a series of tragic events culminating in the massacre of Hussain and his family in Karbala by the forces of the oppressive caliph Yazid.

[6] *Mazar* literally means a grave but is used to attribute more respect to the buried person. The word for a grave of a common person is *Qabr*.

[7] *Janamashtmi* is a festival marking the birth of Lord Krishna. Literally *Janm* meaning birth and *Ashtmi* means the eighth day. *Janamashtmi* falls on the eighth day of the month Bhadon.

[8] *Saawan-Bhadon* is the rainy season.

[9] *Fatiha* is a prayer for the dead which involves reciting several verses of the holy Quran.

the tall grass again. The surroundings were filled with silence. Only the scream of a peacock came from afar. After that, the silence became deeper. The *doha*[10] of Amir Khusro that I had just recited at his grave lingered in my mind.

Gori soe sej pe aur mukh pe daaro kes
Chal khusro ghar aapne, sanjh bahi chaundes

(The maiden sleeps on her bed and her tresses cover her face,
Go back to your home, Khusro, it's evening everywhere.)

After this I had to wait for 30 years before I could go to Dilli again. It was only then that a way to visit this settlement could be found. One visit, second visit, third visit—each one included a mandatory visit to Hazrat Nizamuddin Aulia's neighbourhood. However, now the entire landscape had changed. The same hustle-bustle and crowds rubbing shoulders. Each shop had heaps and heaps of roses. There was some jostling to cross the threshold and enter the mausoleum. And yes, the plinth on which Ghalib's grave rested was gone. The grass had vanished. In its place was a massive marble platform enclosed by beautiful mesh walls. Inside, the grave was also made of marble. Adjacent to the grave had risen a huge Ghalib Hall. During each visit the commotion seemed only to increase. And each time, I immensely missed that sad Bhadon evening and the derelict grave amidst the wild grass. O Allah! Where is that evening hidden and where is that grave lost? Where shall I look for it?

And now when I remember the silent and sad evening which has become for me the very metaphor for the lost Dilli, the scream of the peacock from that evening reverberates in my mind. This reminds me of something D.H. Lawrence once said. He said that the chirping of a few birds contains within its sound the signs of good things to come. And the sad sounds made by some other

[10] A *Doha* is a couplet that exists independently in its form and meaning. Each line has a measured metre of 24 *matras* (moraes).

birds transport us to the past. He named birds from his country and listed which bird calls are the bearers of good news from the future and which carry the listener to the past. I think our peacock is a strange bird. Its scream contains glimpses of past and future like the play of shade and sun. When the month of Saawan would pass without rain and one day suddenly the clouds start looming and the screams of peacocks may be heard from afar, my *nani amma*[11] would say, 'The peacocks are screaming. It'll rain.' Later, when *Saawan-jhari*[12] would start, and on some evenings after raining the entire day there would be a pause and from afar a lost peacock's scream could be heard, it would be laden with such sadness. It seemed to come from some threshold of the past and pull us towards ancient times.

And at this moment when this lonely lost peacock's sad scream tearing through the dusk of that sad evening is resonating in my ears, it seems to be dragging me to many, many parts of the past. And I am amazed at how many times in its centuries-long journey Dilli has been plundered and resettled. But I am trying to find out when it was settled for the first time. Who were the settlers, who were settled? This search has taken many researchers to Indraprasth. But was that settlement really Dilli? It was Inderprasth or Inderpuri or Inderpat. Read the Mahabharat and you will know how it got settled. Like the bickering and rioting and Partition that led to the creation of the two countries; the same had happened then. Dhritrashtra had told his nephews that better than this daily bickering they could take away their share and settle their own country. For this purpose I give you Khandoban.

It was then that the Pandavs said their final goodbyes to Hastinapur and arrived in Khandoban. But Khandoban was just a

---

[11] *Nani* means maternal grandmother. *Amma* (mother) is added as an honorofic.

[12] *Saawan-jhari* refers to unremitting, incessant rain that occurs during *Saawan*. *Jhari* literally means a volley.

wilderness—thick forests, no sign of humans, and lots of snakes. It is fantastic that the Mahabharat records the name of every type of snake, how poisonous each one was, and how it came to be found there. Arjun stood with his bow and arrows. Krishna ji was his reinforcement. But all those snakes could not have been tidied up by Arjun's bow and arrows. The Pandavs had some good fortune and received additional reinforcement from *Agni Dev.*[13] This burnt all the snakes to ashes. Only one snake was spared because that day it was not in Khandoban, and was visiting another forest. On being spared a terrible end what stratagems it employed and how it took revenge—that is a different story. The fact is that the forest was cleared and a new town was founded. What a town it was! When seen from afar the parapets of its ramparts seemed to look like a cluster of white clouds. On the ramparts were stationed, row upon row of soldiers armed with arrows and swords. The ramparts also had gates that seemed like mountains. They were surrounded by trenches as wide as the sea. Adjacent to these were lush orchards which echoed with the cooing of cuckoos and peacock screams.

News of this new city reached far and wide. Scholars, artists, pundits, astrologers, merchants and artisans were attracted to it, and Indraprasth became a lively city. But how could such a lively city have been destroyed? It was not even invaded. And how could it be invaded, when all their enemies had already been trounced in Kurukshetra? Well, there is no historical account of that era. But there are many legends, as many stories and legends as there are mouths telling them. Bashiruddin Ahmed retrieved one such legend and recorded it in his volume *Dehli: the Abode of Governance*. I will leave those who investigate to their devices and will just reproduce what has been said. The nuisance of the Kauravs had ended. And now the Narrator[14] wrote peace for the Pandavs. King Yudhishthir sat on the royal throne and ruled. The Pandav brothers

---

[13] *Agni Dev* is the Vedic god of fire.

[14] A reference to God as the author of the story of life.

were living a tranquil life. All seven blessings were within their reach. And do not even ask about the spread at their banquets. All kinds of cuisines and all possible tastes! But it so happened that one day when food was being served, an ominous fly came from somewhere and sat on the food. In the sacred ambience of Inderpuri! That too in the royal palace, whose cleanliness the gods used to swear by! King Yudhishthir was stunned. He was so revolted that he stood up without eating. He felt disgusted with Inderpuri. Nay, his heart was repulsed by the world itself! He left the royal palace, said his final goodbye to the city and began his last journey. With him the other Pandav brothers and Draupadi also said goodbye to their city. All the verve, all the glory of Indraprasth went away with its precious darlings. The happy bustling city was deserted within a few moments. O cursed fly! Woe to you! What a bustling city it was that your greed destroyed!

Then the world forgot all about the city, so much so that it does not ever again find mention in any chronicle. What befell the city after the Pandavs? It was as if it was erased from the very pages that record existence, like a wrong letter. The only reference that comes up is that ages later it was somewhere here that a small king named Dehlu settled another town. It was called Dehli after his name. It was Dehlu's name that gradually got distorted to Dehli and then became Dilli. So this is the actual beginning and preamble of Dilli. Dilli was inhabited when Indraprasth was abandoned. It is said that the site of the old fort in Dilli is the actual site where the city state of Indraprasth used to be located.

King Dehlu settled a town whose name came to be Dehlu and then people started calling it Dehli. What happened after that? Nothing is known. Yes, in one of the *kabitt*[15] songs sung by the

[15] A *Kabitt* is a quatrain in which moraes or syllables are not counted. In the present context, it also refers to a series of kabitts that were sung as adulatory songs about heroes and kings by the Bhatts.

Bhatts[16] there is a reference to the city remaining desolate for 792 years. Only after this period was it inhabited again. When exactly was that? About this, history speaks, and this town once again emerges from behind the curtains of oblivion. In the year AD 1052, King Anangpal made it his capital city and rehabilitated it with much fanfare. This is the period when Mahmud Ghaznavi returned from India after carnage and plunder. And now the King Anangpal of the Tanwar Dynasty can breathe easy. He makes Dehli his capital and builds a wall around the city. Temples are built. Bunding is undertaken. Reservoirs are built. Above all, a fort named Lalkot is constructed. What an imposing structure Lalkot is! Standing on the left and right sides of the gates are two lions with chains hanging from them. Plaintiffs have total freedom to pull the chains. Their complaints would be heard and justice would be delivered. This was how the 'chain of justice' tradition commenced in India.

There is no idea as to how long Anangpal ruled. However, his progeny flourished and the Tanwar Dynasty ruled for more or less a century. After almost 100 years, let us say, in AD 1151, the Chauhan Dynasty gained strength and one of its kings, King Bisal Deo, attacked Dilli and conquered it. But soon the conquered and the conquerors reconciled. Reconciliation was brought about on the condition that the Tanwar ruler would marry the princess of the Chauhan dynasty. The son born of this wedlock would then sit on the throne of Dilli. So the marriage was solemnised. The son who was born was called Prithviraj. He was the son of the daughter of Bisal Deo, the apple of the eye of both dynasties.

Bisal Deo did not have a son. He adopted his grandson. When his eyes began to close[17] he made him his heir. Thus, the thrones of both Dilli and Ajmer were bequeathed to Prithviraj alias Rai Pithora.

---

[16] Bhatt is a Brahmin surname. It was often also used to denote learned scholars and poets of the courts.

[17] When he was about to die.

So, gentlemen! Drum beats for Rai Pithora—two capitals, one king! He has one foot in Ajmer and the other in Dilli. And his reign begins from the Himalayan Mountains and extends to the Bindhyachal Mountains and the Narbada River in the south. People forgot all about Anangpal's Lalkot. Now the Pithora rule built its own Lalkot with such grandeur that its clamour spread in all four directions. Shahabuddin Ghauri attacked with ferocity but had to taste defeat at the hands of Rai Pithora. Rai Pithora's dominance was established far and near.

But woe be to love! The passion of Rai Pithora led to his collapse. Now listen attentively,[18] how his ill-fated love blighted Rai Pithora's life and what fruits it bore. Raja Jai Chand had a daughter named Sanjogta, with the countenance of both the sun and the moon. Bhatts would go around singing paeans to her beauty. Chief among them was the Bhatt in the court of Rai Pithora, Chandra, who drew out the contours of her beauty with such flair that her picture was etched in Rai Pithora's heart. The arrow of passion pierced his heart.

But it always happens in passion that a twist develops. And from then onwards a tale of trouble begins to be written. Here the twist was that Sanjogta was the daughter of the enemy, King Jai Chand. Jai Chand was the King of Kanauj and a rival of Rai Pithora. How was that so? It was so as he belonged to the Rathore dynasty and was its prized descendant. But one of the daughters of Bisal Deo was also married in the Rathore dynasty. Jai Chand was her offspring. Thus, he was also a maternal grandson of Bisal Deo. Indeed, he was the elder grandson. But the grandfather had adopted the younger grandson and bequeathed the throne to him. It was this that ate up Jai Chand.

So how would fate bring together Sanjogta and Rai Pithora? As it happened, one of Rai Pithora's old maidservants played

---

[18] The words of the author are '*Ab zara gosha-e-hosh se suno*'. A rough literal translation would be, 'Now listen from the conscious corner of your being'.

the role of a go-between. She used a thousand stratagems to get inside Jai Chand's palace and close to Sanjogta. But she did not really need to do all that. Sanjogta had already heard stories of Rai Pithora's bravery and had fallen passionately in love with him. So the fire of passion smouldered equally on both sides. It just needed a reason to blaze. This spark was provided by Jai Chand himself.

King Jai Chand wanted to show that he was a bigger king than all others. Towards this end he had drums beaten to announce an Ashwameda Yagya. Ashwameda Yagya is a sacrificial ceremony of a horse. The kings from far and near come to take part in this ceremony and thereby acquiesce to the higher standing of the host king. And yes, along with this he also announced the *swayambar*[19] of the princess Sanjogta. This meant that Sanjogta would come into the full court with a garland in her hands and put it around the neck of whomever she fancied from amongst the kings present.

King Jai Chand invited many kings for the celebration and, as custom demanded, had to assign different tasks to them. The object was to humiliate Rai Pithora, so he was to be assigned the task of guarding the entrance to the court.

The Ashwameda Yagya was observed grandly. All the other kings came, but Rai Pithora did not arrive. So King Jai Chand had a golden statue made of Rai Pithora and propped it up at the entrance of the court.

At the same time Rai Pithora had his own scheme. He took along 100 Chauhan warriors, disguised as beggars. They left their horses in the jungle and mingled with those celebrating the *swayambar*. Among them was Rai Pithora himself.

Princess Sanjogta walked into the court with a garland. She passed by all the kings one by one. She saw each one's face. The

---

[19] *Swayambar* is a corruption of *Swayamvar*. It refers to a ceremony where princesses could select their grooms from among invited princes and kings. *Swayam* means self and *var* means groom.

person for whom her eyes were searching was missing. When she came near the entrance and her eyes fell on the statue, she swiftly put the *jaimala*[20] around its neck. Immediately there was an uproar. At that very instant Rai Pithora swung into action. He burst into the court, and catching hold of Sanjogta's wrist, made out of there in an instant. He made her sit with him on his horse and swiftly got away. His Chauhan warriors rode behind him. Now the Rathore warriors realised what had just taken place. Their pride and honour had been challenged. They mounted their horses and pursued the Chauhans with their swords drawn. They caught up with them in a little while. Iron clanked with iron, and spears were crossed. Rivers of blood flowed. But the Rathores were no match for Rai Pithora. He reached Dilli, killing and slaughtering. Next day he was in Lalkot.

Jai Chand was humiliated. He was writhing in the embers of disgrace. He began to look towards Shahabuddin Ghauri as the only way to trounce his enemy. What a harsh father was he! It did not occur to him that his daughter's home would be broken. And without foresight, he could not understand that once an outsider knows the path to the inside, why would he be content with only Dilli and Ajmer? For Ghauri it was a godsent opportunity. He was already determined to take revenge for his defeat. Now that he was being prompted by an insider he stood up firm.

But wait! There was another occurrence at this time. Now the historians would not regard this incident as real, would they? Anyway, the historians do not even take any note of Rai Pithora's love for Sanjogta. They go only by events. However, the world during that era has attributed Rai Pithora's ruin to both—this love and the incident that I am going to describe now.

---

[20] *Jaimala* is a garland made of flowers used for ceremonial purposes. *Jai* is an honorific and salutatory word while *mala* literally means a threaded necklace of beads or flowers.

It was said that besides his enmity with Jai Chand, Rai Pithora had also earned the wrath of Basak, the King of the Earth. Basak Nag[21] was the brother of Shesh Nag.[22] Hindu mythology says that he has no tranquility in his temperament. He keeps wandering under the ground. If he is here today, tomorrow he may slither away to another place. If he went and stayed under the palace of a king, it was an honour for that king.

One day some astrologers of Dilli presented themselves at Rai Pithora's court. With folded hands they said, 'O great King! Our knowledge of astronomy tells us that King Basak is residing under Lalkot. If, by some ploy, he can be made to permanently settle here, then the Chauhans need have no fear or threat. They will always rule.'

Rai Pithora was pleased to hear this. He asked them to suggest a way. The astrologers told him to have a long iron nail forged and to hammer it right into the hood of the King Basak Nag. Once the nail was hammered into his hood, how would King Basak slither away? Rai Pithora liked this scheme. An iron nail was ordered to be made hastily. What a nail it was, it was a pillar of iron! The astrologers made their calculations, assessed the location of King Basak's hood, and had the nail hammered into it.

After this, the astrologers were at rest but Rai Pithora remained anxious as to whether the nail had been hammered correctly into the hood. He ordered the nail to be pulled out so that he could assure himself that the hood was within the range of the nail. When the nail was dragged out its tip was dripping with blood. Rai Pithora ordered that it be hammered back into the same place immediately. But the astrologers beat their heads and said, 'O great king! What an outrage you have unleashed. And now what will

---

[21] See footnote 22.

[22] Nag literally means a cobra. Shesh Nag is considered to act as a seat or bed for Lord Vishnu. Shesh is also called Anant or the one who never ends. It is said that when the entire universe is destroyed, Shesh (literally, the remainder) would still remain. Basak Nag, also known as Vasuki, is Shesh Nag's brother. Basak Nag and Shesh Nag are worshipped in the snake worshipping cults.

come of hammering the nail back? By now King Basak will have slithered to no one knows where.'

And listen, at this very moment Shahabuddin Ghauri was coming towards Dilli rumbling like a storm. Beating and killing on his way, he reached the borders of the Chauhan Empire. And here Rai Pithora was sitting with Sanjogta, oblivious to it all. He had attained Sanjogta, it was as if the world, all of creation, was his. What was there to worry about now? Paying no heed to his reign or governance, he was cosseted with Sanjogta. When news of the attack by Ghauri reached, there was pandemonium in the royal court. Who would go to give the news to the king? Chandra Bhatt, who was close to the King, assumed this responsibility. He crossed seven thresholds to reach the King and told him of the attack. Now, Rai Pithora came to his senses.

On the slightest gesture by Rai Pithora, numerous Rajput warriors collected under his banner. It was a battle to the end. The sun came overhead and there was a pause in the fighting at noon. Rai Pithora sat under the shade of a tree to catch his breath. One hundred and fifty small and great kings were gathered around him. Each placed his hand on the hilt of his sword and picked up a *bida*[23] of betel leaf, put it in his mouth, drank *sharbat*,[24] placed a leaf of holy basil on his tongue, put a saffron mark on his forehead and swore to fight until the last breath. And truly, they fought till the last breath and displayed their dexterity with the sword. But the day did not bode well for Rai Pithora. By the time the day was ending the game of chess was set to become upset. The Rajput army was in chaos and Rai Pithora himself could not save his life.

At the same time, in all Rajput grandeur, Queen Sanjogta was awaiting her fate. News was reaching her at every moment. When

---

[23] *Bida* literally means a bundle. The betel leaf is eaten especially on auspicious occasions in many parts of India by 'bundling' several ingredients including areca nut pellets into it.

[24] *Sharbat* is a sweet drink made out of fruits or flowers.

the contours of the battle changed she ordered a pyre to be made ready. The moment the news of Rai Pithora's end arrived, she got off the royal throne and went and sat on the burning pyre.

Here this narrative of passion concludes, and with it the Chauhans' sun sets too.

3

New Culture, New City

Lo, the entire topography of Dilli is transformed. Neither do the doors look the same nor do the walls. Where has Lalkot vanished? Have the heavens devoured the tangle of temples or has the earth consumed them? The trend in construction is entirely different now. A high and mighty minaret is standing tall. A magnificent mosque. The style of the text engraved on these is quite different.

It has been found that Rajputi grandeur was due to the might of Rai Pithora. His passing away is not merely the passing away of a king; an entire culture and the might of the Rajputs drowned with him. It was 1193 AD when Rai Pithora was killed. Not even a year had passed before the message of King Jai Chand's death was also received. Kanauj was also appropriated by Ghauri; other Rajputs did not even matter.

The twelfth century came to an end. Now the thirteenth century has begun. Dilli is being coloured in an entirely different hue. Those who have vanquished their opposition in the city have come from far-off lands. Their ways are different. Their language is different, religion and faith are different, lifestyles are different, and their architecture is different. And the city is changing accordingly. Shahabuddin Ghauri left after murdering and pillaging, but he left his lieutenant Khan Qutubuddin Aibak behind to manage the affairs after him, and when Shahabuddin died he was formally designated a king; from Qutubuddin he became Sultan Qutubuddin. He is the one who built Qutub Minar. It is another matter that it was completed by Sultan Altamash. Actually, the new colour and form of Dilli truly came into its own during the rule of Altamash. He is the one who made Dilli the seat of power of the new dynasty. Otherwise, Qutubuddin did not leave Lahore until his very last days. It is in this city that he died. When Altamash took the reign of this dynasty in his hands, he made Dilli its seat of power. Then he built and adorned the city in such a manner that it became a cultural hub. He completed building the Qutub Minar and Quwwat-ul-Islam mosque. He built the Hauz-i-Shamsi. He constructed new palaces and new settlements. Do not think that Qutub Minar is named so with reference to Sultan Qutubuddin Aibak. No, the name came into currency with reference to Khwaja Qutubuddin Bakhtiyar Kaki.[1] This is why common people began calling the minaret *Qutub Sa'b ki Laat.*[2]

Look at another amazing feature of Dilli. All kinds of victors have come and triumphed here but for some years a beautiful princess also sat on the throne. She also ruled in her time with great verve. This was Razia Sultana—the daughter of Altamash. But love proved to be the undoing of this Sultana as well. She fell in love with a *sardaar* named Yaqut. So much so that she married him. Poor Yaqut was dark soil of Abyssinia, his status was that of a slave. The pride of the other Turk sardaar was roused and the fire of rebellion raged. For this game of love Razia lost both, her throne and her life.

The reference to Razia Sultana cropped up in the middle of the discussion but actually the reference that ought to be made is that

---

[1] A Sufi saint who lived in the locality known as Mehrauli in the vicinity of the Qutub Minar in the early thirteenth century. His dargah is popular even today.

[2] *Qutub Sa'b ki Laat* is the pillar of Qutub.

of Kaiqbad, because the discussion is with regard to Dilli and not its various Sultans. After Altamash the one who settled another Dilli is Kaiqbad. It was from this point onward that a strange custom began: whoever came to power built their own separate mosque of one and a half bricks[3] and their own separate Dilli. Qutubuddin Aibak and even more than him, Altamash devastated the Dilli of Rai Pithora and settled their own Dilli. Kaiqbad abandoned the Dilli of Altamash and settled a Dilli in his own style. This Dilli got the name of Kilokhari. It had a pleasant location. The Yamuna was flowing right next to it. Sultan Kaiqbad built a majestic palace here; he planted gardens. Then the ministers of the court also built their villas here. Right before one's eyes, the verve of the older seat of power was sucked to this new city. When the era of Sultan Alauddin Khilji came, he left the happily-settled city of Kaiqbad. The Siri area was quite close and he laid the foundations of a new town here. So now the vitality of Kilokhri got transferred to Siri. Kilokhri was destroyed; Siri was settled. When a new capital was designated it was logical that a new palace be constructed. A large palace was built in Siri which was called *Qasr-e-Hazaar Sutoon.*[4] But the life and energy of Siri was tied solely to the existence of the Khiljis. When they went, they took with them the vitality of Siri and Qasr-e-Hazaar Sutoon.

After the Khiljis, came the Tughlaqs. They also settled their own Dilli. To cut a long story short when Ghiyasuddin Tughlaq took the throne he also founded another new city nearby. He named it Tughlaqabad and left the stamp of his lineage on it. What a palace he built; when the rays of the sun fell on it the city shone like gold so brilliantly that one could hardly glance at it. In fact, the bricks used to build this palace were gold-plated. But Tughlaqabad did not bode well for Tughlaq. Just when the palace was completed, the King died. And what a strange way to die!

---

[3] Idiomatic reference to cut oneself adrift from the community.

[4] *Qasr-e-Hazaar Sutoon* is the Palace of thousand pillars.

He was on a military expedition to Bengal. As he was returning, his son, who was the crown prince and later became famous as Muhammad Bin Tughlaq, built a small palace on the outposts of the city for the king to rest in and freshen up before he entered Tughlaqabad. But the palace was built in such a strange way that the moment His Majesty set foot in it, it came crashing down on top of him.

So, Tughlaqabad was destroyed right after it was settled; actually, even before the construction had finished. And consider the son who could not stand being enthroned in this capital and this palace. He came to the old city to be consecrated and immediately decided to construct his own city as per his own vision. But what a king he was! He settled Dilli himself and then destroyed it. And, destroyed it how!

The story from destruction to settlement will go on. But while we are at it let us also glance at the map of Dilli now. All this reflected the excessive ways of the kings that whoever sat on the throne built a palace. All around the palace the nobles constructed their chalets. And His Majesty thought that he had settled a separate Dilli. But the story goes like this—one Dilli was the one that breathed its last with Rai Pithora and got obliterated along with its culture. After that the victorious outsiders stepped inside the ancient settlement and began to cast it in a new mould. And so now a new map has been drawn of Dilli. The city is prosperous and settled. The inhabitants happy and living abundantly. The citizenry is diverse. Some are Hindu, others Muslim; some Turks, some Afghans; some Hindi, some Irani. Social life is full of cultural richness. The city is marked by peace and contentment. Alleys, streets, and markets are bustling. The caravanserais are full of patrons. The opium taverns are even fuller. One motley crowd of the thirsty throng the opium joints, another kind of crowd gathers by the wells, ponds and pools. The paths in the markets are neat and clean. Shops of jewellers abound right next to each other. All kinds of shopkeepers, all kinds of artisans are sitting at their stall counters.

The local and external colours are mixed and create a unity. A new society is making an appearance. A new culture is emerging. The court has its own grandeur. The Sufi retreats have their own dignity. The street and alleyways have their bustle. Markets have their crowds. There is a poet who has one foot in the court and another in the Sufi gatherings at the retreat. The streets, alleys and markets have not been spared his steps either. The fame of his Persian poetry is established in the court and travels far and wide till Shiraz.[5] Due to this he was bestowed the title of Trumpet-of-Hind. But as became evident, he was fluent in an entirely different language.

On one corner of a street, a woman has set up a cannabis house. The smokers of marijuana and cannabis come here and initiate gambling matches. When the poet passes them by, the woman stands up and greets him. She fills up a hookah and presents it to him. The poet puts the hookah pipe in his mouth and takes a couple of drags; he sweet-talks the woman for a bit and then continues on his way. One day the woman from the cannabis house asks him a strange question:

> Oh, Sir! May you be protected! You have composed so many ragas, and written so many ghazals and songs. On the request of a wretched servant woman from the inn you even wrote *Khaliq-e-Bari* [6] for her boy. Please compose something after the name of this servant girl too!

The mood was just right. The wish of the cannabis shop woman was granted immediately.

Auron ki chaupehri baaje, Chhammo ki aathpehri
Bahar ka koi aaye naahein, aaein saarey shehri

---

[5] The ancient Persian (Iranian) city of Shiraz was once famous for its writers and poets, and its refined culture.

[6] *Khaliq-e-Bari* is a rhymed dictionary written by Amir Khusro of Persian and Arabic words with their Hindvi meanings. (https://rekhta.org/ebooks/khaliq-e-bari-ameer-khusrau-ebooks)

Saaf-soof karkey aagey raakhey jin mein naahein tausal
Auron ke jahan seenk samawein, Chhammon ke wahan moosal

It's midday for the others, but for Chhammo it's midnight
Whether there is any outsider or not, all the citizens come
They clean and keep the bathing pan for the medium
Where only a twig can go for others, Chhammo's can take an entire pestle

God knows who this woman servant was, on whose request the Poet had written the entirc Khaliq-e-Bari.

Khaliq-e-bari sarjanhaar
Waahid ek bada kartaar

Khaliq-e-Bari's creator
Is the only one big doer

He got thirsty while walking. He saw that at the well four water girls were drawing water. He went near them and asked for water. One of them said, 'May you be protected! Are you not Amir Khusro who has written songs and whose riddles *keh mukarni* [7] are famous?'

Yes, Bibi. I am Khusro. I am thirsty. Give me water to drink and earn virtue.
No, not like this! Say something for us first!
O, Bibi! Now what shall I say for you?
Okay... then say a few words on *kheer.*[8]

Another one piped in and said, 'Let's have you say something on the spinning wheel too.' A third one said, 'Say something about a drum!' The fourth demanded something on a dog. The poet was really annoyed. But he began immediately with ease.

---

[7] *Keh Mukarni* or *Keh Mukri* are a kind of riddle composed by Amir Khusro in which the narrator, a woman, says (*keh*) something to a woman friend that involves a double entendre. The friend guesses if the answer is her lover but the original narrator denies (*Mukarni*) it. See http://www.angelfire.com/sd/urdumedia/kemukar.html for examples.

[8] *Kheer* is a dessert made by thickening milk with rice.

Kheer pakai jatan se, charkha diya jala
Aaya kutta kha gaya, tu baithi dhol baja [9]

Burned the spinning wheel, cooked kheer with care
A dog came and ate it, while you sit and beat the drum

Now give me water!

Then he composed a riddle on the request of some Tom, Dick or Harry. On someone's request he would compose an *anmel* [10] or a *dhakosla.* [11]

Bhadon paki paheli choo-choo padi kapaas
Bi mehtarani daal pakaogi ya nanga hi so rahoon [12]

Riddled ripened in bhadon, the cotton fell down dampened
Madam sweeper will you cook pulses or shall I go to sleep naked

Is all this merely about mirth and laughter? To us it seems like the appearance of a new language. This had to happen. After all, no culture is born dumb, it brings with it its own language. With a new culture a new language is also growing and being nurtured; in other words, Urdu is now gaining stature.

But all this was taking place in the streets, alleys and markets. What was happening in the courts? The time of Ghiyasuddin Tughlaq was over. It was now the period of Muhammad Bin Tughlaq. First he settled Dilli and then uprooted it. Tired, he gave up and he settled it again. Suffice it to say that he arranged for Dilli's security. He got a wall built around it. He also built a palace called Qasr-e-Hazaar Sutoon. He named the city that he established

---

[9] See footnote 11.

[10] *Anmel,* literally meaning 'not matched', is a non-rhyming poem-riddle. They are often abrupt and seem nonsensical but may have some deeper meaning.

[11] *Dhakosla* literally means 'sham' or 'deceit'. Similar to *Anmel,* they are also nonsensical. They may or may not rhyme but have a perfect metre scheme.

[12] This verse is a wonderful example of an *Anmel.*

Adilabad, because he thought himself to be a just[13] king. But you know what happened subsequently? While he was storming the Deccan he liked a city, Deogir, so much that he thought of making it the seat of his throne. He got a drummer to make a public announcement in Dilli ordering people to leave Dilli for Deogir—the new Adilabad and the new capital. It is said that after this order by the ruler, Dilli was emptied of its inhabitants such that in the end only two men, one lame and the other blind, were left in the city. But Khaleeq Ahmed Nizami, in his book *Auraq-e-Mussawar*,[14] says that this is an exaggeration. 'Sultan established only an administrative centre at Deogir and Dilli continued to enjoy the same status. There were palaces here in which the royal family was still stationed, the cantonment was still here and so was the mint.' But in the same breath he also goes on to say that, 'the scholars, jurists, and the elites of the city left behind them a vacuum in the city. According to Syed Muhammad Gesudaraz[15] the Sufi gatherings of the city became so desolate that except for the shrines of Qutub Sahab and Sheikh Nizamuddin Aulia others did not even have anyone lighting a lamp in the evenings.' So Dilli was now a dark 'City Desolate'.[16] The riches and the people of the city were now in a decline and had reached Daulatabad.

But the new city neither suited the people nor their ruler. A drought came to pass causing much misery and suffering to the people. They began the torturous move once again. The journey to Daulatabad had been agonising. From there the journey back

---

[13] *Adil* means 'just' or 'righteous'.

[14] *Auraq-e-Musawwar* literally means 'sheets of paper used by artists'. The title is a reference to a couplet by the poet Mir in which he compares the sights of the streets of Dilli to the work of artists. (https://rekhta.org/ebooks/auraq-e-musawwar-ahd-e-wusta-ki-dilli-khaleeq-ahmad-nizami-ebooks)

[15] Syed Muhammad Gesudaraz was a Sufi saint of the Chishtiyya order and a disciple of Nizamuddin Aulia.

[16] *Shehr-e-be-charagh* literally meaning 'a city with no lighted lamps' indicating that it was not just dark but dark because there was no one to light a lamp.

to Dilli was equally miserable. Slowly, Dilli settled back into its earlier state of bliss. The streets and alleys were buzzing once again. The markets were once again bustling. And yes, have a look at those traditions and institutions which had given birth to this new culture. Above all were the Sufi *khanqah*.[17] At the time of Muhammad Bin Tughlaq there were about 2,000 such places for Sufi gatherings. These had their own culture which remained untouched by the court. Nor had the philosophical style of the religious scholars tinged with their orthodox beliefs found a way to get to these places. One belonged to the family of Shariyat while the other to the family of the everyday practices—miles away from religious and cultural contestations. Hindu-Muslim, rich-poor anyone who wished to come to this 'court' was welcome to benefit from it. There was no compulsion of knowing and speaking Persian. Here Hindvi was in currency. They did not have any quarrel with the art of jesting. Music had taken the form of *samaa*[18] and had permeated these places.

Among these shrines the one that slowly gained a central position was that of Shiekh Nizamuddin Aulia. It was so popular that from morning till late in the night there was always a big crowd of the devotees there. Among these devotees there were Hindus as well as Muslims. Sheikh was not a votary of practising any kind of distinction between them. It is said that one day he was strolling on the terrace of the gathering hall. On the banks of the river Yamuna which flowed nearby he saw some Hindus worshipping as they sang and played musical instruments. Sheikh recited this line:

Har qaum rast rahe dine wa qibla gahe

Each people have their path of faith and a direction they turn to

---

[17] *Khanqah* are Sufi shrines or residences.

[18] *Samaa* literally means 'to listen'. In Sufi traditions *Samaa* is an exalted form of prayer and is said to involve arriving at the truth through love and acceptance by tradition.

His disciple, Amir Khusro was otherwise of Turkish origin but completely dyed in the colour of Hindi. One *Basant*[19] morning on his way to the Sheikh's gathering he passed by the Kalka Temple. He was already feeling very happy to see mustard blooming all around and men and women dressed in bright yellow clothes. When he heard the priests singing in devotion at the temple he felt a strong sway in his own person. He arrived in front of Sheikh Sahab with mustard twigs and flowers adorning his turban, still under the influence of the experience. The guide smiled at seeing the devotee thus and instructed that arrangements be made to celebrate Basant at the khanqah. So this is how the annual Basant fair began at a Sufi's khanqah. The guide was happy and so was the devotee. What to say of the community kitchen here? It was as if a *sada brat*[20] was on. It was as if no one in the city will go to sleep hungry. But Sheikh himself would fast. What would he have eaten anyway—a *roti* and a little *daal-tarkaari*.[21]

But because of its grandeur this khanqah posed a challenge to the royal court. Look at Ghiyasuddin Tughlaq. What got into his mind that when he was returning from a mission in Bengal he issued an advisory that the well-being of Sheikh Nizamuddin lies in leaving Dilli before the arrival of His Excellency. This message reached the Sheikh. The unruffled spiritual leader uttered, '*Hunuz Dilli door ast*'.[22] And lo! What peril befell that Ghiyasuddin Tughlaq could not reach Dilli at all. The palace that his son had built outside the city to welcome him collapsed on him and he was flattened underneath. The king on his way to Dilli had to proceed to the eternal world instead.

---

[19] *Basant,* literally 'spring'. *Basanti,* the adjective form, also refers to the bright yellow colour of the mustard flowers.

[20] *Sada brat* is a community meal in the Sikh tradition that goes on over days and nights.

[21] *Roti, daal-tarkaari* is a simple meal of leavened bread with a preparation of pulses and a vegetable.

[22] It is still a long way to Dilli.

So these were the khanqahs of the Dilli of this era. Now hear about the madrasas. At the time Dilli had 1,000 madrasas. Many received state patronage. The expenses of many others were taken care of by the elites. There were also madrasas that took no gifts from either the state or the elites. Their condition would be marked by scarcity. But they had such teachers that students were attracted and came here from far and wide. One madrasa was the Madrasa Firozi which had been established by Firoz Shah. What to say of the grandeur of this madrasa—all around it was such greenery and flowers. The trees were laden with fruit. And in the midst of all this was the impressive building of the madrasa. Adjacent to it was a tank, famous by the name Hauz-e-Khas. A little apart from it were the living chambers for students and teachers and a guest house for the guests. All expenses for board and lodging were paid by the state.

In the city there were also sarais in good numbers. And then there were gardens and orchards, tanks, wells and step-wells. What a huge tank was the Hauz-e-Shamsi! There was a raised platform and a grand building right in the middle of this tank. There were rooms for the Sufis nearby. You can imagine how this tank had become the centre for cultural activities.

The most and best gardens were planted by Firoz Shah Tughlaq. He was responsible for 1,200 gardens being planted around Dilli. And not merely gardens. This king had 30 tanks, 100 bath houses, and 150 bridges constructed in and around the city. Along with this he had built 100 sarais, 30 seminaries and 40 mosques. And yes, 50 of those bridges were built across rivers. One way to look at it is that with his welfare activities he even compensated as much as possible for the destruction caused by Muhammad Tughlaq. Muhammad Tughlaq was a strange king. A collection of contradictions. In helping the needy he was the Hatim[23] of his own time. In matters of killing and murder, he was

---

[23] Arab chief who was famous for giving liberally in charity.

the Halaku Khan of his time. A hundred tales each of notoriety and goodwill are associated with him.

It bears mention that in this environment the effect of religious conflict is seen very little. It is almost as if the new culture that was emerging was founded on religious tolerance. The Sufis were in any case the flag-bearers of religious tolerance. Hear about Sheikh Hamiduddin Nagauri who got very upset when one of his disciples once called a Hindu, Kafir. He said, 'My dear, what do you know of the spiritual condition of this person!' Sufis apart this is quite apparent in the behaviour of the rulers as well. Khaleeq Ahmed Nizami cited Jalaluddin Khilji from Barni.

Har roz hinduwan, mandal zana wa bauq zana dar zer koshak man mi guzrand

Everyday the Hindu women go to temple, they blow the conch and pass by under my palace.

And this king did not prohibit them from passing by the palace. Instead some Hindu festivals used to be celebrated at court. Holi was celebrated in the court of Muhammad Tughlaq. And one of the engagements of this king was to hold discussions with yogis.

Firoz Shah Tughlaq continued with the good traditions of Muhammad Tughlaq even as he made amends for the bad traditions associated with him. In 1352 he established a new settlement called Firozabad. But this settlement had no influence on the razzle-dazzle of Dilli. In fact it so happened that the population of the city had increased so much that the need to build a new settlement was palpable. The king had been responsible for a lot of construction work. Since he was very fond of hunting he also constructed a hunting lodge called *koshak shikar*. It not only had a palace but also a museum which had on display all kinds of birds and animals.

Firoz Shah bade farewell to the world having earned a lot of goodwill. But his successors turned out to be unworthy. It was back to abandon and debauchery, and fighting and killing for the throne. In this chaos an evil came and left Dilli damaged and in disorder. This was the invasion of Taimur Lang. His army murdered and killed on the streets of the city. According to Bashiruddin Ahmed, 'So many corpses were dumped in the alleys that there was no room to even walk.'

Lord Taimur camped in Dilli for 15 days. Those were the 15 days of *qayamat*.[24] The entire city was swept of all its riches. When Taimur went back he took away all the treasures of the city with him.

The fourteenth century was coming to an end. How much had Dilli risen in stature? New settlements were inhabited, each better than the other. Above all was the fact that a new society was born and a new culture had made an appearance. A new language had added to its magnificence. But the city was utterly destroyed. With what pride was Dilli settled and in what an exemplary way was it destroyed. This is 1398 AD. Taimur has left after unleashing doom. Dilli is now a desolate city. It remains to be seen when and in what colour will it be settled again.

---

[24] Qayamat literally means doomsday. Figuratively used for describing periods of great difficulty or mayhem.

4

From Dilli, towards Agra

For 15 days Taimur wreaked havoc and got his royal kettledrums[1] beaten in the city. He looted the city voluminously; he beheaded people and slit throats as if they were vegetables. And then he scooted. It was a typhoon that passed. Now the town is devastated and ruled by anarchy. Unjust city, ruinous rule. Whoever does not care for his neck can go and occupy the throne. A raging rebellion will rise against the occupant of the throne. If he is able to flee with his head intact then consider that person fortunate. Khizr Khan was lucky that he was not murdered but died due to medical reasons. His son Mubarak Shah sat on the throne. The old and continuing tradition of this seat of power was that whoever sat on it would settle his own Dilli and build his own palace. Mubarak Shah also followed suit. As soon as he was crowned he laid the foundations of a new town, Mubarakabad. But a new city takes time to be built and settled. On the other hand time was passing by quickly in Dilli. Mubarak Shah had very little time in his share. The new city was uprooted before it could settle. Mubarak Shah was murdered. He could not sit on the throne in the half-built city. But yes, his grave was located there.

---

[1] Kettledrums were usually beaten by players accompanying armies. The practice was considered a royal prerogative and meant to be an aggressive tactic.

After this Muhammad Shah, son of Farid Khan, sat on the throne. Helped by his good fortune he escaped being murdered. His intelligence had something to do with it too. Surrounded by his attackers, he permitted them to enter through one door while he exited from another. He saved his life by the skin of his teeth.

Dilli spent half a century in this tumultuous disorder. It was in this disorder that a Lodhi found strength and occupied the throne. And behold, now for some the will and coinage of the Lodhis would prevail over Dilli. Whether they could do anything else or not, but for sure they would leave one and a half gardens and two and half monuments as a memory of their legacy. But the feat of shifting the seat of power from Dilli to Agra is also documented in their name. Anyway, that happened later. But first Behlol Lodhi sat on the throne and he continued to occupy it for 37 years. In other words, he occupied the throne in 1451 AD and bade farewell to it in 1488 AD. But he was neither murdered nor did he have to flee. He died of medical reasons. Without a moment's delay, his son Sikandar Khan Lodhi immediately took to the throne. But he was destined to have not a day without trouble. Every day brought a new rebellion or revolt. He never got a chance to sit in peace in Dilli, and for this reason he grew weary of the city. He resolved to leave Dilli and establish his capital in another city. A draw of luck foretold the name of Agra.

So now the entire century has passed in turmoil. And as the new century began the capital shifted from Dilli to Agra. This took place around 1504 AD. But misfortune befell him at the very beginning of this venture. The city experienced an earthquake so intense, it felt like the day of judgement had arrived. Sikandar Lodhi, however, was stubborn and resolute. He stood his ground. He remained in Agra and as a result, for a long time in the future even the Mughals did not give any importance to Dilli. They remained captivated by Agra.

Despite this, Dilli remained indispensable to the rulers. According to the *Waqeyaat Darul Hukumat Dehli*, 'by convention a coronation would not be considered complete until a formal crowning ceremony took place in Dilli.' And look at Sikandar Khan's nerve; he took the entire business of the regime away from Dilli to Agra and settled a new city there by the name of Sikandra. He ruled from there. It was there that he fell sick. And there that he died. But his dead body was brought to Dilli to be buried. Sikandar Shah was buried in Dilli and not in Sikandra.

But how many days were the Lodhis fated to sit on the throne of Agra? Ibrahim Lodhi followed Sikandar Lodhi on the throne. After that the dynasty came to an end. Babar had left Kabul and was killing his way to Dilli. From this side Ibrahim took an army of brave fighters and went forward to confront him. A battle ensued on the grounds of Panipat. Ibrahim was killed and Babar won the battle.

So the era of the Lodhis ended. With their gardens and their tombs the Dilli of the Lodhis was also consigned to the story of the past. Now the Mughals will rule here and will adorn this city. On 24 April 1526 Zahiruddin Babar entered the city proclaiming victory and took grandly to the throne.

After his coronation, he gave the city a once-over. He attended sessions at the mausoleums of Khwaja Bakhtiyar Kaki and Hazrat Nizamuddin Aulia. He went sightseeing at Hauz-e-Khas and Hauz-e-Shamsi. He visited the Qutub Minar. He saw the gardens and tombs of Behlol Lodhi and Sikandar Lodhi. Then he left for Agra in a boat. Babar was the second Mughal after Taimur to have set foot in Dilli. But this Mughal had a different disposition. He had not come here to loot, snatch and behead. He had come to establish a dynasty. His trip to Dilli may have been brief but his progeny would go on to build and adorn this country and this city. The devastation caused by their forefathers would be compensated by them in full.

As long as Babar ruled he stayed in Agra. He died there but afterwards Humayun bestowed royal status upon Dilli when he became the ruler. Here he resolved to build a Dilli after his wishes.

It was called '*Deen Panah*'.[2] The site marked for this city was the one believed to be where Indraprasth had once stood. The fort began to be constructed but destiny did not allow Humayun to live in this city and its fort. It was Sher Shah who was destined to stay and settle here. Betrayed by his own brothers, Humayun was defeated bitterly by Sher Shah; he drifted and wandered and eventually reached Iran. The construction of the still incomplete fort was finished by Sher Shah. He made his own addition to the fort and called it Sher Mandal.

It was 15 years later that fortune turned for Humayun. His enemies were beaten. He became fortunate and successful. Now he turned his face against Agra and sat tenaciously in Dilli. He turned Sher Mandal into his library. But Sher Mandal carried the signature of Sher Shah. He could not really flourish there. Sher Shah had divested him of his power over India. Sher Mandal took away life from him.

Humayun had a deep interest in astrology. It was due to this interest that he had been planning to build a provision room at Sher Mandal. One evening he was informed that on that night *Mushtari*[3] and *Zehra*[4] are going to meet in the skies. Humayun went to the top floor of Sher Mandal to see this sight. After having seen it, when he started climbing down he heard the sound of the azaan being called out in the nearby mosque. Out of reverence he sat down on a step of the staircase. After the azaan was over he began to stand up with the help of his stick. The stick slipped on the smooth marble floor and with that the King tumbled down the staircase. He was badly hurt and did not survive the fall. On On 24 January 1556, the note of death arrived.

Humayun had wandered about before coming to Dilli. Then he lived here and died here. He was buried here. Humayun's tomb

---

[2] *Deen Panah* means sanctuary of faith.

[3] *Mushtari* is Jupiter.

[4] *Zehra* is Venus, morning star.

is one of the famous monuments of Dilli. If there is a tomb of a Mughal king in Dilli it is this. In fact, the most famous and well-known Mughals preferred not to die and be buried in Dilli. Babar died in Agra and was buried in Kabul. Akbar too preferred to die and be buried in Agra. Jahangir was buried in Lahore. For Shahjahan, Agra became a compulsion after Mumtaz Mahal. He went and slept beside her in the Taj Mahal. Aurangzeb went to the back of beyond to Aurangabad to be a patch on the earth. The subsequent kings who lie in Dill figure nowhere in this account. None of them have a tomb built for them that can be counted among the tombs of Dill. All that is left in this account is the last Mughal Emperor Bahadurshah Zafar. During his last days he was taken as a prisoner to Rangoon, where he died saying:

Do gaz zameen bhi na mili ku-e-yaar mein
Did not get even two yards of land in the land of the beloved

Oh, yes, the discussion started with Humayun who had made Dilli his base. But his son did not follow in his father's footsteps. Akbar bestowed glory upon Agra and built majestic forts there; one in Agra, one in Fatehpur Sikri. Then, alluding to him, Agra became known as Akbarabad.

So after the transfer of the seat of power all the verve of Dilli descended on Agra. According to Bashiruddin Ahmad, in Dilli, 'there were only some elderly left from the time of Humayun who continued living here. They died here and became a part of this earth.'

Think of Agra as Dilli's *saukan*.[5] At any rate Dilli must have had many *saukans* but two of them were heavyweight adversaries. One was Deogir and the other was Agra. But with Deogir the charm of the new was short-lived.[6] In just about nine days Sultan

---

[5] *Saukan* or *Sautan* means husband's mistress or other wife.

[6] The author uses an idiom often used in this context—*nai nau din, purani sau din*. Literally, it means, 'the new lasts nine days while the old lasts a hundred'.

Muhammad Tughlaq grew tired of it. All his whims and desires ended in these nine days. He had slung[7] his subjects away from Dilli. But the nine days of Agra got stretched a little. Akbar disregarded Dilli and embraced Agra such that he made Agra Akbarabad. All this while he lived in Lahore for 13 years and ruled from there. *Yak na shud, do shud.*[8]

Anyway, after this it was the turn of Emperor Jahangir. He followed in the tradition of Akbar and sat tight in Akbarabad. After that Emperor Shahjahan sat on the throne. This king embellished Agra like no other. To top it all he built the incredible building that is the work of a lifetime, Taj Mahal. But with that the King's heart grew weary of Akbarabad. In his weariness he had a brainwave that now that he had built many palaces and tombs, he should also show everyone how to build a city. This reminded him of this long-forgotten settlement that had been favoured by his great-grandfather. Taj Mahal was complete by this time and Jahanabad began to be built. And how it was built!

Agar firdaus bar ru-e-zamin ast
Hamin ast we hamin ast wa hamin ast
If the heaven be somewhere on earth
It is right here, right here, right here

All the other past and future arguments slipped into the background. Now only the Dilli of Shahjahan shall rule.

---

[7] The term used here by the author is *danda-doli* which is a game played by children; two or more children lift up a child by the limbs and swing him/her. Here the usage is meant to be jocular.

[8] *Yak na shud, do shud* is an idiom literally translated as 'if one wasn't bad enough, we now have two'. Or a bad situation going worse.

5

City Settled, World Settled: Jahanabad

Having stayed too long in Agra, let us go back to Dilli. Who knows at what moment Sikandar Khan bade adieu to Dilli and started towards Agra. Subsequently, all the kings made Agra a pillar of their throne. The first Mughal king too ruled from here. Of course, Humayun favoured Dilli and settled his new town Deen Panah in the midst of this ancient city. But then how long did Humayun live and how long did he remain in the city? Akbar made Agra his base once again and he did so with such grandeur that Agra became Akbarabad. Then came Jahangir. He too ruled from Akbarabad alone.

And then began the era of Shahjahan. Even Shahjahan's coronation took place in Akbarabad. He spent an age in Akbarabad, built and adorned the city. Above all he built the Taj Mahal. Thus he put his own stamp on this city. Even then Akbarabad remained Akbarabad; the grandfather had put such a strong stamp of his name on the city that even after the Taj Mahal was built, that stamp remained. Shahjahan grew weary of this city and was reminded of the city of his great grandfather. He made up his mind to go to Dilli and build a city after his own heart.

So gentlemen, now Dilli's fortune made a turn. It is time that a new Dilli is inhabited in the midst of the old Dillis. This Dilli will have such vigour and brilliance that all the preceding Dillis and the Dillis to follow will fade before it. It will be called Shahjahanabad which will get shortened to Jahanabad. But the name Dilli will also remain in currency. You could call it Dilli or Jahanabad as you wished.

So the designs are ready. The plans begin to be implemented. The foundations of the new town are about to be laid. Building will commence from the fort. If a king lays a foundation of a city it is obvious that he will first construct a house for himself. So the construction of the fort started. At first Izzat Khan was appointed the chief of building. This contract provided that the famous Ustad Hamid and Ustad Ahmed would supervise the operations. This was in 1638 AD (or 1639 AD, according to another tradition); the date was the 9th day of Muharram, 1049 AH. This was the date on which the foundation of the court was laid.

This is the historical narrative. Now I'll narrate the folklore related to the arrangements made for the construction of the fort and the incidents that took place as that happened. Nasir Nazir Firaq[1] heard these from the Dulhan Nani[2] who had been associated with the fort, and who said that marble, red stone and all kinds of materials for the fort came from many countries. The chief of building gave the dimensions of the brick to a contractor and ordered for such bricks to be prepared. They were not to be underdone, and should be red in hue. The contractor agreed, took one lakh rupees and got busy with the order. After a few days he came back crying and howling. He said, 'I am ruined. The heat in

---

[1] Nasir Nazir Firaq (1865-1933) was a writer known for his fiction, and essays describing the cultural life and royalty of Dilli.

[2] *Dulhan* (literally, bride) is often used as a life-long term of endearment for daughters-in-law. *Nani* means maternal grandmother. Dulhan Nani being referred to here is Banni Begum – an old woman of the royal family who narrated the events recorded by Nasir Nazir Firaq in his book *Lal Qile ki Ek Jhalak* (A Glimpse of Red Fort).

the kiln was too high. The bricks are now just *khangar.*[3] The king will now have the women and children of this subject worried.'[4]

The chief of building tried to comfort him and told him not to worry. He immediately sent an application to the king asking permission to use *khangar* instead of granite in the foundation. He said that *khangar* can absorb a lot of water and will keep the foundation strong. The application was accepted. The contractor happily got to work. Listen to what happened next in Dulhan Nani's words, 'Fat was boiled in large iron pans and copper tubs and then the bricks were fried in them like fritters. When the bricks had absorbed a lot of fat they were taken out and left to cool and then placed in the foundation with stucco mortar. The stucco was composed of limestone from Narnaul, urad lentil flour, red lead, jaggery, linseed oil, flax, wax, and strained bel sharbat.'

The work went on night and day with such opulence. 'The red fort, the houses inside it, villas and porches were being built. Gems were being polished for the *takht-e-taaus.*[5] All kinds of conveniences were gathered in the wilderness. Thousands of labourers, architects and artisans were stationed in *khema*[6] and *chholdaari*[7] tents, and in huts. Stones are being brought from far-off hills loaded in carts. Fifty or even a hundred oxen are harnessed in each cart. In the din made by the chisels of the stonemasons you can hear nothing else.'

Ten years later, the construction was completed. Mukarramat Khan, who was the chief of building then, sent word to court. On the 24th day of Rabi-ul-Awwal 1057 AH (accordingly 1648 AD) His Excellency came with all his regal opulence to relish the fort. 'From top to bottom it was made of stone which was red in colour like a rose. Then there were the stylised side panels of marble.

---

[3] *Khangar* are overdone or burnt bricks.

[4] An idiomatic reference to impending punishment to the person responsible for wrongdoing.

[5] *Takht-e-taaus* was the peacock throne.

[6] *Khema* refers to large luxury tents.

[7] *Chholdaari* are small tents meant for servants.

Pleasant looking towers, walls and decorated arches. So attractive were the buildings, gardens, the water channels in the gardens that if we were to write a detailed commentary on each one we will end up establishing an office to accomplish the task. The fort, when seen in its map on paper, looks like a rectangular flower.'

Next, the court was convened in the Diwan-e-Aam. In front of the Diwan-e-Aam a *shamiyana,*[8] which was called *dal baadal,*[9] was erected. In front of the Diwan-e-Khas another *khema* called *saha mandal.*[10] Both these tents had been created after hard labour of seven years. Instead of the regular throne another one especially made for the occasion was used. It was this throne that was named *Takht-e-taaus*. What a magnificent throne it was—six feet long and four feet wide with six heavy legs. The takht and the legs, everything was made of solid gold. At the back two peacocks stood with their tails spread wide open as if they were just about to begin dancing. Their tail feathers were studded with sapphires, rubies, diamonds, emerald, and topaz. Between the peacocks there was a parrot made of emerald. The shamiyana over the takht was glittering with gemstones. A silver pavilion was placed a little further away from here. According to the *Waqeyaat Darul Hukumat Dehli*, 'Outside the pavilion first there were the warriors, the rich, and the illustrious princes. After them rulers, noblemen from various countries, and minor aristocrats were standing in order of their stature. But all these obedient courtiers kept their eyes fixed on the ground and their hearts set to follow the orders of their sovereign. In each arch two soldiers with special rifles in velvet covers and flags stood at attention like statues. In the outer courtyard the other officers, jagirdars, and mansabdars stood awaiting any orders. In the next pavilion there were three

---

[8] *Shamiyana* is a fabric canopy erected to provide shade. *Shaam* literally means 'evening', and *Shaamiyana* thus means 'like evening'.

[9] *Dal Baadal* means cluster of clouds.

[10] *Saha Mandal* means magical circle.

black giants from Abyssinia, their eyes bloodshot, wearing brocade uniforms, loaded with weapons, a mace on the iron shoulders, the flags in their hands fluttering like clouds. In the third rank there were the officials in charge of the clerical and dispatches sections; scribes and accountants were present with their pen-stands tied to their waists and their bags at the ready. In the next arches soldiers standing quietly next to the silver railings as high as themselves displayed their bare swords. Indeed, outside the pavilion, after every 30 yards there was a silver railing. Stationed next to it, were the brave special soldiers of the king wearing their sparkling uniforms, with golden and silver flags in their hands. Among them the Turks were on the right, Afghans on the left, and Rajputs in front. From here till the gate, beyond the riders, the adorned soldiers stood in sharp contrast. All the visiting courtiers could proceed further only after identifying themselves at each security post. There was so much anxiety and apprehension that it was difficult to keep one's wits about oneself. Once the courtiers reached the court they had to bow in acknowledgement at three places. When the herald made an announcement directing them to pay their respects with deference and according to their turn—*Jahanpanah Badshah Salamat! Aalampanah Badshah Salamat!*—hearts thumped with terror in the chest.'

This was the description of that day. At night the moonlit celebration was unleashed which had its own excitement.

The celebration went on for nine days. Thus was the opening of the fort of Shahjahan. The fort would now be called Lal Qila and enjoy an eternally famous stature.

The King's house having been built, it was now time to build Allah's house. That is the Shahjahani mosque right in front of the Shahjahani fort. The fort was ready in 1648 AD. The construction of the mosque was completed in 1650 AD. But this Masjid was not built so easily. It also has a story. Nasir Nazir Firaq's Nani Dulhan had the penchant to turn every incident into an entire story. So this is in her own words. At the time when the foundation of the mosque was being filled, the architect vanished along with the plans. Ultimately hope of finding him alive was abandoned. In a bid to find his body the wells were stirred with bamboo. One year passed, the second passed and then the third year passed. No news still of the architect. When three years had passed, the architect appeared one day suddenly, went to the court and stood there with folded hands. 'My lord, I'd like to say something if my life be spared. The building of the mosque was getting very heavy. It was dangerous to build such a heavy building on a new foundation. The rain water would seep into the foundation and with it the doorways and walls would have sagged. With that the arches and beams would have slumped. Considering this, I made a sacrifice and went into hiding. Now that the foundation has survived three rainy seasons it is as strong as a pillar of iron. The building that is erected now will continue to stand tall for centuries.'

The king was convinced. The slip was forgiven. A robe was bestowed. Construction began. In 1650 AD the mosque was ready. Meanwhile another tale was spawned. It was such a high platform and such a tall and grand building that anyone who saw it was amazed. But someone expressed a doubt and said the mosque did not face the *Qibla* [11] properly. With the help of a compass they checked the direction of the Qibla. It was true that the mosque did not exactly face it. Obviously, everyone concerned was quite troubled. In this chaos a dervish appeared from somewhere. He asked, 'What's the story?' and was told what had ensued. He said, 'No problem at all,' and saying this, he walked to the building and placed his back against one corner of the mosque and pushed a little. The entire structure shifted a bit and stood facing the Qibla perfectly. People enquired about the dervish but he had vanished and was never seen again.

How grand was this mosque built on the Bhojla Hill about 100 yards from the Red Fort! It sat on a platform about 30 feet from

---

[11] *Qibla* is the direction of the Kaaba, the building in Mecca city which Muslims face while praying.

the level ground. A platform of 1,400 square yards made of red stone. On its three sides there were over 30 steps—35 on the east, 29 on the south and 33 on the north. With three grand entrances, the mosque was constructed over six years. The opening of the mosque took place on a strange morning. Shahjahan decided that he will go to pray in the mosque he had built. It was Eid and the royal entourage left for the mosque. From the gate of the fort to the gate of the mosque there was a long queue of vehicles. Right in front were the herald and the usher. Behind them were the princes. The grand entourage entered the mosque, and namaaz was offered. After this namaaz the mosque was open to all namaazis. The doors were open to the citizens. Namaaz began to be offered here five times a day.

Wah dilli ki Masjid-e-Jama
Jis mein baraq farsh-e-sangi hai

Great is the Jama Masjid of Dilli
That has the white stone floor

Now the God's house has also been constructed. But one house had actually been built before both the King's house and the God's house. This was Matia Mahal. When a plan for the construction of a building was made the labourers and architects had camped on the site and made temporary residences for their own use. This was the form of Matia Mahal. According to Mulla Wahidi,[12] 'it was a temporary residence in which the supervisors of the implementation would sit and monitor the construction of the Red Fort, the Jama Masjid and the rest of the city.'

While the construction plan keeps expanding, the face of the city is also undergoing transformation. From the Lahori gate of

---

[12] Mulla Wahidi (1888-1976) was a celebrated writer, publisher, and politician. His real name was Syed Muhammad Irteza. He was also a chronicler of the cultural history of Dilli. Like Intizar Sahab, Wahidi also reluctantly moved to Pakistan after the Partition.

the Red Fort there are unbroken rows of tents and huts such that an entire market has come into being. Barley, wheat, all kinds of cereals, all kinds of vegetables, all kinds of dried fruits; one could buy anything here that one's heart desired. The king decreed that in this market, which became famous as Urdu Bazaar, all kinds of goods should be made available so that artisans and labourers who had come from faraway countries should not lack for anything.

One of the ways in which Shahjahan accomplished the construction of the city was by dividing it and giving different parts to his offspring. They were instructed to draw money from the royal treasury and build houses, palaces, mansions, gardens and markets, and thus adorn the city. The princes, princesses and the *begums*[13] began to participate in the construction of the city according to their own individual tastes. The eldest princess Jahanara, the favourite daughter of Shahjahan, constructed a market which became famous later as Chandni Chowk. Starting from the Lahori gate of the fort it stretched for about 1,520 yards; it was four yards wide with a canal in the middle, and verdant trees were planted on both sides of the canal. But Jahanara did not rest merely at this. At a little distance from the market she had a garden planted and a serai built. The garden gathered fame as '*Begum ka Bagh*'.[14] The serai was so grand that a thousand travellers could stay there. All the expenses of boarding and lodging were the responsibility of the princess.

Shahjahan had a wife named Fatehpuri Begum. She had a mosque constructed further from this market. The Fatehpuri mosque, as it came to be called, marked the other end of the market. Another Begum called Akbarabadi Begum had a market built which vied with the Chandni Chowk[15] in splendour. It also had a canal flowing

---

[13] *Begum* means royal woman.

[14] *Begum ka Bagh* means Garden of the Begum.

[15] *Chowk* is an open or enclosed space at the intersection of two or more roads. *Chowk* are often bazaars or market places sometimes with an installation like a fountain, a clocktower or a statue in the centre.

in the middle and a row of trees along the banks. Named after the canal, the bazaar came to be known as Faiz Bazaar.

Both these markets came into being in 1650 AD, a little apart from each other. In a very short time these marketplaces became so popular that shoulders would rub against shoulders as one walked here. The other markets were also not any less dazzling—Khaas Bazaar, Khanum ka Bazaar, Urdu Bazaar, Chowk Saeed Ullah. But see the divine order that the change of era got the better of all these. The only name that remained was that of Chandni Chowk.

Other than the bazaars the city had *darwaze*,[16] *khidki*,[17] *muhalley*[18] and streets. All the streets were pretty as paintings. There were 14 gates and 14 windows. The 14 darwaze were the Kashmiri Darwaza, Mori Darwaza, Kabuli Darwaza, Lahori Darwaza, Ajmeri Darwaza, Turkman Darwaza, Khairati Darwaza, Raj Ghat Darwaza, Kalkatta Darwaza, Kela Ghat Darwaza, Patthar Ghati Darwaza, Badar Darwaza, Nighambod Darwaza.

About the Nighambodh a writer has said well that,

Takhta-e-aab-e-chaman kyun na nazar aae sapaat
Yaad aae mujhe jis dam wo nigambod ka ghaat

Why shouldn't the flat bier next to garden and water be visible to me
The moment the memories of Nighambod Ghat come to me

What of this writer, the reference to this ghat can also be found in the Mahabharat because the city of Indraprasth is connected to it.

Now let us also count the windows. Khidki Zinat-ul-Masjid, Khidki Nawab Ahmed Bakhsh Khan, Khidki Nawab Ghaziuddin Khan, Khidki Naseer Ganj, Nai Khidki, Khidki Shah Ganj, Khidki Ajmeri, Khidki Darwaza, Khidki Syed Bhola, Khidki Baland

---

[16] *Darwaza* is literally 'door'. In the present usage, it means a large gate-like structure for the new city.

[17] *Khidki* is literally 'window'. In the present usage it refers to a smaller entrance in the walls surrounding the city.

[18] *Muhalley* are enclaves or neighbourhood.

Balagh, Khidki Farash Khana, Khidki Ameer Khan, Khidki Khalil Khan, Khidki Bahadur Ali Khan, Khidki Nigambodh.

Apart from the 14 gates and 14 windows there were 36 residential enclaves in the city. Each enclave had high mansions, labyrinthine alleyways and according to Mir:

Haft aqleem har gali hai kahin
Dilli se bhi dayar hote hein

Does each alley open into seven continents anywhere?
Cities such as Dilli do exist

And what kind of houses were there in these alleys? In their courtyards were small lawns, tanks, fountains; there was a basement furnished with fans, and a main gate.

Chujannat bar zameenash har makaane
Bod dar har makane bostane

Every house is like heaven on earth
Each house has a garden

A city is not built in a day. Shahjahanabad took seven years to be settled. Those succeeding it will build it further and embellish it. According to their wishes they will stitch on gussets and loops on to its fabric. This was an initial map but even in this initial stage it looks quite finished and polished, and happily settled. The fortune of this city has turned after a long time. Taimur had destroyed it. From among his progeny emerged the worthy descendent who resettled it. A poet describes the history of the city thus,

Shehr Shahjahanabad az Shahjahan aabad

City Shahjahanabad was settled by Shahjahan

The city developed in such a way that its shape appeared like a bow. The river Yamuna and the fort can be imagined as the two ends of the wire on the bow. It was surrounded by a wall whose diameter, according to one estimate was five and a half miles and according to another estimate it was 10 miles long. After every hundred steps there was a turret. There were gardens here and there, open grounds, well-settled enclaves, big mansions in the enclaves, long spacious bazaars—Faiz Bazaar, Khaas Bazaar, Khanum ka Bazaar, Urdu Bazaar, and the queen of Bazaars, Chandni Chowk. The bazaars were bustling with people and the shops were stocked with hundreds of varieties of goods.

Nashista har taraf gauhar faroshey
Barawarda zoriyaa haakharoshey
Fatada har taraf sad laal-e-rakhshan
Bod dar har dukan kaan-e-badakhshan

Everywhere the sellers are sitting with gems and jewels
Their loud call to the visitors for attention compels
Everywhere rubies and lustrous stones lie strewn
Every shop looks like a Badakhshan[19] mine

There is nothing wrong if the couplet that is written on the front of the *aiwan-e-aam* [20] is engraved on the crest of Shahjahanabad.

Agar firdaus bar ru-e-zamin ast
Hamin ast we hamin ast wa hamin ast [21]

If the heaven be somewhere on earth
It is right here, right here, right here

[19] Badakhshan (now in Tajikistan and Afghanistan) was a region of importance on the Silk Route. It was famous for lapis lazuli and rubies.

[20] The couplet is actually engraved under the cornice of the Diwan-e-khas. 'Aiwan' literally means entrance or approach. In Mughal architecture it could also mean a roofed room on the outside of a courtyard.

[21] This very famous couplet is by Amir Khusro and the poet was referring to Dilli, while it now famously refers to Kashmir because according to folklore Jahangir recited it when he went there.

6

This City was Plundered a Hundred Times

From time to time numerous cities were settled on the land of Dilli. But not one of these cities was loyal to its founder. While talking to the writer of the *City of Djinns*, a frail old English woman remembered the era gone by when New Delhi was founded. She remembered her father who was strongly against the idea of the new construction. He used to say that the money being wasted on the new construction could be better spent on something more worthy. In reality he had heard this old saying about Dilli which he never forgot. The saying was more in the form of a prophecy according to which whoever built a new city on the land of Dilli, would very soon have to lose it. So when the entire story of the construction of New Delhi began, this English gentleman would sadly recite a Persian couplet which mentioned the prophecy and fall silent. The frail old English woman was also saddened by her recollection. She said, 'My father was right. Whoever settled a city on this land had to wash his hands off the city. Pandav Brothers, Prithvi Raj Chauhan, Firoz Shah Tughlaq, Shahjahan—in short, this happened to anyone who settled a city on this part of the earth. This had to happen to us too, so it happened.'[1]

---

[1] *The City of Djinn*s, by William Dalrymple, Penguin Books India, 1993.

If this was the history of Dilli, how could Shahjahan be an exception? And when fidelity is not an ingredient of the *ghutti*[2] of this city then why should the lack of it be considered a fault of Jahanabad or indeed its peculiarity? Still, it is amazing how rapidly times change and how hastily Jahanabad turned its sight away from its founder.

Just 10 years ago Emperor Shahjahan had set foot in his city with such pomp and splendour. What a magnificent entourage it was! The king graced the Peacock Throne. What a display it was with which the court was convened, and what a spectacular moon-lit celebration followed! This was 1648 AD. Now it was 1659 AD. That court, the moon-lit celebrations are now all historical tales. Today a new coronation and a new court are being arranged. The one who founded this city is sitting imprisoned in Agra. Here in Jahanabad a new procession is on and a new celebration is being arranged. It is so spectacular that the celebrations arranged for Shahjahan dim in comparison. This is the celebration of the crowning of his rebel son.

The rightful heir to the throne, Darashikoh had been defeated. Aurangzeb has emerged the victor. With this victory Aurangzeb became Auranzeb Alamgir.[3] He stepped into Jahanabad with great show and pomp. His procession began moving towards the Red Fort with a dazzling display. Tambourines and heralding drums pulsate at the head of the procession. Swaying elephants are queued up behind them. On each elephant's back there are runners made of bead-worked brocade. Their feet are shackled in silver chains. Royal flags unfurl on their backs. Following them is a queue of horses. Gold and silver saddles are tied on their backs; the reins are studded with precious stones. Behind them are

[2] *Ghutti* is a liquid concoction given to infants in South Asia. Exact ingredients can differ but in value it is like gripe water. In the present usage, it is suggestive of something that becomes part of the constitution of an entity because it is administered so early in life.

[3] Alamgir is a decorative title meaning 'ruler of the creation'.

soldiers with naked swords in their hands. Next are the rows of the noblemen. Go past these rows and you see Aurangzeb riding on a grand elephant. On his right and left, at the front and back are fully armed soldiers. Gold and silver are being showered on him from above.

The grand retinue enters the fort. How beautifully the Diwan-e-Aam has been prepared! The awnings and terraces are wrapped in silk, brocade and velvet covers. Lanterns are hung on the arches. The peacock throne too is resplendent. The peacock feathers are studded with sapphire, emeralds, topaz and rubies. Hung above is a canopy. The courtiers are wearing glittering dresses. Behold, Aurangzeb Alamgir takes the throne! The crown is placed on his head. Now he is Emperor Aurangzeb Alamgir.

A new era of the Mughal Empire began with this coronation and the vibrant culture of Jahanabad was enhanced. But now the colour of blood has tinged this grandeur. The new city was still unacquainted with this colour. Dara, of course, had to be beheaded. But death was hovering over the head of a Sufi too. Aurangzeb's rein proved lucky because it gave Jahanabad a martyr. The city had received mausoleum shrines and khanqahs of the Sufis in inheritance from the earlier Dillis; it was now provided with a martyr's shrine thanks to Aurangzeb. The stairs of the Shahjahani mosque had begun to be occupied by hordes of bizarre people. But one of them was the strangest. He was possessed, lost in the knowledge of supreme centredness, free from the material world, bereft of clothing. His nakedness became his most distinct identity. Darashikoh was a God-ordained devotee of the sages. He saw this possessed person and was smitten by him. The possessed man also had such deep love for Darashikoh that the friendship of the prince and the faqir became exemplary. Religious leaders and jurists have always challenged Sufis and the possessed. Where would they have had the heart to tolerate this stark naked crazed man who sat picketing the stairs to the mosque? But they could do nothing while Darashikoh prevailed. After his death they got their chance. They began complaining to Aurangzeb that Sarmad speaks against the *Shariya.*[4] Without doubt this was ground for capital punishment. Aurangzeb was even more uncompromising than the religious leaders. Moreover, Sarmad's connection with Dara throbbed like a thorn in his heart. Eventually he got into an argument with the faqir. He asked, 'Why do you go around naked?'

Sarmad gave him this portentous reply,

Aun kas ke tura kar-e-jahan bani daad
Mara hamein asbab-e-pareshani daad
Pushaand ne libaas har ke ra aib-e-deed
Be aibaan ra libaas-e-aryaani daad

The entity that bestowed kingship
That became an instrument of distress for all of us
Whoever he thinks is flawed, he covers with cloth
The one without blemish is attired in nakedness

How could Aurangzeb have tolerated such a reply? He took a decree from the jurists and beheaded Sarmad.

In the area adjacent to the mosque there was already a mazar of Harey-Bharey Shah. Next to it a martyr's mazar was built. God knows who Harey-Bharey Shah was! It is said that he was the teacher of Sarmad.

Whether it was the colour of Sarmad's blood that did it or Aurangzeb's own discriminatory policies which assured that he could never sit on the throne comfortably, a time came when his time in Jahanabad was over. Captivated by the idea of attacking the Deccan he left for the journey of the black miles.[5] The charge on the Deccan took more and more time and Jahanabad's lustre

---

[4] *Shariya* is Islamic law derived from Quran and Hadith (words or practices of the Prophet Muhammad).

[5] The author uses *kos* instead of miles. *Kos* is a unit of distance equivalent, roughly, to three kilometres or two miles. The author probably uses the word *kaley* (black) to figuratively refer to the journey as ill-fated.

kept getting dimmed. It had to get dim. How long can a centre of power with an unoccupied throne retain its vitality? When the king left the city, so many things left with him. All kinds of nobles and plebeians, dubious and dapper, dullards, braggarts, who had added to the charm of the city left—some along with the Emperor, others when required by him. Jahanabad became increasingly desolate. You could say that Dilli's water had flowed to the Deccan and the return was not in sight. There was an already existing tradition of songs of separation in the city. These songs now acquired added sting.

Dilli Shehr suhawana aur kanchan barsey neer
Sab ke kanth bator ke le gaye Alamgir
Sahab ki minti karo aur man mein rakho dheer
Ab ke bichhdey jab milein jab paltein Alamgir

Where gold rained like water; city of Dilli was pleasant
gathering along everyone's voices, away Alamgir went
Please implore the Sahab and keep your hearts patient
Farewell now, we hope to meet only when Alamgir returns

But Hazrat Alamgir was never to return. He was to become a patch of land in the Deccan itself. He left Dilli for the Deccan, and he left the Deccan for his heavenly abode. Jahanabad's fortunes returned only after the final journey of Aurangzeb. After Aurangzeb his son, prince Muazzam Shahalam Bahadurshah sat on the throne. After remaining desolate for 12 years, Dilli started being inhabited and acquiring its lost cheer once again. But how could the old vigour ever be restored? Hazrat Alamgir had left taking along with him the power and dignity of the Mughal Empire. The empire had become infected with mite. The throne had been shaken. Nobody could ever sit on this throne firmly again. Among the heirs no one showed the strength or capacity to control conspiracies and run the affairs of the empire. Before long the awful time came when Dilli had to face a major devastation, of the kind that it had seen during the assault by Taimur. Except that it was possibly worse.

Aurangzeb died in 1707 AD. Suffice it to say that within 30 years of his death the situation became so bad that Nadir Shah came charging and wreaked havoc in Dilli.

Shamat-e-aamal ma soorat-e-Nadir giraft

Trouble caused by one's own action took the shape of Nadir

A massacre was unleashed on the city on the orders of Nadir. People's throats were hacked like vegetables. Nadir took a breather and his soldiers stopped only after over 1,00,000 people had been killed and stacks of dead bodies lay everywhere.

Nadir Shah left after pillaging and killing. But this city which Shahjahan had built with such joy was distraught, and ruination now knew its address. Not many days had passed since the Nadir Shahi destruction when another Nadir Shah charged and attacked Dilli. This was Ahmed Shah Abdali. Nadir Shah plundered Dilli in 1739 AD. Seventeen years after this, in about 1757 AD, Ahmad Shah Abdali attacked it. After Taimur and Nadir Shah he was the third bandit who robbed Dilli to his fill and massacred the people indiscriminately. But this time around, the bloody incident also contained an ironical aspect. The leaders of Dilli had invited this disaster themselves. They thought that this brave man would rid the Muslims of India of the larceny of the Marathas. They thought that he was a saviour. This 'saviour' did crush the Marathas but trounced the Muslims of Dilli too. He came back again. Then he came back the second time. Shah Madar kills those who are already dead.[6] Then this pillaged Dilli was looted by the Marathas and the Jats as well. Mir describes the condition of the city after this, thus:

---

[6] '*Marey ko maarey Shah Madar*.' The author uses this idiom invoking ironical reference to claims of magical prowess by a faqir who actually possesses none.

One day I went for a walk. I passed by a new ruin of the town. I cried at every step and learnt a new lesson. I was astonished more as I walked ahead because I could not recognise the spots. I couldn't place which part of the town it was because there were neither any buildings there nor any people. Demolished houses, fallen walls, khanqah without the Sufis, taverns without the drunkards ..... Where were the markets that I could mention them? Neighbourhoods had been destroyed, the streets were non-existent, everywhere there were signs of terror.

This entire scene was described by him in verse like this:

Ab kharaba hua Jahanabad
Warna har ik qadam pe yan ghar tha

Now Jahanabad is a ruin
Otherwise there was a house at every step here

First the water of Dilli flowed towards the Deccan. Now it flowed to Lucknow. All kinds of virtuous and sharp people left this city for that city. Only poor Mir Dard[7] remained sitting on his *takiya*;[8] all other well-known poets left their dwellings and moved to Lucknow. Even Mir Sahab left the ruin and introduced himself thus in Lucknow:

Kya bod-o-baash puchho ho purab ke saakinon
Ham ko ghareeb jaan ke hans hans pukar ke
Dilli jo ek shehr tha aalam mein intekhab
Rehtey they jahan muntakhib hi rozgaar ke
Is ko falak ne loot ke viraan kar diya
Ham rehne waale hein usi ujdey dayaar ke
Aisa ujda dayaar jo baar baar ujda, baar-baar viraan hua
Ye nagar sau martaba loota gaya

---

[7] A Sufi poet, Mir Dard is considered one of the four pillars of Dilli's poetic tradition along with Mirza Mazhar, Mir Taqi and Mirza Sauda.

[8] *Takiya* is literally a pillow or something to rest on. It is used to refer to the resting place of a Sufi where they would live, teach and guide their followers from.

Oh you ask for my native place, the eastern listeners
You laughingly call me out thinking that I am poor
Dilli which was the specially chosen city in the entire creation
Only the most select of this profession lived there
It was made desolate by the plundering fate
We are the natives of that desolate land
It was uprooted again and again, made desolate repeatedly
This city was plundered a hundred times

Nadir Shah, Ahmed Shah Abdali, Marathas, Jats, Rohilas, whoever got a chance did not leave any stone unturned. They plundered the city excessively. As they say, a poor man's wife is everyone's sister-in-law.[9] Dilli was now a poor man's wife. The presence of a king or his absence amounted to nothing. He was himself at the mercy of someone or the other. Should he have saved his own life, or should he have worried about Dilli? And what king anyway? If even one had managed to sit stable on the throne, he could be named. It was all a fast-moving lane of kings. They were removed right after the moment they took to the throne. And they were given such a frightening *chhathhi*.[10] Mutinous nobles had Ahmed Shah poked in the eyes with thin iron rods to blind him and then they imprisoned him. It is not known when this great king bid farewell to the world and where he was buried. After him came Alamgir, the second. He was misled by a treacherous nobleman Ghaziuddin that a very sagacious faqir had come to Firoz Shah Kotla. That he was so miraculous that whatever he touches turns to gold. This emperor was like clay in anyone's hands. He paid no attention to royal etiquette. Bereft of any guards he went out with tricksters. When he reached Firoz

---

[9] A common Hindi saying referring to supposedly sexually permissive relationship between a woman and her husband's younger brother.

[10] *Chhatthi* is a ritual to mark the sixth day of birth. Here the reference to a person's *chhathhi* is to be reminded of his humble and precarious position.

Shah Kotla, there was no sign of the faqir. The murderer killed him with a dagger, beheaded him, and left the body on the sandy bank of Jamuna to writhe to death. This was Emperor Alamgir, the second. Later Shah Alam, the second made a grand appearance on the throne of the empire. What befell him was that one day a captain, Sardar Qadir Rohilla—whom he had teased a lot—sat on his chest and blinded him by poking his eyes with spindles. When the city got rid of the Rohillas after some frantic praying, it was surrounded by the Marathas. When the Marathas lost a bit of strength the English tightened their grip.

In 1802 AD, Lord Lake defeated the Marathas and took hold of Dilli. Now the Emperor Shah Alam came under the shadow of the East India Company's influence. He spent four years of relief under this cover and then he left this world, leaving Dilli and the Mughal Empire to their own devices. After him his son Akbar Shah, the second took the throne. But according to the writer of the *Waqeyaat Darul Hukumat Dehli*, 'he was *Akbar*[11] only in name'. In reality he was more fastened and bound than even his father. During his reign, the English enjoyed even greater control.

The English dominance was not legitimate. But at least it got rid of the recurring nuisance of invasion. Now Dilli was at peace. And according to the narrative in the *Waqeyaat Darul Hukumat Dehli*,

> The control over the fort remained unaffected. The kingdom continued to be held in esteem. Great Kings and Nawabs still wore earrings signifying their allegiance [12] to this doorstep and continued to consider it an honour to be conferred a title here. The emperor's coins remained in currency in all the provinces. Gifts and presents, and taxes and tributes continued

[11] *Akbar* literally means 'great' or 'senior'.

[12] It was a Sufi custom in the Chishtiya order to wear an earring to show their allegiance to their guide. Jahangir began to wear an earring to display his allegiance to the Sufis. This practice was later emulated by the nobles and nawabs. The origin of this practice probably lies with the Nath yogis who wore huge earrings.

as per tradition. Although, there was no comparison with the grandeur of Alamgir's time. This was merely an empty envelope. But whatever was left of it one had to think of it as a gain and something to be thankful for.

Truly this was something to be relieved about. *Nadirshahi*, *Ahmedshahi*, *Marathagardi*, these catastrophes were all eventually relegated to the past. The next catastrophe that was to befall was still some distance away. In this intervening period, Dilli breathed easy. It gathered its scattered and disorganised state of affairs. Days and nights became festive and celebratory once again. One should learn from Dilliwallahs the spirit to live. If one wishes to see how a culture survives after being caught in the midst of storms and outbreaks, and if you wish to see how it defeats every trick of time and reaches its pinnacle, then let us go to see Dilli in the nineteenth century.

7

Before Dawn Breaks

The watchwoman cried, 'Beware!' The ushers answered in loud voices, 'Allah and his Prophet are aware.' Then one of the ushers shouted, 'Do *mujra*[1] to *Jahanpanah*[2] *salamat*.'[3]

The palanquin-bearers came along with the *hawadaar*.[4] The Emperor sat astride. The hookah-bearer came to stand along the throne with the hookah. The Emperor took the pipe of the hookah in his hand.

The herald and the usher with gold maces in their hands walk in front shouting, 'Step forward, step ahead! Jahanpanah, long live the Emperor.'

The soldiers wear red broadcloth angrakha shirts. They have black turbans on their heads, guns with red covers on their shoulders, shields on their backs and swords hanging at their waists. In front of them the horses, gold and silver musical instruments, velvet banners, plumes on the horses' heads make a jangling sound as they walk. The water-carriers walk sprinkling water on the way.

After arriving at the royal court, the emperor sits on the throne. The proceedings of the justice court have begun. The amirs,

---

[1] *Mujra* is an elaborate, ceremonial salute.

[2] *Jahanpanah* means Protector of the World.

[3] *Salamat* means healthy or safe.

[4] *Hawadaar* was a portable throne for a ride.

ministers, chiefs, the superintendent, judges, chiefs, scrivener—all stand respectfully—with their official papers under their arms. The prosecutor brings forward the application of the plaintiff. Decrees are being passed and orders are being written.

This was the routine. During the festivities, the grandeur of the royal processions was much more magnificent. Cannons were fired as the Emperor's procession began to move. First of all two elephants with emblems appeared. After that elephants with umbrellas, golden pinnacles at their crests and silver sticks underneath. After that the elephants bearing the insignia of honour emerge. Then more elephants and camels; on one of the camels, kettledrums are being played continuously. Then the platoons of soldiers appear. The Royal Dignitary platoon,[5] the Colt platoon, the Black platoon, the Agri platoon. Decorated horses in formation. The thrones, one with a shade, one ventilated, each glorious in its own way. *Raushan Chauki*[6] is being played. Frills made of gold tissue are being waved. The singer sings ballads. Soldiers called *dhaliyat* stand armed with shields and swords. Special guards with guns on their shoulders walk in the procession. And now the elephant with the royal seat is visible at last. The Emperor is sitting on the seat which is resplendent with diamonds and pearls. A yard away is the ride of the reigning queen. Behind her the princes. Behind them the rides of amirs, nawabs, governors and maharajas. Then the procession of the cavalry. Then the drum elephant. And at the end, the elephant with alms. The drummer plays the drums as alms are distributed among the poor. The markets are full of people bowing in ceremonial salutes. The herald keeps calling, 'Pay respect! Long Live the Emperor!'

This is not the procession of the Emperor Shah Jahan, nor is it of Hazrat Aurangzeb Alamgir. This is a procession of the final era when the Mughal Empire had been destroyed to bits and the

[5] The Royal Dignitary platoon consisted of Western soldiers in Western uniform.

[6] *Raushan Chauki* was an honorary musical performance as the royal person retires for the day.

riches of Dilli had been looted. The Emperor was a puppet in the hands of the British, making do with the amount designated as his pension by the East India Company. Authority and power lay in the hands of the company. The king was only a front. The company had no objection to the kingdom existing only in the name. Bring out ceremonial processions, move astride horses, have festivities, hold courts, bestow robes of honour—none of it concerned the company. In fact whenever the British officers attended the court they would also observe all the royal ceremonial rituals.

So what was left of the sultanate now? All the same, royal gestures and rituals lingered. Not a bit had changed there. Grandeur and clamour as before, Elegance and splendour as ever. The royal procession would leave with the usual pomp. The court would be convened with the same grandeur. However there was a difference; earlier it was a show of the power and glory of the Mughals, now it was a display of the Mughal royal culture. The Mughal Empire was not an empire anymore, it was now a royal culture. Akbar Shah, the second and Bahadur Shah Zafar had preserved and enhanced and glorified this culture much in the same way that Jahangir and Shah Jahan had preserved and glorified the empire. Royal traditions were all continued. If something was added, it was by way of further refinement.

It was the era of Emperor Akbar Shah, the second. Two washermen got into a brawl with each other on the banks of the Yamuna. Both knocked at the Red Fort for justice. The Emperor held, 'Tell the washermen that our reign does not extend over the river, it is inside the fort. Go to the *firangis*.' So these kings were well aware of the state of their reign and where authority lay. Nevertheless they would hold splendid courts and pass grand royal rulings, and the people of Dilli would accept their rulings with courtesy. Whatever was the emperor's current position, for the people of Dilli he was still Jahanpanah, and the Red Fort was the *Qila-e-Mualla*.[7]

---

[7] *Mualla* is literally Exalted. *Qila-e-Mualla*, the Exalted Fort, was the name given to the Red Fort.

Mufti Sadruddin still held the position of the Grand Chief at this time. He received an appropriate salary from the Company—more than a thousand rupees. From the Emperor's treasury the same mufti's monthly salary was fixed at two and a half rupees. When Mahboob Ali Khan Khwaja became minister he stopped this salary. Mufti Sadruddin made a case in front of the Emperor and the Emperor finally reinstated his salary. The *firangi* commissioner of Dilli asked Mufti Sahab, 'Mufti Sahab, you are paid a salary of more than a thousand rupees by our government. Why did you bother with a court case for a mere two and a half rupees?' Mufti Sadruddin answered, 'Commissioner Sahab, the two and a half rupees are consecrated, we are proud of it.'

Confident that at least the people believed the Mughal king to be the Emperor and the shadow of Allah, he sat with dignity and splendour in Red Fort, preserving the traditions he had inherited from his ancestors. Expenses were constrained as there was just the pension fixed by the Company to depend on, and a few gifts and offerings—for the rest Allah sufficed. But royal hands were habituated to giving. The long tradition of giving alms and gifts continued; the culture of the fort could not be imagined in its absence. During festivities it was mandatory to weigh the Emperor in gold and silver. This gold and silver would then be distributed among the poor and indigent. Moreover, the courtiers were bestowed robes of honour. It was also essential to have the elephant of alms for the poor in the royal procession. The elephant would move alongside the procession and alms would be distributed among the poor. Here at the fort, food was cooked in big vessels with much clangour, and trays were decorated with different kinds of dishes and distributed in the city.

What to say of the variety of food. The Mughal *dastarkhwan*[8] of this time is not the same spread that Zahiruddin Babur had

[8] *Dastarkhwan* refers to a cloth that is spread on the floor or table and then the meal is laid out on it. The word is also used to denote the spread itself.

brought with him. So many tastes have been introduced that its diversity seems to mirror the diversity of the Mughal culture. There are too many dishes to be named or counted! Just for this, one needs Munshi Faizuddin's book-keeping skills. In his name let us at least count the plates of pulao, since that is the speciality of the Mughal spread. *Yakhni* (Mutton stock) *Pulao*, *Moti* (pearl) *Pulao*, *Noor Mahali Pulao*, *Nakti*[9] *Pulao*, *Raisin Pulao*, *Nargisi*[10] *Pulao*, *Zamurdi* (Emerald) *Pulao*, *Laal* (Ruby or Red) *Pulao*, *Muzaafar* (Saffron) *Pulao*, *Faalsaai*[11] *Pulao*, *Aabi Pulao*, *Sunehri* (Golden) *Pulao*, *Roopehli* (Silver) *Pulao*, *Murgh* (Chicken) *Pulao*, *Baiza* (Eggs) *Pulao*, *Ananaas* (pineapple) *Pulao*, *Kofta* (meatballs) *Pulao*, *Biryani*[12] *Pulao*, *Chilao*[13], *Saarey Bakre ka* (Whole Goat) *Pulao*, *Bont Pulao*.

While we are at it, let us hear from him about the kinds of *rotis*[14] as well. *Chapatis*, *Phulkas*, *Parathe* (shallow fried breads) *Buttered Breads*, *Besani Roti* (gram-flour breads with condiments in it) *Leavened Bread*, *Naan*, *Sheermal* (a sweet bread), *Oval Bread*, *Fried Bun*, *Kulcha*, *Baqarkhani*, *Ghausi Bread*, *Almond Bread*, *Pistachio Bread*, *Rice Bread*, *Carrot Bread*, *Sugar-Candy Bread*, *Cotton Bread, Gulzar Bread*, *Tunki Bread* (a thin sweet bread) and *Qumash Bread*.

When there is a celebration, the ritual of *Tore Bandi* is a must. This ritual would continue for 10 days, which meant that all kinds of food will be cooked for 10 days and then distributed after being arranged on trays. Tora cannot be of more than 22 spreads or of less than two spreads. According to the level of regard in which

---

[9] *Nakti* is a kind of sweetmeat.

[10] *Nargis* is a kind of flower.

[11] *Faalsaai* means coloured purple with *Faalsey* (small sour berry-like fruit).

[12] The word *Biryani* derives from the Persian word *Beryan*, which means fried, grilled or roasted. In this context it could be a reference to a richer variety of pulao.

[13] *Chilao* refers to rice cooked with oil, cumin and caramelised sugar.

[14] *Roti* is flattened bread.

they are held, the ushers can be seen distributing Tora meal spreads from house to house.

The king is generous, and the begums more generous than the king. For them money was like dirt on their hands. In their estimation, gold coins were the same as *cowries*. When the rains started they would buy velvet mites for the little princesses. One rain-insect would cost one gold coin. Once the velvet mite of a princess died, she cried so much that her eyes got all puffed up. When the elder begum saw this she ordered her servant to go to the market and buy 10 velvet mites. The servant received 10 gold coins and ran toward the bazaar. Shortly he came back with 10 velvet mites but reported, 'The price of the insects had doubled in the market today. I had to borrow 10 gold coins, only then could I buy the velvet mites.' The begum was pleased and thought that the servant was loyal. He had not cared for the gold coins and had found a way to bring the velvet mites. He was bestowed the remaining 10 gold coins and eleven rupees in reward.

One of the begums had a daily morning routine of opening the jewellery bundle and taking out a *ser* [15] and a quarter of jewellery from it. She would give the jewels to the goldsmith's boy and instruct him that the gems had to be separated from the ornaments in such a manner that none of them should have even a scratch on them. After working hard the entire day the goldsmith's son would present the gems carefully separated from the ornaments to the begum on a tray. After satisfying herself that the work had indeed been done well, the begum would tell her servant, 'O Gulchehra, hand over these gems to the superintendent of the store for jewels.' Then she would address the goldsmith's son, 'Goldsmith, take these ornaments. You have earned this for your hard work. Come again tomorrow morning.'

These begums lived in a world of their own. Why stop at the begums, the Red Fort was another world in itself. Right in the

---

[15] *Ser* is a measure of weight of around seven kilograms.

middle of the city of Dilli, here was a world which was as much part of the city as it was separate from it. There were some rules of etiquette, rituals and manners which were specific to the Red Fort. For certain others it can be said that they belonged to Dilli, however when mixed with royal manners they became part of the culture of Red Fort as well. Eid, Baqreid, Shab-e-Barat, the last Wednesday of the month of Muharram, and then Holi and Dussehra. Dilliwallahs already celebrated these festivals. In the Red Fort, they acquired a royal magnificence. However, the festival of *Nauroz* was probably brought here by Emperor Humayun. Nauroz was a seasonal festival of Iran, but when Iranian culture acquired Islamic colour, some of it rubbed off on this festival too. It was believed that the day Ali was born it was Nauroz, and the day he became the Caliph it was also Nauroz. Whatever be the way in which this festival was celebrated in Iran, at the Red Fort it acquired its own colour.

The fort would be painted each year for Nauroz in the colour indicated by the astrologers. You could call it the Naurozi colour. The Emperor appeared dressed in Naurozi attire and this ensured that the entire court donned the same colour. The princes, noblemen, nawabs, all wore clothes of the Naurozi colour. When the dastarkhwan was chosen, it was also of the Naurozi colour. The spread included seven types of pulao, seven types of sweets, seven types of fruit, and seven types of vegetable curries. Besides these there was barley roti, *saag*[16] and *sattu*.[17] This was the dastarkhwan of Hazrat Ali over which the Emperor would pray. First he would taste a bit, and then bestow it upon the princes and nobility as a consecration. Everyone would perform the ceremonial salute and accept the sacred offering to taste it. Thereafter it was the turn of

---

[16] *Saag* is a Potherb, or a leafy plant cooked as a vegetable preparation.

[17] *Sattu* or flour of dry roasted cereals and gram. It can be eaten as porridge, or a drink, or as stuffing in other dishes after garnishing it with a variety of ingredients.

the women. The women made the Diwan-e-Khas luminous with their presence on Nauroz. The begums and princesses also partook of the sacred offering. Whatever was left was then distributed among the rest of the fort's inhabitants.

Some *shagun*[18] had over time become associated with Nauroz—swaying fans, gold and silver tossed liberally, and finally the game that became a tradition especially with Nauroz, the royal egg fight. With this game the Nauroz celebrations would come to an end.

The last Wednesday arrived. The court would be convened very early in the morning. Gold and silver rings would be brought to the court arranged on a tray. The king would himself wear two gold and two silver rings. Then he would give two to the crown prince, one each to all the princes, and the rest to the nobility.

In another similar tradition, water was poured into a small pitcher, and a gold coin was put in it wrapped in a piece of cloth. The pitcher would then be thrown away after circulating it around the head of the emperor as an offering. When the pitcher broke, the sweeper woman would grab hold of the gold coin. A little hay would be burned and the Emperor would step across it. Now the distribution of pitchers would begin. Each pitcher had in it a little money. First the begums and princes received them. Then they were sent to the houses of the nobles. Whoever received the pitchers stood up and broke them. The money in the pitchers would then be given to the sweepers.

Bara-wafat[19] came. On the first of the month of the Rabi-ul-Awwal, a Qawwali performance would be held in the Moti Mahal. The Emperor participated in it. In the end sugar-coated cardamoms would be distributed. Food would be given to the elders and *malangs*.[20] This would be done not just on one day but

---

[18] *Shagun* is a perfunctory ritual.

[19] *Bara-wafat* is the 12th day of the month of Rabi-ul-Awwal in the Islamic calendar. The day of the Prophet Muhammad's birth and death.

[20] *Malang* is a person who doesn't care for material things; a Sufi mystic; a crazed faqir.

on 12 days. On the twelfth day lamps and candles were lit, and sweets were distributed.

On the eleventh day there would be a display of fireworks. Sumptuous spreads would be laid out. Supplication would be made in the name of Hazrat Ghaus-al-Azam, and food distributed.

Ramzan, Eid, Baqreid, Shab-e-Barat—these were the major festivals. The festivities were organised accordingly. When Muharram came all celebrations would stop. Courts would not be held, nor would there be festivities or singing or music. The court or the peakock throne would be forgotten; now the Emperor would sit dressed as a dervish, a small cloth bag usually used by faqirs hanging around his neck. The bag had in it sugarcoated cardamom seeds, aniseeds, and poppy seeds. The emperor's state on the sixth day of Muharram was something to be seen. Two banners with silver palms would be prepared. One had a red and the other a green *patka*.[21] The emperor held the one with green cloth in one hand and the one with the red in the other. A silver chain hung from his waist. Two Syeds would drag the Emperor by the chains for two or three steps. The chain would then be put around his neck. On the eighth day of Muharram, the Emperor played the waterman of Hazrat Abbas. He wore a red *khadar*[22] *lungi*,[23] with a leather bag filled with water on his shoulder. From the bag he filled earthen pots with sharbat and served the children.

On the day of *Aashura*,[24] a special Aashura namaz was offered in the Moti Masjid. The dastarkhwan was laid out in the Diwan-e-Khas with shirmaal and kabab along with chopped mint, ginger and radishes. The Emperor stood and prayed over the food. This was distributed to all those present in supplication.

---

[21] *Patka* is a cloth used for tying around the waist as a belt.

[22] *Khadar* or khaddar, i.e., thick, coarse cotton cloth, hand-spun and hand- woven.

[23] *Lungi* is a length of cloth tied around the waist and worn like a long skirt.

[24] *Aashura* refers to the first 10 days of the month of Muharram. Also, the tenth day of Muharram, which is the day of martyrdom of Imam Hussain.

The sacred relics arrived from the Jama Masjid—the robe and shoes of the blessed Prophet, the Holy Quran written in the hand of Hazrat Ali, earth from Karbala. These were taken around the court accompanied by the playing of musical instruments, and thus they were returned to the Jama Masjid.

Gota [25] was distributed at the shrine in the palace. *Taziya* [26] were raised. Dirges were recited. Drums and cymbals were played.

So these were the festivals of the Muslims. Then there were the festivals of the Hindus. In the fort these festivals were also celebrated with pomp and gaiety. On the day of Dussehra the royal court would be convened. First a *Neelkanth*[27] would be set free. Then a falcon would be brought from the mews. The falcon would be made to perch on the arm of the Emperor. In the evening embellished and decorated horses would be paraded before the Emperor.

On the day of Diwali the Emperor would be weighed in gold and silver. This gold and silver would be distributed among the poor and destitute. Then a buffalo, a black blanket, mustard oil and seven foodgrains mixed together, along with silver and gold were given away in supplication. At night there were lights and naubat drums were played.

But one festival was specially attributed to the Fort. This was Raksha Bandhan and also referred to as Saloney. The story went like this—a few aides-de-camp took Shah Alamgir the second, to old Kotla on the ploy of meeting a miraculous dervish as part of the conspiracy of Ghaziuddin-Haidar. He was killed there. The killers threw the dead body on the sandy banks of the river Yamuna and left. A Hindu woman happened to pass by. She saw the dead

---

[25] *Gota* is a type of lace, silver or gold in this case.

[26] *Taziya* are shrine-like structures made of bamboo and paper, etc., built in symbolic representation of Hazrat Imam Hassan and Hussain. These are kept for the 10 days of Muharram and then taken out in a mourning procession on the tenth day.

[27] *Neelkanth* is the Indian Roller Bird.

body and recognised that it was the Emperor's. She sat near the head of the body and guarded it. Emperor Shah Alam was grateful to the Hindu woman and from then on considered her a sister. For as long as he lived he treated her as a brother would. And after being called a sister, the Hindu woman performed all the traditions of being a sister. So on the day of Saloney she came to the Red Fort every year with trays full of sweets and tied a Rakhi on Shah Alam's wrist. The emperor in turn would send her off with gifts of gold coins.

Shah Alam's successors honoured this relationship by keeping alive this tradition. Saloney was thus celebrated in the Fort with a lot of festivity.

But all this was the description of the men's quarters. Were there only the Emperor, the princes and nobility in the Fort? There must have been princesses too. Certainly, they were! The begums—the elder begum, the younger begum, princesses, teenage girls, baby girls. And there were their female servants and guards, beauticians, seamstresses, black women, Turkish women and cooks. Each had their customs, their culture and mannerisms, their beliefs, their superstitions and their own rituals. To appreciate these it is essential to know where these begums had come from in their palanquins. They had come from Iran, Turan,[28] and Rajputana. Some were Sunni, some Shia, and some Hindu. They mingled so well after arriving in the Fort that a composite feminine culture emerged here. But the old influences also continued alongside. For example, *Bibi Ki Sahanak* was observed with such devotion and arrangements. Who is this Bibi? Hazrat Fatima Zahra. The supplication was made behind seven veils.[29] Not even a male bird could flutter its wings nearby. In brand new earthen platters plain boiled rice would be kept; it would be topped with yogurt and sugar. The platters were stacked on the dastarkhwan along with bangle sets, small packets

---

[28] Turan, now obsolete, referred to the present Central Asian region.

[29] A metaphorical reference to utmost care to seclusion.

of henna and *missi*[30] wrapped in red paper and tied in *kalaawaa*,[31] seven types of vegetables, and one and a quarter rupees each for lighting lamps. The pious women prayed to the Bibi.[32] Each woman put henna on her little finger and wore a red stole over her head. They would all then sit on the dastarkhwan and eat *chuna*.[33] Their mouths did not get cut because they were virtuous women. They passed the test of virtuousness. Now they had the right to eat from the *Sehnak*.[34] And they performed this right with such finesse that the vessels were cleaned out in moments.

So the Sehnak has been eaten. All the women rubbed their teeth with missi, applied perfume, picked up a pair of bangles, received the money for lighting lamps, and took leave.

Actually offerings and supplications were very popular in the Fort. It was inevitable. The begums took vows frequently. They had great faith in the Sufis, *majzoobs* (those immersed in remembrance of God) and dervishes. They would retreat in mystic seclusion to shrines for 40 days, pray there and offer entreaties. This was not a new trend. The tradition had its roots in the past over many generations. Majida Qudsia Begum, mother of Muhammad Shah Rangiley, dearly wished that her son should ascend the throne as emperor. This was at the time when Muhammad Shah was still a toddler and was called Roshan Akhtar.

A ritual called Naurata has long been associated with the shrine of Hazrat Nizamuddin Aulia. The popular belief was that a man or woman supplicant who spent nine nights keeping vigil at the shrine would have his or her wish fulfilled. Qudsia Begum

---

30 *Missi* is a tooth powder made from varied ingredients such as clove, cinnamon, black pepper, salt, neem, camphor and even coal.

31 *Kalaawaa* is yarn dyed in red and yellow, and sacred in Hindu traditions.

32 *Bibi* is a respectful term of endearment for young women. Here it refers to Prophet Muhammad's daughter Fatima.

33 *Chuna* is limestone. Small quantities are eaten with the betel leaf (paan). Larger quantities can cut the flesh.

34 *Sehnak* is a dish prepared in supplication and distributed in the name of the Prophet's daughter Fatima.

vowed to carry out Naurata. A camp was established in the shrine courtyard and the Begum stayed there. Every night she sat by the doorstep of the Hazrat and spent the entire night awake. On the ninth night, Roshan Akhtar woke up muttering from his sleep in his mother's lap. 'Revered mother, I had a dream.'

'My dear life, I am all yours! What did you dream of?'

'I saw that at the doorstep of God's favourite, a sesame seed is lying. I picked up the sesame seed and ate it. It was very tasty and fragrant.'

'Congratulations dear, may you live long! Hazrat has bestowed upon you whatever is left of the sultanate of Hindustan—the size of a sesame seed.'

Mirza Jahangir was *noor-e-nazar*[35] of Emperor Akbar Shah, the second. Arrogant about his status as a royal prince he spoke rudely to a high-ranking British official. He was put under detention and then banished to Allahabad. His mother Mumtaz Mahal vowed to offer a floral canopy and a cover to the shrine of Khwaja Bakhtiar Kaki if her son were returned safely. And lo! Having been released, Mirza Jahangir indeed returned. Now Mumtaz Mahal fulfilled her vow and ordered a floral canopy to be made. The makers of the canopy made an addition of their own, a fan, and hung it by the canopy. A huge crowd gathered to share in the happiness. After the feasting was over, the emperor was pleased and declared that a fair be held every year in the month of Sawan. The fair gained popularity as *phoolwalon ki sair*[36] and became extremely popular.

---

[35] *Noor-e-nazar* is literally 'sight of the eye', a term of endearment for a son or a daughter.

[36] *Phoolwalon ki sair* is literally a 'stroll of the flower-sellers'. The festival was celebrated for the last time under Mughal patronage during the 1857 siege of Delhi by the British. The British continued patronising the syncretic festival until the 1942 Quit India Movement. Prime Minister Nehru deputed Yogeshwar Dayal, a Dilliwallah and doyen of the syncretic culture of the city to revive the festival. In 1962 the festival began to be celebrated once again under the tutelage of *Anjuman-e-Sair-e-gul-e-faroshan* (Organising Committee of the Stroll of the Flower-sellers) and has continued uninterrupted since then.

These Bibis also had strong faith in good and bad omens. According to them, once such a bad omen occurred which boded danger for the Sultanate. This took place at the time of the coronation of Bahadur Shah Zafar. Akbar Shah, the second passed away from this world at two o'clock in the night. Since Bahadur Shah Zafar was the heir apparent, he had been waiting for the emperor to breathe his last so that he could ascend the throne. No sooner had he heard about the emperor's death that he put on royal garments. The astrologers respectfully told him that it was not auspicious to have a coronation at night. But Bahadur Shah Zafar was too eager to become the emperor. He found a solution to this by ordering that lamps and candles be lit. It was in this light that he ascended the throne.

The astrologers' foreboding became well-known. Eventually the begums heard of it and began worrying. This was a bad omen. Innumerable apprehensions rose in their hearts. Within a year, when there was a famine and a crowd of the hungry looted the boats carrying cereal sacks, they felt their apprehensions had been borne out.

These women of the court also prayed and fasted a lot. Fasting was particularly prevalent among them. The ones who did not fast were pointed at and taunted by saying things like: 'eating fast, cheating God', 'paan in hand, worms in mouth', 'on the fast eaters such ruin befell, their shoes are torn and tattered quilts!'

Whether they cooked or not during the rest of the year, during Ramzan the begums and princesses prepared food with much enthusiasm. Right after noon they would sit next to the ovens and bake all kinds of breads. Pots and pans would be set up on earthen stoves, and dishes would be prepared for breaking the fast.

But while praying, fasting, offerings and supplication had their place, fun, play, laughter and jest had their own. The bibi who sat looking so serious and authoritative during the Sehnak, one has to go and have a look at her in the women's garden. Look at them leap, or dive into the pool. While jesting with each other they are not conscious that the smaller parts of their dresses are proving too small; they are unconscious that their bodices are coming apart at the seams. Every princess seems to be bursting out of her outfit.[37]

Anyway, some order is in effect here also. They look greedily at the trees laden with fruit but none dare touch it. They await the gesture of the Emperor. The moment he gestures (to allow them), they tumble up the trees. The groups of princesses raiding the trees seem to be worse than locust swarms destroying standing crops.

Night falls, the moonlight glows. The activities of the princesses intensify along with the moonlight. The game of hide and seek begins. This game is the favourite of the princesses. Here hide and seek is being played and there a group rides small boats in the reservoir. Everyone is dressed in red. Their earrings are wreathed in *bela* and *motia*.[38] In the small boats, bathed in moonlight, are these princesses or fairies?

All other pleasures have their own place and the *huqqa* [39] and *gilauri* [40] had their own place too. These were an important part of female culture in the Red Fort. In any case there wasn't just one kind of gilauri. Numerous were the types of betel leaves: Samosa Gilauri, *Luqmi*[41] Gilauri, *Taawizi*[42] Gilauri. And there was a type superior to gilauris: 'beera'. A woman singer was so fond of gilauri that she began to be referred to as *Terhmuhi Khanam.*[43] She always had a gilauri in the side of her mouth, making one cheek appear a bit swollen which gave the impression of the mouth being crooked. Once the Red Fort residents started calling her Terhmuhi Khanam everyone followed.

---

[37] *Jama se bahar hona* literally means 'to be not contained by outfit'.

[38] *Bela* and *Motia* are kinds of jasmine.

[39] *Huqqa* is an instrument used for smoking tobacco, wherein the smoke/ vapour passes through water before inhalation. Hubble.

[40] *Gilauri* is a rolled-up betel-leaf seasoned with different ingredients.

[41] *Luqma* means morsel.

[42] *Taawizi* means amulet.

[43] *Terhmuhi Khanam* is literally Madam with a crooked mouth. (Terha literally means crooked and Munh is mouth or face).

This feminine culture had its own etiquettes, manners and tones. And the language—it was the same as that of Dilli. But in the Qila-e-Mualla it got wings of politeness and became Urdu-e-Mualla. Munshi Faizuddin was brought up in the fort and there he became an adult. Hear from him how these bibis used to speak.

> O Gul Bahar, Nau Bahar, Sabza Bahar, Champa, Chameli, Gul Chaman, Nargis, Maan Kanwar, Anand Kanwar, Chanchal Kanwar, Mubarak Qadam, Nek Qadam! Where have you flown. See, they are frolicking about, jesting in the garden. Wait the cunning strumpet, witch, whore, prostitute, dupe, disgraced! So out of control! No shame in eyes! Everything has been put into the drawstrings and worn! No attention is paid to work! Always on their feet! Never rest on the ground like a cat with burnt feet. They keep gathering all the cobwebs of the garden.[44] I am drinking gulps of blood.[45] See how I will straighten you with a plank. Aunt, you keep rolling your eyes. Cry at the slightest of excuses. What was so extraordinary, strange, life of Adam, liver of Nemat's mother, urine of eagle, rare about it that you wept so bitterly? She is your younger sister, what if she took it away from you? Come here, I will buy you another. Well, let me see that mischief-maker. She has been overcome by the devil. She has kicked up a row, turning her blood into water. She cannot be amused by the mention of any topic. O so and so porter, go and bring this for the Madam. Begum Sahib, I just went looking for it. It is not available at any shop. How come the materials have disappeared from the market? This bastard piece of flesh, illegitimate, good for nothing, glutton. You sit here only like a wet cat and evade working. Have you got these thick wretched, ruined cucumbers for swallowing and stuffing yourself? You only gobble it. While eating you say 'in the name of Allah', when asked to work you recite 'I seek refuge from Allah'. This is the

---

[44] *Jaaley lena* is an idiom that means 'going where no one goes'.

[45] *Lahoo ke ghoontpina* is an idiom that means 'to have extreme patience in the face of extreme suffering'.

effect of our salt; not their fault. Well, don't be upset, patch up now. Spit out the anger. Stop fussing so much. I do not like such flattery. It is good to fight or hold on to enmity with each other. The breads baked on one *tawa* [46] are the same, doesn't matter if they are small or big. To me both the eyes are equal. Would you take this with you to the Paradise? Who is she to show me Hell? Well, if you don't cool down, let it be. I keep that on the point of my shoes. If you sulk, we'd get away from you.

That was the routine talk of Dilli's women. The begums of the Red Fort do not seem to have set any diamonds or pearls in it? The only difference is that once some of the city girls had come to the Red Fort in a ceremony. While talking to each other they repeatedly used *tu*.[47] A little princess was also present in the gathering. She explained to them that *tu* should not be used. It is rude. That they should address each other using *tum*.[48] But the girls continued as if they had not heard her and kept addressing each other as *tu*. The young princess found it very unpleasant. She said to Dadda,[49] 'Dadda, please take me away from here. I cannot bear to hear this *tu*-calling.'

So, the language of Dilli and that of the Red Fort had only the difference of *tu* and *tum*. Such was the difference between the culture of Dilli and the Red Fort. For the rest, all was bread baked on the same tawa—no real difference between the small and big rotis.

---

[46] *Tawa* is a iron hot plate to cook flat bread.

[47] *Tu* is literally 'you', but used when addressing someone who is very close or inferior.

[48] *Tum* is a more formal and respectful word for 'you'. *Aap* is the word for 'you' in Urdu that is even more formal and reverential.

[49] *Dadda* means elderly nanny.

8

The Streets and Markets

The Red Fort stood glorious in those days and was called Qila-e-Mualla. Come down from the Red Fort and have a look outside. What a city has settled all around it! It takes time for a city to be settled and Jahanabad took six years. But the city had begun to take shape with the very first building, Matia Mahal. And it is of great significance that the Red Fort was constructed later. First Matia Mahal was constructed. You can imagine Jahanabad to be a blend of the Red Fort and Matia Mahal. This blend can be seen everywhere and at every level—at the level of culture, at the level of living standards, and at the level of the streets and markets. In fact, the thing about markets was that there was a surge of people there, shoulders rubbing against each other. Shopkeepers and grocers, astrologers and fortune-tellers, vendors, water carriers, artisans, acrobats—everyone was engaged in their trade. But somewhere in the background the Red Fort is visible. Why in the background, the big bustling markets with large crowds were a gift of the Red Fort itself. Chandni Chowk, Saadullah Khan Chowk, Faiz Bazaar, Khaas Bazaar, Bazaar of Khanam, Urdu Bazaar these were the big bazaars which owed their existence to the favours of princes, princesses, the nobility and the ministers of the Red Fort.

What an excellent market Chandni Chowk was! What did the poet see in it that he immediately became its fan?

Dil mera jalwa-e-aariz ne behelne na diya
Chandni Chowk se zakhmi ko nikalney na diya

My heart was not allowed to be pacified by the sight that presented itself
It did not let the wounded come out of Chandni Chowk

Just have a look at the layout of this market. Right in its middle a canal flows, on both sides dense and shady trees of mango, jamun,[1] goolar,[2] moulsari,[3] neem,[4] peepul and banyan. Under their shade different kinds of carriages travel—*palkis*,[5] *nalkis*[6] and chariots. These had their own splendour. Golden sheaths were moulded to the horns of the bullocks drawing the carriages. The brass rings in their necks ringing. On and off, on that path a royal ride passes by. How grand the royal elephants are, with golden litters on their shoulders, bags of brocade and banaat hanging on the sides. Rows of shops on both sides of the central passage are filled with materials, and shoppers do business in figures of thousands. In front of the shops, colourful curtains tied to bamboo sway gently. There is colour everywhere. The entire market is painted with colours and fragrant as if nestling in flowerbeds. The flower-seller roams around carrying baskets full of flowers. The water-carriers wearing *lungis*[7] of *kharwa*[8]

---

[1] Jamun is a large flowering tree that has a berry-like deep purple fleshy fruit.

[2] Goolar is the Indian fig.

[3] Moulsari is a medium-sized tree with dense foliage and fragrant flowers.

[4] Neem or margosa.

[5] *Palki* is a kind of palanquin with an enclosed chair that can carry one person.

[6] *Nalki* is an open but roofed palanquin which was used by more well-to do people or grooms, putting their finery on display. Whereas, a Doli was an enclosed palanquin used by the middle class for women or the elderly.

[7] A *lungi* is a sheet or length of cloth worn like a skirt, tied at the waist with a knot, by men in Asia.

[8] *Kharwa* or coarse red cotton.

carry waterskins[9] on their shoulders, clank bowls and run about. They repeatedly call out, 'Sire, may I give you a drink of elixir?'

The shoppers buy at a pace such that bargains worth thousands are made in no time. Every buyer is a man worth thousands. A pampered son makes a request to his beloved mother, 'Mother dear, today I intend to go to Chandni Chowk.' Mother takes out one lakh rupees from the cash-box and hands it over to him saying, 'Son, may you keep going to Chandni Chowk for aeons! For one lakh you cannot get any article worthy of mention. But my hand is a bit constrained. For the time being this is it.'

Come out of Chandni Chowk. Go towards Faiz Bazaar. The sight here too is equally soothing. A canal in the middle. Green, lush trees on both its banks. Shops on both sides, filled with all and every kind of materials. Some were of the opinion that this was a market superior to Chandni Chowk because foreign products were sold here. Indeed, products imported from Iraq, Khorasan and even European cities were sold here.

At the Khaas Bazaar the abundance of aesthetically planted trees made it seem more like a garden and less a market.

Come to Chowk Saadullah Khan. But who was Saadullah? His full name was Mulla Saadullah. He was from Lahore. He did so well in royal service that he became the Prime Minister. The Shahjahani Masjid was constructed under his supervision. Along with the mosque, he also established a market. What a wonderful market it was; amidst the shops, here and there, pulpits could be seen. On one side a bargain was struck, and on the other a sermon delivered. Annually, each at their appointed time, the banners of Ghazi Mian and Madar Sahab were also raised.[10]

---

[9] Waterskins (*Mashak* in Urdu) are goatskin bags with only one opening used to carry water by the 'Bhishti' whose occupation was to carry and offer water for drinking or watering plants, etc. The word Bhishti is derived from 'Behisht' which is Persian for heaven.

[10] *Chhariyan* were public processions comprising red and green flags/banners that were held in the honour of revered North-Indian saints: Shah Madar (b.

The craft of textiles was a particularly flourishing one in Jahanabad. Therefore, in all these bazaars the shopkeepers selling cloth were the busiest ones. The cloth was exquisite and fine, each bale better than the other.

A kind of person was commonly seen in all the markets. People were fond of them. These were the astrologers and fortune-tellers. At every street corner some astrologer or fortune-teller would be found sitting on his spread. A crowd of people, especially women shrouded in burqas, would gather around them. Then there are *qehwa*[11] houses which were tumultuous with poetry.

But all the markets, streets and chowks pale in comparison with the Jama Masjid Chowk. What a magnificent mosque was built by Shah Jahan! It has now become the heart of Dilli; a heart where religion and culture may be seen coming together in an embrace. This was the central place of worship of the city as well as its cultural centre. Inside there are rows of people praying, bowing and prostrating. And outside on the steps egg-fights[12] are being

---

15th century) and Ghazi Miyan (b. 11th century). The procession (called 'Barat' or wedding procession) used to be received by the Mughal emperor with *malidah*, a sweet preparation, and *pharaira*, a cloth embroidered with gold and adorned with silver *katora*, or cups. While the Malidah was distributed among the people, the pharaira were later offered at the shrines of the two saints in Makanpur, near Kanpur, and Bahraich respectively. Celebrated even today, the processions contain many syncretic rituals observed by both Hindu and Muslim devotees. The veneration of the warrior-saint Ghazi Miyan (who ironically is said to have been the nephew of Mahmud Ghazni) is especially considered by some scholars as an Islamisation of the Hindu cult of marriage. (*See Conquest and Community: The Afterlife of Warrior Saint Ghazi Miyan* by Shahid Amin (1980, Orient Blackswan)

[11] *Qehwa* is a preparation of tea, popular in Kashmir and other areas of Central Asia.

[12] The author uses *andey ladana* in Urdu. This sport was also called Beza Bazi (Beza is Arabic for egg). The players would come with eggs, of specially bred hens, which had hard shells and more sharply pointed ends. The eggs were made to collide and the owner of the egg which would not break in the collision would win the fight.

organised. The *Dastan-e-Amir Hamza*[13] is being narrated. Pigeon-breeders and those fond of red titmouse sell their favourite birds. The foodies enjoy haleem and kababs. A variety of entertainments on the many steps. The steps are shared by them all.

The mosque has three gates and accordingly three staircases. In front of them those days, there were three markets. The southern gate opened to the Chitli Qabar Market. On this side there are 33 steps. At sunset these steps started teeming with activity. On one step peddlers have spread their fare, on another step a flummery seller is selling flummery drinks. The kabab sellers are roasting kababs on the skewer. Another step forward and cock sellers are crowing like pure breed cocks even as they display different kinds of birds to lure bird enthusiasts. Turn your attention away from them and you can see on the next steps boys getting into egg-fights.

Now, come to the Northern Gate. This gate opens to the Payewalon ka Bazaar. This side has 39 steps. Kabab sellers can be seen sitting here, too. But the real occupants of these steps were the jugglers and storytellers. The sun has started setting. And lo, a storyteller appears. He starts reciting the Dastan-e-Amir Hamza. A crowd begins to gather around him. At some distance, another storyteller has begun the story of Hatim Tai. A few steps down from there and you will find another storyteller narrating the story of Bostan-e-Khayal. Every storyteller has gathered a huge crowd around him. But besides storytelling other things are also happening here. On a step a juggler performs in the middle of a large crowd. He is performing a show of Bhanmati[14]—turning the old into young and the young, old.

---

[13] *Dastan-e-Amir Hamza* refers to the Epic of Amir Hamza. It is a series of intertwined fantasy stories (oral and written) on the adventures of Prophet Muhammad's uncle, Amir Hamza. The recitation of the stories originated in Persia but spread to other parts of central and south Asia, including India, where the epic was recited in many other languages apart from Urdu.

[14] Bhanmati or Bhanumati, was Duryodhana's wife in the Mahabharata. It is said that she had a magic box or *Bhanumati ka pitara* from which she could pull out things that had magical powers.

Now come to the eastern gate. It opens to the Khaas Bazaar. In front of this gate there are 35 steps. These steps were famous for their evening market. And Muhammad Shah paid great homage to it.

Piri mein kis tarah na karun sair jahan ki
Din dhaltey hi hota hai tamasha guzri ka

How can I stop perambulating the world in old age
The show of the evening market begins with the sunset

No sooner than the sun has set that the evening market begins to burgeon on the steps of the mosque. If you want to see the spring of colours, go to the streets and see it in the evening market. The drapers are selling colourful cloth, the bales separated, swinging on clothes-lines. Nearby, the connoisseurs of birds are carrying colourful birds in cages. What attractive colours and sweet voices they have! From pigeons to titmouse, and from titmouse to horses, you may buy here any animal of your choice.

Upon these very steps some preachers may be seen giving sermons. A quack may be seen selling medicines. And yes, those fond of poetry, too, will be here in their gatherings. And these are the same steps which Sarmad had made his dwelling. Khaliq Ahmad Nizami narrates that one evening Sarkhosh, Nasir Sarhindi and Bedil were reading poetry. From somewhere Sarmad happened to pass by. The crazed person came to a sudden stop when he saw them engaging in poetry. And then he recited the following couplet:

Der ast ke afsana-e-Manzoor Kahun shud
Aknu sar nau-e-jalwa wa-hamdar-o-rasan ra

It has been a long time since the story of Mansoor became old,
Now I present my head for the trial of detention and hanging.

And then he went on his way.

And yes, Mir used the language and dialect spoken on these very steps.

Now, just have a look at the backyard of the mosque—shops of pulses and cereals. Further, from these shops, Chawri Bazaar. What a market it is! Sire, here hearts are being traded. Let us just say that this market is the market of beauty.

Chawri qaaf hai ya khuld barein hai Raasikh [15]
Jhamgatey hooron ke pariyon ke pirey rehtey hein

Raasikh, what is Chawri, a Caucasus or the Heaven above?
Here keep assembling crowds of *hoors* [16] and fairies.

Evening has fallen and with it the crowd has been increasing at Chawri. The flaneurs of Dilli have emerged all foppish and dandy, and are walking in long stylish steps. Hey, where are you headed? Where else except towards the street of the slayer, Chawri? Stepping foot in Chawri, they see friends wandering aimlessly. Tilted cap on the head, dipped in perfume, garlands of jasmine flowers wrapped around the neck or wrists, their feet on the ground, but eyes fixed on the belvedere. The water-carriers dressed in lungis of coarse red cotton are active. And more active are the hookah-carriers.

Those markets were built by the begums of the Fort and the princes. But which inventor of cruelties instituted this market?

In these markets a creature has its permanent presence and a voice can always be heard. Girdle of red coarse cotton around the waist, water-skin on shoulders, metallic bowl in hand, the bowls between the fingers continuously creating a sound which is repeatedly heard. 'Sire, shall I give you a drink of elixir?' This is the *saqqa* [17] who is always on his feet. Filling bowls to give drink of water to the thirsty.

But this was just one sound. In those markets many more voices would be heard. The fingers of Laila and the ribs of Majnoo,

---

[15] Raasikh Azimabadi (1729-1823) is the poet of this couplet. His family was from Dilli but he was born and lived in Azimabad (today's Patna).

[16] *Hoors* or heavenly nymphs.

[17] *Saqqa* refers to a water-carrier.

bet the cucumbers are sweet and soft; buy *khirnis* [18] from the Qutub folk. Buy khirnis of the fall! Purple-purple faalsey, make sharbat with them! Black beetle jamun! The shopkeepers would sit at their fixed places, but there were also sellers who walked along selling their products. Each seller would announce their wares and the announcements were no ordinary announcements; vendors would become quite poetic in praising their wares. These were the vendors. Compared to the markets they peddled more in the streets and could be seen loudly advertising their wares. These vendors would begin going around in the streets and alleys as soon as a city got settled. They did not do it by themselves; indeed they were required to do so by the decree of the king. While building the city, Emperor Shah Jahan realised that Bazaar Barhaq, Faiz Bazaar, Chowk Saadullah, and Chandni Chowk are all splendid markets in their own right. But would the people living in the streets and alleys keep standing all the time in the markets? And the housewives of the city were veiled women. How would their needs be fulfilled? Thus, a royal decree was made that arrangements be made for selling all types of wares such that the women living in houses in the streets and alleys would make purchases without having to cross their thresholds. The vendors ventured out, peddlers set up their businesses, and reached every neighbourhood compound and began calling out.

In this atmosphere, a Mughal businessman arrived in Dilli from Kashmir with apples. Although the long journey had spoiled the apples, the businessman was keen to somehow offload them. He happened to hear the vendors making their loud calls and was struck with an idea. He sliced pieces of those apples which were not entirely spoilt, and arranged them in a tray. With this tray, he sat on a sidewalk in Chandni Chowk and began calling out.

Mun qaash farosh-e-dil sad para-e-khawish aam

---

[18] *Khirni* is a berry-like fruit which tastes a little like raw dates but sweeter. The trees fruit for a very brief period during the peak of summer.

I am selling my heart that I have sliced into a hundred pieces

No sooner had the words left his lips, they became famous among the residents. His words left Chandni Chowk to reach the Red Fort in a strange manner. Shah Jahan had composed a line:

Lakht-e-bard az dil guzard har ke za pesham

Whosoever follows me wins a piece of my heart

A gentleman of the court who had interest in poetry told the king about the words of the businessman and completed the couplet:

Lakht-e-bard az dil guzard har ke za pesham
Mun qaash farosh-e-dil sad para-e-khawisham

Whosoever follows me wins a piece of my heart
I am myself selling my heart sliced in a hundred pieces

Shah Jahan became so happy that he called the Mughal businessman to the court and gave him riches.

Anyway that was the age of Shah Jahan. Persian was still in use at court. But in the streets and the markets it was the era of Taksali Urdu. The vendors were now fluent in this language. How interesting that the vendor did not name the wares he was selling but instead conjured in his mind a simile and then called out with such pride that the listeners, young and old, understood exactly what he was selling and leapt in his direction. The vendor would say, 'crystal bits' and people would guess that pieces of ice were being sold. He would say, 'jugs of cream', and the foodies would lick their lips imagining *qulfi*.[19] The vendor would say, '*pedey*[20] from Allahabad' and people would know that guavas were being praised.

---

[19] *Qulfi* or kulfi, sweet frozen thickened milk.

[20] *Pedey* is plural for peda (literally a ball of dough), also the name of a sweet made from soft but thick condensed milk.

Then there were vendors who would use metaphors and similes but would also gave away the names of their wares.

Nirmal talao ke doodhiya
Kapoodey ki bel ke bataasey
Kaanton se hariyaale
Shah ji ke talao ke
Doodhiya singhadey le lo

Milky-white from a gentle pond,
Sugar drops on a vine
Their thorns fresh
From the pond of Shahji,
Buy milky-white water chestnuts.

Bin kadahi ka halwa shakarqandi

Sweet potato halwa made without frying

Balushahi,[21] juicy pieces of sugarcane dabbed with *keoda.*[22] But the watermelon vendor seems to have sworn not to name his product:

Laal ka dala, laal ka dala
Laalon mein aaja chhilkon samet
Qand ke dale hein, rangat ke ghade hein

Lump of ruby, lump of ruby
To the beloved children bring these with the skins,
These are lumps of sweet tubers, these are pots of colour

---

[21] *Baalushahi* is a disc-shaped sweet made from flour and clarified butter with a crumbling sand-like (baalu) consistency.

[22] *Keoda* is a fragrant flower whose essence is used while preparing meat and sweet dishes.

A voice can be heard coming from far: 'purple-purple with green umbrellas, reared by *dhekli*'.[23] It was found that this was in praise of the brinjal.

Red turban on head, a large serving tray in hand, arranged on the tray are gilauris wrapped in thin silver foil. Standing at the Chowk the vendor keeps calling out:

Kundan ko sharmaati hai
Joban ko chamkaati hai
Achhey munh ko suhati hai
Gori jab chabaati hai
Honton aag barsaati hai
Le lo gori ke liye gilauri

It makes pure gold shy away,
Make youth gleam
It looks fitting on a handsome face
When the fair one chews it,
fire rains from her lips,
buy gilauri for the gori

Dildaar ki ek shaan hai
Ye paan uski jaan hai
Aur jaan bhi ek paan hai
Le lo merey paan ki gilauri

It is the opulence of the beloved,
The betel leaf is his life,
And the beloved is also a betel leaf,
Buy my betel leaf gilauri

[23] *Dhekli* is a kind of manual irrigation.

Bada-bada paan hai
Laal-laal shaan hai
Badakhshan ki dukaan hai
Ye paan hai, ye paan hai

The betel leaves are big,
Red is the mark of privilege
This is a shop of Badakhshan,
This is betel leaf, this is betel leaf

These voices held strange magic. As the vendor arrived in the streets children came out and gathered around them. Their calls made the vendors a success. Dilliwallahs were generous to begin with. And then they were fond of shopping. Though the house had every kind of fruit in it, they still would not turn away the vendors empty-handed. As it is, prices were low. Things used to be sold for the price of cowries. Wheat, a rupee for a *mun*.[24] Ghee, *four aanaa*[25] for a ser. Gur and sugar, a *taka* for a ser. Give two paise to the *naanbai*[26] and take *paraantha*[27] dripping in ghee and a full bowl of spicy meat curry. The vendors did not stop at selling only eatables but brought all kinds of supplies with them. Without crossing the thresholds of their houses, standing behind the doors, the women observing purdah could buy entire dowries for their daughters. Indeed, it was for the convenience of these ladies that Shah Jahan had decreed the practice of vending in the streets and alleys of the city.

And these streets, these alleys, these houses, what were they like? What was the way of the noblewomen and noblemen residing

---

[24] *Mun* or *Man* or *Maund* is a measure of weight. One mun is equivalent to 37.324 kg.

[25] *Aanaa* is a unit of money. Sixteen aanaas made a rupee. Even when this aanaa system was discontinued in favour of paise, a 25-paise coin (a quarter rupee) continued to be popularly called four aanaa.

[26] *Naanbai* or a bread chef.

[27] *Paraantha* is a shallow-fried flat bread.

in those houses? Streets, lanes and mansions, some were associated with the names of the rich and the noble, some were famous for their association with occupational groups like Mohalla[28] Churi Giran,[29] Kucha[30] Charkhey[31] wala, Kucha Batashey[32] wala, Muhalla Dholi wada, Kucha Qabil[33] Attaar,[34] Kucha Ghasi Ram, Kucha peepal Mahadeo, Reodi[35] walon ka katra[36] (Sweet Cracker Sellers' Compound), Bazaazon ka katra, (Drapers' Compound), Kucha Bulaaqi[37] Begum, Chhatta[38] Shahji. And what a variety of mansions were built—Mansion of Bakhshi Bhawani Shankar, Mansion of Hakim Miyan Jaan, Mansion of Sher Afghan Khan, Mansion of Aazam Khan, Mansion of Sada Sukh Pundit.

The houses on a street were such that each jostled with the other for attention. The roof of one house was joined with that of another. The roof of the second house was joined with the third. Ruffian boys looting kites found this most convenient. The moment a kite snapped these boys made a note of where it was headed and then began running on the terraces. From one terrace to the second, from second to the third, where could the kite escape? The window of one house opened into the window of the second house, and the second into the third, which made it easy for the women observing purdah to take a round till the end of the street if they liked. Thus, they walked about the entire mohalla while also observing purdah.

---

[28] *Mohalla* means neighbourhood.

[29] *Churi Giran* were bangle sellers.

[30] *Kucha* means street.

[31] *Charkha* is a spinning wheel.

[32] *Batashey* are puffed sugar candy.

[33] *Qabil* means talented.

[34] *Attaar* was the perfume maker.

[35] *Reodi* is a crunchy sweet made of jaggery and sesame seeds.

[36] *Katra* is a closed-gated compound of houses, all facing a square open space.

[37] *Bulaaq* is a nose ring.

[38] *Chhatta* is a covered compound/lane.

And how were these houses? High gates. Very thick nails fixed in their doors. On both sides of the threshold there were two stone seats. Inside the gate a small foyer, past the foyer a large courtyard with earthen floor, a water reservoir in the middle of the courtyard, in it a fountain, and arranged all around it pots of flowering plants, and then, two and half, or three trees—a pomegranate, a *karaunda.*[39] If the mansion belonged to a Hindu then the courtyard would also include a sweet basil plant. Step forward from here—there was a long arched passageway, inside it another portico. Thick curtains were hung upon the arches of the portico which protect the house from the cold in winter and from the sun on summer afternoons. On the sides of the portico were two-sided upper storeys and small rooms. Right next to the reservoir, basements and rooms were covered with scented Khus grass. On summer afternoons curtains made of khus are hung in the house, and water was sprinkled on them. Within the room there was an arrangement for *farshi*[40] fans. The air of the fan, the fragrance of the sweet-scented grass, and the coolness—the image that is conjured from this description is the map of the mansion. The mansions were so huge that after the 1857 apocalypse when they were demolished, entire neighbourhoods got settled in their place. If you shrink this map a little, it will be the house of a middle-class nobleman. In the same way that the mansion is trying to become the Red Fort, the houses of the nobles are copying the mansions.

In every mansion and every house of a reasonable size there were men's and women's quarters. A *Diwan Khana*[41] was essential to the men's quarters. Each Diwan Khana reflected the means of its household. Those people whose means did not allow them to have a Diwan Khana would make do by utilising their foyer as one.

---

[39] *Karaunda* is a small flowering tree with small berry-like fruits which are pink when ripe and very sour. They are used for pickling.

[40] *Farshi* or moveable fan.

[41] *Diwan Khana* is a drawing room or parlour.

Leave alone the women's quarters in the palaces and mansions, even the women's quarters in well-to-do homes epitomised a world unto itself. Pious women would rarely step outside it except on the occasion of wedding ceremonies. And for such occasions *doli* [42] were used. But there were also women who never set foot outside the foyer of their houses until they died. They came sitting in a doli and when they ventured it was only after they had spent an entire lifetime in the house, leaving it only in a coffin.

Now imagine the houses where the women's quarters were small and the men's quarters were also small. So small that in the evening the owner of the house had waterskins sprinkle water outside the door in the street, laid out *mooda* [43] stools, and put a hookah right there in the middle of the street. A florist went past shouting, 'These are bowls of Gujarati motia. Take flowers of jasmine, beaded necklace of the cute girl.' A gajra[44] would be bought from the florist and wrapped around the pipe of the hookah. Lo! the gathering is now fragrant. The pipe of the hookah is doing rounds and with its gurgling sound the gathering is warming up.

[42] *Doli* is a sedan chair.

[43] *Mooda* is a stool woven with thatch and thin rope.

[44] *Gajra* is a small garland of flowers, worn as a bracelet or in hair.

9

Rituals and Songs Abound

Separate quarters for women and men in houses meant that social life in Jahanabad was divided into two compartments. The two domains were separate. Male pride lay in eating in the women's quarters and rinsing one's mouth in the men's quarters. While the rules of feminine shyness dictated that even the sound of a good woman clearing her throat should not be heard in the men's quarters. Even at a time when there was no possibility of unknown men being present in the men's quarters, the women of the house would not take a step in that direction. It was only if a poetic or some such gathering was arranged that they could peep through the gaps of the *chik.*[1]

The *diwan khana* [2] was the pride of the men's quarters. What a fine layout a diwan khana had! Divine words or inscriptions were displayed on the walls randomly; one or two shields and swords were hung on the wall along with sketches of the elders of the clan. Chandeliers adorned the ceilings. There would be a mat on the floor, which would be covered by a snow-white *chandni.*[3] On

---

[1] *Chik* are curtains made by tying, tubular pieces of thin bamboo together.

[2] The *Diwan Khana* was a room where guests were entertained in the house of a prominent person. These were almost like public spaces or institutions that depended on (and contributed to) the reputation of the host.

[3] *Chandni*, literally, 'moonlight'. Here however, they refer to spotless white sheets spread on the floor for everyone to sit on during a gathering.

its right and left there would be Iranian carpets. Round cushions rested against walls. In the middle, spiralling hubbles were kept randomly. A few spittoons were also kept here and there. A round tray decorated with *gilauri*[4] covered in delicate silver foil would be rotated from one person to another. So too plates of cardamom and crystallised sugar lumps. These were animated gatherings. Sometimes there would be poetry recitations, at other times, proper *mushairas*;[5] sometimes *dastangoi*[6] would be arranged, at other times, music or dance performances. If not all this, then one could see a game of chess being laid out. If not chess, then *chausar*.[7] *Ganjefa*[8] if not chausar. The hubble pipe would be passed from one elder to another.

Now we move to the women's quarters. This world was colourful. The liveliness in the household depended on creating a furore. At times it was the dirge of sad occasions and at others it was a wedding song. Celebrations and grief go hand in hand throughout human life. But the women of Jahanabad transformed celebrations and mourning into something else with their rituals and songs. All the celebrations and dirges were accompanied by a string of rituals.

When celebratory events are being described one must not forget a character called the *domni*.[9] She would be seen at the forefront at celebratory events. The moment a bride sat for

---

[4] *Gilauri* refers to a little bundle created when several ingredients including tobacco are wrapped stylishly in a betel leaf (*paan*). It was considered fashionable and refined to eat gilauris which would stain the mouth and lips red.

[5] *Mushaira* is a gathering of poets (*shaair*) and the audience where each poet recites his or her poetry to robustly expressed praise from the listeners.

[6] *Dastangoi*, literally, 'storytelling'.

[7] *Chausar* or *Chaupar* is a board game played with three long dice.

[8] *Ganjefa* was a card game popular in those times.

[9] *Domni* refers to a woman from the Dom community. Considered 'untouchable' in the caste system, historically their caste occupation was to dispose of dead animals or work on cremation grounds. Later, the term came to refer to diverse occupational groups, prominent among which were music and other performing arts.

maanyun[10] the domnis would place a drum in their midst and start singing.

Naajori ghoonghat khol
Ghoonghat mein terey chandar basat hein
Laal lagey anmol
Naajori ghoonghat khol

O anxious one, lift your veil
your beloved, the moon resides in the veil
studded with red coral
O anxious one, lift your veil

This was called the *Suhag ghori*. Then there was the *sehra*[11] which the domnis would sing after the *nikah* before taking their reward.

Hariyaley hamarey banne ke liye sehra goondh la mori maalaniya
Beley chameli ki kaliyan sehra goondh la mori maalaniya

Make a sehra of flowers for our young groom, O my dear flower seller!
Make a sehra of buds of jasmine, O my dear flower seller!

One custom, second custom, third custom! There is no sign of the rituals coming to an end! And there is a special song associated with each custom. The domnis enjoying themselves. They never stop singing. Considered the climax of the celebrations, the *Mandha*[12], as it is known in Dilli parlance, is sung at the time when the bride leaves her natal home.

---

[10] *Maanyun* is a practice of separating a bride-to-be from the household and its chores a few days prior to the wedding. Confined to a room or a corner in the house she is given a ritual massage with pastes of turmeric and sandal in preparation of the wedding.

[11] *Sehra* is headgear for a groom (or bride) that has a veil of garlands of flowers covering the face. Also, a rhyming poem read out at weddings at the time of nikah blessing especially the groom but also the union in marriage.

[12] The word *Mandha* is a corrupted form of *Mandhap* or *Mandap*, which is a canopy under which the most important rituals of Hindu marriages are performed.

Harey-harey baans kata morey babul
Neeka mandha chhawaao rey
Dehliyaan parbat bhaein
Babul angna bhaya bides rey
Le babul apna ghar
Ham chaley piya ke des rey

Get green bamboos cut, my father
Get a nice canopy made of them
The doorstep has become steep as a mountain
The courtyard of my natal house is now foreign
O father now keep your house
I am off to my beloved's home

So the bride is now sitting in the palanquin. Fistfuls of two and four aanaa coins as well as flowers made of silver are being showered upon the palanquins. A new stream of rituals will begin when the palanquin alights at the doorstep of the groom; new songs will then be sung.

Banne dekh teri banni hai suhaag bhari
Taaron bhini raat rey, rahiyo jaise chandar ki kiran khari

Groom, see your bride is full of conjugal bliss
It is a star-lit night, keep standing as the moonbeam does

The wedding is over. Everything has gone off well. But the string of rituals will still not stop. And lo! Now the bride[13] is expecting. There is a tumult of congratulations and blessings. And then the rituals begin. At the beginning of the seventh month, the girl's family dash to bring a *sadhauda.* Sadhauda means seven things—seven vegetables, dry fruits, and delicacies. The name indicates that this ritual reached Muslim households from Hindu households. As the ninth month starts, the bride's natal family is all aquiver

[13] The daughters-in-law would endearingly be addressed as *dulhan* (bride) for years, especially by the elders and the servants in the family.

with anticipation as they bring the *naumaasa*.[14] This includes a set of clothes for the bride, a comb, tooth powder, perfume, flowers, a silver mirror, a silver bowl for keeping oil and a red stole. It also included seven kinds of dry fruit, gifts for the sisters, and money for *panjiri*.[15]

Naumasa is over. The time of childbirth is imminent. The child is born accompanied by wishes, prayers and supplications. The sisters of the groom begin singing.

Biran bhaiya mein teri maa jaai
Holar sun ke badhawa le kar aai
Chhati dhulai kaudi loongi to lat dhulai rupiya
Paanv dhulan ko chiri loongi to khasam chadhan ko ghoda

Dear brother, I too am born of your mother
came with congratulatory gifts when I heard the bother
to wash the bosom I'll take a cawry, and to wash tresses, a rupee
I'll take your turban to wash my feet, and your horse for my husband to ride

From now till the sixth day of the birth there will be continuous vigil around the new mother. Black seeds will be thrown into the hearth so that the new mother is protected from the evil spirits and the newborn from the evil eye. The birth attendants sing all this while.

Aaj janam liya mere raaj dulaarey ne paalna banaungi
Ghee khichri babul jab rang sughad
jachcha ko mein tarey dikhaungi
Ri paalna banaungi

My prince is born today; I will make for him a cot

[14] *Naumaasa* or of the ninth (nau) month (maasa).

[15] *Panjiri* is a sweet crumble made of wheat flour or semolina and dry fruit especially for expectant and new mothers.

Give ghee and *khichri*[16] father;
I'll show stars to the midwife, such a pleasant complexion he has got
Listen, I'll make for him a cot

Once childbirth is over, the attendants start singing another song,

Albele ne mujhe dard diya
Saanwaliya ne mujhe dard diya
Paayaliya ne mujhe dard diya
Jaye kaho ladke ke bawa se unchi naubat dharwao re
Albele ne mujhe dard diya payaliya ne mujhe dard diya
Jaye kaho ladke ke nana se rang bhari khachri laao re
Albele ne mujhe dard diya payaliya ne mujhe dard diya
Jaye kaho ladke ke maamu se hasli kadey gharao re
Albele ne mujhe dard diya payaliya ne mujhe dard diya
Jaye kaho ladke ki khala se kurtey topi laao re
Albele ne mujhe dard diya payaliya ne mujhe dard diya
Jaye kaho ladke ke bawa se bhand nachwaao re
Albele ne mujhe dard diya payaliya ne mujhe dard diya
Albele ne...

The dandy gave me pain
The dark handsome one gave me pain
The anklet gave me pain too
Someone go tell the father of the boy to get a drum placed high
The dandy gave me pain, the anklet gave me pain
Someone go tell the grandfather of the boy to get a colourful cart
The dandy gave me pain, the anklet gave me pain
Someone go tell the uncle of the boy to get a necklace and bracelet made
The dandy gave me pain, the anklet gave me pain
Someone go tell the aunt of the boy to get him stitched a dress
The dandy gave me pain, the anklet gave me pain
Someone go tell the father of the boy to get the bhands to dance

---

16 *Khichri* is a cooked mixture of rice and lentils.

The dandy gave me pain, the anklet gave me pain
The dandy gave me...

Chhatti,[17] the sixth day of birth is celebrated with great vigour. Many customs are performed. But there is just one ritual which will be completed only once evening falls. The ritual of watching stars.

Evening falls. A *takht*[18] is placed in the front portion of the portico. The much made-up and adorned new mother with her infant in her arms appears. Two women walk by her side with uncovered swords in their hands. The midwife walks in the front with a four-sided lamp made of wheat flour in her hands. The new mother carries the baby in her arms and the Quran over her head. Standing on the takht she glances at the sky with stateliness and counts seven stars. The women standing by her touch the tips of their swords and make an arc over her head. The idea is that no djinns or fairies would be able to pass over her head.

Now the father of the child, the husband of the mother, makes an appearance with a bow and arrow. Standing on the bed of the new mother he says, 'In the name of Allah' and then aiming at the ceiling fires the arrow. As if hunting a deer.[19]

Jachcha jab dekhne ko aai tarey
Sitarey chargh gardon ney utarey
Hua farzand ye sabko mubarak
Kaho ladke ka bawa mriga marey
Chhatti ki dhoom jo pahunchi falak tak
Qamar aur mushtari donon pukarey
Khuda ney kya khushi donon ko di hai
Damamey baj gaye, goonje naqqare

---

[17] *Chhatti* or Sixth.

[18] *Takht* is a small wooden cot.

[19] Reference to the Orion constellation which is called *Mriga* or *Harnu* (deer) in Hindi.

When the new mother came to see the stars
The circular heavens made stars descend
The child is a blessing to all
Say! The boy's father has hunted a deer
When the gaiety of *chhatti* was heard in the skies
Moon and Jupiter both called out
What bliss has the God bestowed on both
Kettledrums are playing, ceremonial drums reverberate.

Now the vigil begins. The deep frying pan is on the fire all night. Sweet fritters are being fried. Allah's *Rehem* [20] will be cooked, a halwa made of rice flour. Allah's blessings will be read over the Rehem. And then supplication will be made to the revered Fatima in a ritual called Sehnak.

The gaiety of chhatti is over. But there are so many stages of rituals pending even after that. The ritual bath on the tenth day and then on the twentieth day. And then *chilla* or the ritual bath of the fortieth day. And the child is much cosseted; lullabies are being sung.

Tu so merey baley, tu so merey bholey jab tak baali hai neend
Phir jo padega tu duniya ke dhande kaisa hai jhoola kaisa hai neend
Tu so merey baley, tu so merey bholey jab tak baali hai neend

You sleep my baby boy you sleep my innocent until your sleep is tender
You'll get involved in the affairs of the world, what then is swing and what's sleep
You sleep my baby boy you sleep my innocent until your sleep is tender

Aajaari nindiya, aa kyon na ja
Mere baaley ki aankhon mein ghul mil jaa
Aati hun bibi aati hun
Do chaar baaley khilati hun

---

[20] *Rehem* or Mercy.

Come, O sleep! Why do you not come?
Come and dissolve in my baby's eyes
Coming, O ma'am! Coming!
I'll keep a few babies entertained.

And they are being fed with so much cosseting!

Miyan aawaey duron sey, ghoda bandhun khajuron sey
Miyan aaway daud ke, dushman ki chhaati tod key
Jag jag jag jag kiya karo
Dood-o-maleeda piya karo

Sire has come from afar; I tie the horse to the date palm
Sire came running, after defeating the enemy
Live with a dazzling gleam
Keep drinking milk and *malida*.[21]

And the baby's teething is still to take place. Later, a ritual to enhance lactation has to be performed; the next step is circumcision; then *aqiqa*[22]—rituals, rituals and rituals!

When the child is a little older the ritual of '*bismillah*'[23] will be performed. 'Bismillah' and 'Iqra bismi rabbikallazi'[24] will be written on silver tablets or silver dotted red paper and the child will be made to read it. And yes, when facial hair appear, there will be a feast of moustaches. In this ritual, sandalwood paste would be rubbed on the moustache of the boy; the sandalwood paste will then be touched to money which would be distributed. A supplication of *siwaiyan*[25] will be offered. Men and women will all eat it. But if the baby is a girl then there will be Sehnak and only the women will eat it.

---

[21] *Malida* is a sweet crumble made from leftover rotis.

[22] *Aqiqa* is an Islamic practice of sacrificing an animal at the birth of a child.

[23] *Bismillah*, literally, 'In the name of Allah'. Here it is used to mean 'initiation'.

[24] The first Quranic verse 'Read in the name of your Lord'.

[25] *Siwaiyan* or vermicelli cooked in sugar syrup or sweetened milk.

Only the facial hair has grown yet. The entire life is still ahead. From cradle to grave there is such a long sequence of rituals. A person is sometimes on a journey and sometimes at home. In either case, there are rituals. While leaving for a journey the family members would tie on the traveller's arm a coin called Imam Zamin's money wrapped in cloth. A mark would be made on the forehead with curd, and a spoonful of curd would be fed to the one who is travelling. When someone stepped out of home a mirror would be shown to their back. This meant to indicate the hope of seeing the face of the person coming back in the same way that the back of the one leaving is seen.

When the traveller returned from the journey the relatives and clansmen would send oil and lentils, money for charity, and platters of *jalebis*. In one tray there were lentils, in their middle was a bowl full of mustard oil and there would be an ornamental box with money for charity. The one returning from a journey would see his image in the oil and then put a few grains of urad lentil into it. The oil was sent to the scavengers. Money would be distributed among the poor. This would be followed by the feast of the Didar-e-Pir. Now who was this Didar-e-pir? It was merely an imagination that Dilli women had of someone who ensured that they would see again those who journeyed alone and far.

But there is also one journey from which there is no return. This journey or what can be termed the last journey, had its own set of rituals and superstitions. No effort would be spared for life at the last moment. Of course there would be prayers, but there would also be occult and magical rituals. A goat's liver would be offered in supplication and would be placed in a square along with its head with vermilion on it. Money would be distributed among children after it had been kept near the head of the person who was ill. Supplication, charity, prayers and wishes; nothing can delay what is destined. The traveller leaves. Those who are left behind are engaged in performing rituals—from the day of burial to *Soyam*,[26] from *Soyam* to *Chehellum*.[27] But in this culture *soyam* was not called *soyam*, it was called *tija* and *chehellum* was called *chaaliswan*.

These rituals were only social customs. But there were also other kinds of rituals—religious, seasonal, and the happy ones associated with Eid, Baqreid, and Shab-e-Barat. Muharram would bring a host of sad rituals along with it. According to Dilliwallahs Shab-e-Barat was a festival for the dead. Supplications would be offered for all the chosen friends of Allah from Baba Adam, Amma Hawwa to Amir Hamza. After that supplication would be offered for the dead in the clan. Especially dedicated supplications were made for two kinds of dead, *Aut* and *Suhagan*. *Aut* were the men who died without getting married. *Suhagan*, women who died after getting married.

Aamad-e-Shab-e-Barat bahu saans se ladi
Koi lipey, koi potey, koi kumhaar ke khadi
Matke achchhey dijo bhaiya, aawengey murdey
Chhorenge anaar aur chhuljhadi

On Shab-e-Barat daughter-in-law and mother-in-law fought
One puts mud and other smoothes it, one waits at the potters
Brother, the dead will come so give us good pots
There will be fireworks and sparklers.

The earthen stoves are being plastered with mud and are being smoothened. Halwa is being cooked. New earthen bowls and platters are arranged on the table. Fireworks are being set off. There is also a myth floating around that anyone who does not see their own shadow tonight will not see the next Shab-e-Barat.

Festivals have their own place just as the seasons have their own. In Jahanabad every season acquired its own traditions and customs. And the women sitting in their homes keep adorning

---

[26] *Soyam* is a ritual gathering on the third day after death.

[27] *Chehellum* is a ritual gathering on the fortieth day after death.

them further with gussets and frills. The restrictions of purdah kept them from crossing the doorsteps of their households but within the households they created their own and an entirely new world. They domesticated the seasons so much that the seasons appeared to have taken birth within the household aided by these women. Once the monsoon drizzle began, the tourists would rush towards Qutub Sahab. What would the women in purdah do? They created the spring of Saawan-bhadon within their homes. Stoles were being dyed light green. Jasmine garlands were made. The moment clouds gathered in the skies, the matriarch of the household would put the deep-frying pans on the fire. All kinds of fried treats and snacks would be prepared. The swing had already been hung in the house, on which adolescent and young girls would swing and sing

Nanhi nanhi boondiyan re saawan ka mera jhoolna
Ek jhoola daala meiney ambwa ki daarpar
Lambi lambipengein re saawan ka mera jhoolna
Chhoti moti sooinyan re saawan ka mera jhoolna
Ek jhoola daara meiney saiyan ji ke baagh mein
Lambi lambipengein re saawan ka mera jhoolna

Tiny-tiny drops, O my swing during saawan
I hung a swing on a mango branch
I swung high on it, O my swing during saawan
Small, insignificant needles, O my swing during saawan
I hung a swing in my beloved's garden
I swung high on it, O my swing during saawan

There is another swing in motion at the neighbours' too. The sound coming from there says

Barse kaari badariya
Meri chunariya bhigi jae
Chunariya bhigi jae rama
Laal rang ki odhi chunariya, hai re bhigo di re
Meri chunariya bhigi jae

Paiyan padun mein baanke chhailaa
Lijo kanthh lagaae
Chunariya bhigi jae

Dark clouds rain
My stole is getting drenched
O Rama! My stole is getting drenched
I wore a red stole, oh you got it drenched
My stole got all drenched
I beseech you my dandy lover
Clasp me close
My stole is getting all drenched

And somewhere the song of separation is also being sung

Rimjhim rimjhim chalein phoharein, ghar ghar ghar ghar badara chhae
Haae sakhi mein kis ko bataaun, morepiya ab lag nahin aae
Chhae ri andhiyari har su, kuk rahi hai koyal ku ku
Bol raha haipapihapihu hu, piya bin mora jiya ghabrae
Naach rahe hein tarey gagan mein, byakul hai man mora lagan mein
Apnepiya ki rah takat hoon, morapiya mohey tarsaae

Pitter-patter go the rain showers, clouds roar as they cast over
O friend, whom shall I tell? My beloved has still not come over
Darkness is spreading everywhere, ku ku the koel is calling
The papiha is also saying pihu, without the beloved I am anxious
The stars dance in the sky, obsessed—my heart is restless
I watch the way of my beloved, beloved keeps me craving

And here is a Saawan song written by Amir Khusro. Many a rainy season have passed since he wrote it but it remains as fresh as ever.

Amma merey baba ko bhejo ke saawan aaya
Beti tera baba to buddha ri ke saawan aaya
Amma merey bhaiya ko bhejo ke saawan aaya
Beti tera bhaiya to bala ri ke saawan aaya

Amma merey mamu ko bhejo ke saawan aaya
Beti tera mamu to banka ri ke saawan aaya

O mother send my father, see saawan is here
Daughter your father is very old, though saawan is here
O mother send my brother, see saawan is here
Daughter your brother is only a baby, though saawan is here
O mother send my uncle, see saawan is here
Daughter your uncle is too much of a fop, though saawan is here.

One voice can also be heard from outside, from the street. Saroli[28] from Mehroli has arrived. This is a street vendor who has brought mangoes to sell. His voice has its own magic. There is no householder woman who does not respond to his voice. Mangoes are being purchased by all of them. Delicacies, mangoes, swings, if saawan brings with it all these things, then which season can be better than saawan? Lo! One more voice is heard! 'Dark swirly, buy salty ones! Salty *batashas,*[29] buy salty ones!' Here is another vendor selling jamuns.

But the voices that wounded and evoked the aching pain of separation were different—the *papiha* [30] saying '*pi kahan*' [31], the *koel* [32] saying 'ku ku', and the screams of the peacocks. Another voice among these was that of the *titiri.*[33] A tale started by the royal women of the fort reached the women of Dilli that the titiri has a hole in its throat. So the water it drinks spills out. Therefore, do not call it the sound of the titiri, instead say it is the titiri's

---

[28] Saroli is a kind of mango.

[29] *Batasha* are round, smooth discs of sugar of different sizes distributed to mark celebratory occasions.

[30] Papiha or the hawk-cuckoo, also known as the brainfever bird.

[31] *Pi kahan* are words used for onomatopoeic effect. Its literal translation would be 'where is the beloved?'

[32] Koel is the Asian Cuckoo.

[33] Titiri or Sandpiper or peewit.

cry. It cries '*titiri hoon, pyaasi hoon*'[34]. It dies while continuously calling out like this. And what does the koel call out? The ladies used to say that koels love mangoes. When the mango trees flower and raw mangoes appear, that's when they start to call. But when the mangoes start ripening the corners of the koel's beak begin to fester. The poor bird craves more mangoes but cannot eat them.

[34] *Tititri hoon, pyaasi hoon* are again words for onomatopoeic effect; they sound like the Titiri's call and may be translated as 'I am titiri, I am thirsty'.

10

One City, Five Commotions

Delhi's temperament, as described by Ghalib, is formed by five commotions. The Fort, Chandni Chowk, every day the *majma*[1] at Jama Masjid, the weekly outing at the Yamuna Bridge, and the annual Phoolwaalon ki Sair fair.

We have seen what goes on in the fort. We have also been acquainted briefly with Chandni Chowk. What remains is the visit to the Yamuna Bridge—but what to say of this river? The sight of its waves filled even a genteel and elderly personality like Shah Abdul Aziz Muhaddis Dehlavi with wonderment. Such beautiful compliments he came up with.

'Flowing through this city the water in Yamuna appears like the canals that run below the windows of heaven.'

Since when, for how many aeons, has this river been flowing with its silvery ripples. There is indeed some magic in it that the city on its banks has seen so much bloodshed and destruction. Yet the people made it their home again and built the city all over again. They considered its water holy, built many ghats on its banks, and made it a focus of worship and holy rituals. One ghat better than the other. The best one, Nigambodh Ghat, after all it is the oldest one. It even finds mention in the

---

[1] *Majma* is a crowd watching a spectacle.

Mahabharata. And no, even before that, according to the Hindu faith, in the beginning of the *Dwapara Yuga*[2] Lord Brahma forgot all the scriptures because of a problem. He arrived here in that disoriented state. So fortuitous was his arrival here that he remembered all the scriptures. That is why the ghat came to be called Nigambodh. Nigam means scriptures. Bodh derives from the word budhdhi, meaning intellect and understanding. According to another tradition King Yudhisthira conducted a massive religious ceremony here. Since then this ghat has flourished. Such attractive people congregated here that, in the words of Sayyad Ahmed Khan, 'their bashful beauty makes even the rising sun crimson red'. But the entire scene has been described beautifully by Zaheer Dehlavi[3]. Look at the scene and you will be able to appreciate what Ghalib wrote about it.

> This morning hour. Tempered with light. The moon in thousands of pieces, like flaneurs, is moving and shining. Everyone looks like a troubled spark. One better than the other. Hundreds of fairies from fairyland. Clean features, moon-like visage, lithe bodies, tender build, flower-like hue, high head, black eyes, black tresses, fulsome breasts, doe-like eyes, waist like that of a cheetah, laden, head to toe, in gold and silver. Golden complexion shining through muslin stoles with precious metal embroidery. In dariya-e-jaman[4] a gathering of beauties with flower-like bodies make it appear like a takhta-e-chaman.[5] As if one river is shimmering within another. As if the moon is revelling in the waves of the river. Thousands of heavenly flaneurs wearing sheer silk saris dive in waist-deep water. Often on youthful fun-filled days there are tugging games being played with each other. One fairy-like, after

---

[2] *Dwapar Yuga* is the third (between *Treta Yuga* and *Kali Yuga*) of the four yuga, or ages, according to the Hindu scriptures.

[3] Zaheer Dehlavi was a Mughal noble courtier of Bahadurshah Zafar. He is best known for his eyewitness account of the 1857 mutiny in a book called 'Dastan-e-Ghadar'. The text includes a description of pre-mutiny Delhi.

[4] *Dariya-e-Jaman* is the River Yamuna (also called Jamuna).

[5] *Takhta-e-chaman* is a flower bed in a garden.

bathing in the Yamuna, is drying her hair. Another is putting on a dry sari and twisting dry the wet one.

This was the scene of the women bathing. Now turn your eyes from there, and you will see another scene at the ghat.

One rotund priest, barely dressed, wearing a loincloth, sporting a topknot of matted hair, tummy portruding, is sitting crossed-legged. Across from him is kept Mahadeo's *batiya*.[6] On the other side there is an idol of Gaura-Parvati. There is a marble Nandia, the bull, as well. On a lotus stool there are some articles used in puja such as the conch, etc. On Mahadeo there lies a bit of milk and a bit of water that has been offered. Some flower petals too. On one side there is a rising mound of money and cowries. Close by, there is a big mound of grain. Beautiful fairy-like nymphs who have just bathed in the river change their clothes and pay obeisance to Mahadeo and touch the feet of Misrji Maharaj. Misrji Maharaj smears a bit of sandalwood paste on their foreheads with his thumb and puts a basil leaf in their mouths.

So, this was Nigambodh Ghat, whose memory torments Mushafi[7] every now and then:

Takhta-e-aab-o-chaman kyon na nazar aaey sapaat
Yaad aaye mujhe jis dum wo nigambod ka ghat

Why shouldn't the floral and water bed be not immediately visible to me
The moment the memories of Nigambodh Ghat come to me

Such was the morning at Nigambodh Ghat. As the evening nears, tourists rush towards the Jama Masjid square. As soon as the sun starts setting the tourists' feet feel compelled to move. The

---

[6] *Batiya* is a stone that has smoothened over time due to contact with water. A reference to the shivalinga, which is the form in which Lord Shiva or Mahadev is worshipped.

[7] Sheikh Ghulam Hamdani 'Mushafi' (1750-1824) was a poet. Considered a great master in Ghazal, he is also credited by some scholars for first using the term 'Urdu' for the language variously called Hindvi, Dakkani, Rekhta, etc.

boulevardiers dress up and move straight, like an arrow, towards the Jama Masjid square. The public is assembled there. It is a thick crowd rubbing shoulders with each other. Saucers make jangling sounds as water bearers scurry around with waterskins on their shoulders. Mister, shall I give you a drink of elixir? There are water stations here named after princes. There is commotion in Chandni Chowk too. But this is something else; even more colourful. Chandni Chowk is a bazaar. The best of them all. Its aura is that of a bazaar. But the Jama Masjid square has become the cultural centre of the city. What a mosque! Inside people are bowing and kneeling. The sounds of namaaz emanate. Outside, the stairs have been taken over by well-dressed dandies. Colourful sharbats, falooda, kulfi, seekh kabab, haleem—the gourmands have a range of flavours to choose from here. Those fond of pigeons and lal padri trade the birds. Storytellers tell their tales. A little apart, poetry lovers gather as well. Wearing embroidered angrakhas they are doused liberally in perfume. Upon hearing a good couplet, they get excited and shower the poet with compliments.

But do not go just by the angrakhas. Look at their entire attire. They wear angrakhas on the top; their caps are four-cornered, five-cornered, sometimes round, but mostly two-sided. They wear pyjamas below that are loose, or narrow and tight. And in the case of a pious old man the pyjama is short and doesn't cover the ankles. This is a shariah-prescribed requirement. It looks like everyone is wearing the same angrakha. Yes, there is some difference in whether the bells are tied on the left or on the right. If the bell is on the left-hand side then one can assume the wearer is Muslim, and Hindu if they are tied on the other side. But that's the only difference in how Muslims and Hindus appear here. Everything else—their demeanour, language, fashion—is the same.

To speak the truth, Dilli's Hindu is no longer the Hindu of the Rai Pithora era. Even the Muslim is not the Muslim who came with the forces of Shahabuddin Ghauri. A lot of water has flowed under the bridge since. However much the swords had to cross then, it is now all over. After that history has taken a new turn. In brief, there is a tiny and muted pause, together with a lot of fusion. Not consciously, but unconsciously, organically. Both the religions are where they are, but on the cultural plane the distance has reduced, and an intimacy has developed. But even on the religious plane the erstwhile ideas of identity no longer abound. The religious festivals of the Muslims have acquired an indigenous hue. In fact, the entire Hijri calendar has taken on local colour. Who these days says Rabi-ul-Awwal or Rabi-us-Saani? Probably only the maulvis and mullas. According to Dilli's common people, Maah-e-Safar is now the month of Tera Tezi. Rabi-ul-Awwal has come to be known as the month of Bara-wafat. Rabi-us-Saani has become the month of Meeran Ji. Jamadi-ul-Awwal is the month of Madaar. Zulqada has become the month of Khaali. Shaaban is the now the month of Shabraat.

So this is how colours have mixed in this environment. And different cultural forms have coalesced towards unity. Seasonal festivals and fairs can no longer be easily identified as either Muslim or Hindu. What have remained are Eid and Baqreid and Holi and, but even here one participates in the other's celebrations. And even if there is no participation, religious sentiments of each other are accorded due respect nonetheless. So there will be no music outside mosques. And sacrifice on Baqreid is not done in a way that it would injure someone's sentiment and become a cause for friction. If, on Holi, someone threw gulaal on a Muslim s/he would not flare up but rejoice.

Here comes the camel-mounted messenger who had gone to check on the new moon; he has returned with good news. Today is the eve of Eid. Cannons are being fired. Drums are being beaten. If the moon is sighted on the 29th day of the month then, according to those from Dilli, it is a young Eid. If the moon is seen on the 30th of the month then it will be called a venerable Eid. Young or old, Eid is Eid. Old and young, children and adults, some by palki, some by nalki, in pomp and glory, and in carriages. Everyone is going to the Eidgah. Even the Emperor , riding atop an elephant, arrives at the Eidgah. Namaaz has been offered. Boom-boom, the cannons go off in salutation.

This is a festival of joy Next, it is Baqreid which too will bring happiness. After that it is the festival of mourning. Common men and elite alike, all houses are filled with sorrow. Children act like they are beggars of the Imam, with green shrouds around their necks, and walking towards the Imambada with their satchels full of sugar-covered cardamom seeds, fennel seeds and poppy seeds. There are water fountains for the thirsty all over. In this ritual Hindus play a prominent role. In this moment of grief, the Emperor's participation is also paramount. On the sixth of Muharram he is handed two elegy sticks, and a chain of silver is put around his waist. Two Saiyed boys hold the chain on either end and pull the king. Thereafter this chain is put around the Emperor 's neck. On the seventh, the royal procession commences at the fort and proceeds towards the Imambada. Lights in front, followed by spreads of henna and malida, musical instruments, and tableaux that have been lit up. Behind these walk the Emperor and the royal women. On the night of the eighth, the Emperor plays the role of Hazrat Abbas as a waterman. Putting a waterskin on his shoulders he offers sharbat to children. On Aashura, there are different rituals in the fort and taziyas form part of different processions in the city. As they pass through Hindu neighbourhoods and lanes, the processions are welcomed with water and sharbats.

After the month of Muharram, it is the month of Tera Tezi. And brings along the ceremony of the last Wednesday. Next month is the month of Bara-wafat. The series of milad congregations that start on the first do not end before the twelfth. On the twelfth night there is a festival of lights. The king pays homage at the dargah. Qawwalis are held. Sweets are distributed. After this, the month of Meeran Ji. On the eleventh there is a lot of celebration.

A bungalow, called Mehndi, is created with bamboo sticks covered in red paper. It is illuminated at night and an offering of sweets is made here.

In brief, every month used to come with news of a festival. Every festival had its own rituals. And at every such happy moment, the participation of the Emperor was customary. And not only in Muslim festivals, even in Hindu ones. In the Saloney festival the participation of the king became important because a Brahmin woman called Ramjani, after identifying the dead body of Alamgir the second, looked after it for one whole night. Shah Alam, after assuming the throne, paid her debt by making her his sister. And for Ramjani, after becoming the king's sister, it was only natural that she would tie a rakhi on his wrist on Saloney. And in this way the Saloney festival found its way into the Red Fort.[8]

But even in other festivals the Emperor would participate with a lot of enthusiasm. And along with him all the Muslims of the city. Muslims were enthusiastic spectators during Dussehra. But it was organised in a special way inside the fort. A special court was held. The Emperor played the part of releasing the Neelkanth bird. Then eagles and soldiers assembled before him. As the day progressed, elephants and horses lined up too. The Emperor even carried out an inspection [of the army].

On the night of Diwali the entire city sparkled with the light of diyas. In the fort as well, there would be a festival of lights, while drums were beaten, and the Emperor was weighed in gold and silver.

And what do you ask of Holi. There would be so much abeer and gulaal the air itself would appear red. Earthen pots were filled with *palaash*[9] flowers. The waterguns are full of coloured

---

[8] Intizar Husain, while directly addressing the reader, appears to be following the conventions of oral storytelling more than the conventions of writing, where linearity is privileged. Like a dastango, a storyteller, he makes use of circularity and repetition probably to refresh the memory of the reader, make connections, and emphasise certain parts of the narrative.

[9] Palaash or Flame of the Forest.

water. Whoever comes to the fort gets drenched. Songs are sung accompanied by the Sarangi, Duff, Manjeera, and Chang.

Mein kaise holi kheloon re
Saanwariya ke sang

How do I play Holi
With the dark one

Groups of revellers are out with drums. Every group will go and stand under the Emperor 's jharokha. The Emperor , his queens and princesses wait for these groups and shower them with prizes. And the Emperor did not merely compose ghazals. At the time of Holi, he composed Horis as well.

Kyon mo pe maari rang kipichkari
Dekho kanwarji doongi mein gaari
Baaj sakun kaise mo soon bhaaja nahin jaat
Thadey ab dekhon mein kaun jo din raat
Shokh rang aisi dheet langar se kaun khele hori
Mukh bandey aur haath marore kar ke wo bar jori

Why do you throw colour at me
Do not, for I will swear at you
If I could have run, I would have
I will now wait here, let us see who can drench me
Who can play Holi with such mischievousness
You have stained my face and twisted my arms

But Holi would come later. Before that it was the time for Basant Panchami. For Hindus, Basant Panchami. For Muslims, Basant Mela. Basant marks the end of winter. This was a festival of the season. But according to Hindu traditions, seasons too are willed by gods and goddesses. So flowers are offered to idols in the temples. Mustard flowers and marigold. Prayers and supplications are offered to Goddess Saraswati. Here at the holy *Qadamgah*[10] too bunches of mustard flowers are offered. Rosewater, orris water and musk is sprinkled. Qawwalis are sung.

On the second day the fair moves to the shrine of Khwaja Bakhtiyar Kaki. From there it moves towards Chiragh Dilli. The next day the crowd arrives at the shrine of Hazrat Nizamuddin Aulia. It was by the grace of all these khwajas that the Basant Mela acquired so much popularity among Muslims. The day after connoisseurs of Basant congregate at the shrine of Shah Hasan Rasul Numa. The day after that everyone flocks to the shrine of Shah Turkman. Five days pass like this. On the sixth day the city's rich and esteemed citizens go to the court to deliver Basant greetings to the Emperor .

Now let me tell you about the seventh day. A shrine of Hazrat Azizi was known to be a sanctuary for drunkards. So the drunkards assemble here on the seventh night. Feasting and drinking. Singing and making music. Absolute ruckus.

In this way the entire city is the colour of Basant. What Hindu, who's Muslim—everyone wears Basanti clothes. The Basant fairs at the dargahs only grew in scale. Today it is Basant of Harey-Bharey Shah. Tomorrow, Basant of Sarmad the martyr. Then singers started celebrating Basant of their masters.

With the onset of Basant, winter retreats. The bitter cold is now gone. Now it's time for the bloom of the pink winter. With the burning of Holi the sunlight becomes crisp. Now it's summer. Dilli's summer, O lord! People run around like mad. The rich rest in the rooms cooled by roosa and khus grass, while the poor shout:

> From where do I get a khus room and iced water?

The loo winds blow. It doesn't seem like it will ever rain. It seems to be raining everywhere, except Dilli. Lo and behold the clouds are here. There is a shower. Travellers begin to feel excited.

---

[10] *Qadamgah* is a place that has the footprint of Imam Raza.

Tormented, they run out of their houses. Groups are running helter-skelter. Some towards Humayun's tomb, some towards Okhla, but most groups are headed towards Qutub Sahab. The amariya there are the best. *Asaadha*[11] is over. This is the bloom of Saawan. It rains unceasingly. But the clouds are yet not done. It rains continuously through the week and Dilliwallahs do not get to see the sun in the day or stars at night. In houses and in the lawns, wherever you look, you see swings. Songs are being sung.

Nanhi nanhi boondiyan re saawan ka mora jhoolna
Ek jhoola daala mein ne ambawa ki daar pe
Lambi lambi pengein re saawan ka mora jhoolna
Chhoti moti sooiyyan re saawan ka mora jhoolna
Ek jhoola dala mein ne saiyan ji ke baagh mein
Lambi-lambi penge re, saawan ka mora jhoolna

Tiny-tiny drops, O my swing during Saawan
I hung a swing on a mango branch
I swung high on it, O my swing during Saawan
Small, insignificant needles, O my swing during Saawan
I hung a swing in my beloved's garden
I swung high on it, O my swing during Saawan.

Sometimes there is heavy rain, sometimes mere showers. This is how Saawan comes to an end. Bhaadon is here. It brings with it colourful commotions. One commotion of Janmashtami, one blossom of Rakshabandhan. But these fairs and commotions happen everywhere. Now, listen about the special festival of Jahanabad. Ghalib had said that Dilli's temperament depends upon five commotions; so now it's time for the fifth commotion. The city's two respectable Hindus, and two respectable Muslims appear in the court and say that 'Your Highness, Saawan is over. Now it's Bhadon season. Heavy rains are over. Showers are still on. Here the Hauz-e-Shamsi is brimming. When is the *sair*

[11] *Asaadha* is the fourth month of Hindu calendar. Corresponding with June-July, it marks the beginning of monsoon season.

going to take place if not now?' The Emperor is happy to hear this and decides the dates for the sair. Only he has the right to decide these dates. After all, this blossoming fair is a gift of the Red Fort. When Akbar Shah the Second's beloved son, the light of his eyes, was barred from the city for firing at a foreign resident, the queen resolved to put a canopy with curtains made of flowers and a cover at the shrine of Khwaja Bakhtiyar Kaki, on the return of her beloved son. Such was God's work that he came back soon. The queen fulfiled her resolve. On this occasion the flower-sellers who made the canopy also attached a fan made of flowers to it. The fan became quite popular at the fair. The Emperor was happy and declared that the fair be held every year in Bhadon. The Muslims would offer the fan at the shrine and the Hindus at the Jogmaya Temple. And both would participate in organising the whole affair. This became a real festival and one more blossom was added to the many attractions of bhadon; such was life in Jahanabad.

So the Emperor decides on the dates of the fair. Announcing drums resound through the city. In neighbourhoods and bylanes the news of Phoolwalon ki Sair is received with much excitement. The tourists quiver as they awake. But they will have to wait for a while. The fair will start only at the bidding of those in the fort. And for the inhabitants of the fort it means celebrating one festival close on the heels of another. They have just celebrated a festival in Saawan during which the procession of the fan passed through Chandni Chowk with much celebration. Faizuddin[12] described it thus:

> A golden fan on the Elephant. Under it strings of pearls, riddled with gems. Above, a peacock made of gold with its belly full of rosewater, which is being sprinkled on the crowd through its paws. In front, staffs of flowers. Drums are being played. Firecrackers burst. Soldiers

---

[12] Munshi Faizuddin Dehlavi was the author of book *Bazm-e-aakhir*. (The last gathering), which is the description of the socio-cultural life of Dilli during Bahadurshah Zafar and his predecessor Akbar II. Faizuddin Dehlavi was born and brought up in the Red Fort and thus, was intimately connected to its everyday life.

play musical instruments. At the back the rich and the nobility come riding on elephants. A crowd of people on either side.

With such grandeur this procession entered the fort and reached the sprawling garden in front of the Moti Mahal. Right in the middle there is a water reservoir. To its north and south there are two marble houses named Saavan and Bhadon.

So this fair is over. Now it's the commotion of Phoolwalon ki Sair. Hush children, the fort's carriages are moving towards Qutub Sahab. Some in palki, some in nalki, in pomp and glory, in carriages. Women seeking alms run behind the carriages. God will bless you, he will; you will get what you desire, you will. You have been endowed, endowed yes. In your purse there is money, money yes. Lord will reward you. Give some, give some.

The next day, early in the morning the carriage of the Emperor moves. Accompanying him are the begums and the princes. Leading them are the *saandni sawaar.*[13] Following them are mounted soldiers. Attendants bellow—Behave! Respectfully bow! His Highness the Emperor!

Such buzzing activity at Qutub Sahab. The elite are the most visible among all. This is the women's section. The men are nowhere to be seen. It is a crowd of moon-like faces. Food is being prepared in cauldrons. Every cauldron has something different in it. Delicacies are being fried. On another side mangoes are being looted. The elite are entranced by the princesses. Light showers. Koels are crooning, peacocks are dancing, the princesses are giggling. Some of them are running around. Some enjoy themselves on a swing. Swinging wildly, and singing to a swift rhythm:

Jhoola kin daro re amariyan
Raen andheri taal kinaarey
Murla jhankarey baadal kaarey

---

[13] *Saandni sawaar* were messengers riding tall female camels which typically made very long journeys at high speeds.

Barsan laagi boondan, phiyan-phiyan
Jhoola kin daro re amariyan
Chaar mil gaiyaan bhool bhulaiyan
Do sakhi jhoolein do hi jhulaaein
Bhooli-bhooli dolein shauq rang siyan
Jhoola kin daro re amariyan

Who put the swing in the mango orchard?
The night is dark by the pond
The peacock is screaming, the clouds are dark
The droplets are falling, phiyan-phiyan!
Who put the swing in the mango orchard?
Four (friends) met each other in this maze
Two friends swing, and two push them
Forgetful they roam around, with a colourful beloved
Who put the swing in the mango orchard?

Some princesses are running amuck. They go to the waterfall, slip on the stones and giggle. The Hauz-e-Shamsi is swollen and inviting.

Suddenly one hears the *Jasoolni.*[14] Beware! The Emperor is now ready to leave. The laughter, playfulness, giggling and fun comes to an end. The entire fort's procession leaves with the Emperor 's carriage.

Now the common people begin to take over the place. Traders and shopkeepers, respectable and elite, rich and poor; everyone comes running to Qutub Sahab. The rich in their buggies, the prostitutes in decorated carriages, the rakish youth on their horses. The commoners, walking or running. Some, drenched in the rain may be seen carrying pots on their heads. You know what's in the pots? A pair of new clothes and a pair of shoes to change into. They will have a bath at Qutub Shah, wear the dry new clothes, and be all dandy.

---

[14] *Jasoolni* was the woman messenger in the royal palace.

With the arrival of this crowd the fair comes alive. Till now it was royal. Now it is common. The tourist appears in his best attire. Paan firmly tucked in one side of his mouth, he wears flower garlands around his neck, and an attar-doused piece of cotton in his ear. The liquor vendor startles the tourists as he calls out to them. They accept the khus-smeared cup decorated with flowers, take a couple of swigs, tip the liquor vendor and move ahead. The free-spirited faqirs and the intoxicated shout:

Kuchh rah-e-Khuda de ja
Ja tera bhala hoga

Give something on the way to your lord
You will be blessed

❖

Bhala kar bhala hoga
Sauda kar nafaa hoga

Do good, good will be done unto you
Enter the trade, profit will be done unto you

❖

Kankar chun-chun mahal banaya
Murakh kahey ghar mera re
Na ghar tera na ghar mera
Chidiyon, chain basera re
Ram-ram karley achchhey bandey
Ye kaya nahin paawega
Maati odhna, maati bichhauna
Maati ka sarhana rey
Maati ka kulboot banana
Ismey kalb samaya rey
Ram-ram karley achchhey bandey
Ye kaya phir nahin paawega

Bit by bit you built your palace
But only a fool will say this house is mine
The house is neither yours nor mine
It's just a temporary shelter for the birds
Recite Ram-Ram, o good man
You will not get this form
Earth is cover, earth is bed
Earth is pillow too
Of the earth, this body is made
It encompasses Creation
Recite the name of the lord, o good man
You will not get this form again

One Hussaini Brahmin is standing and shouting. 'The beloved, the truthful, the exalted is divine. He has given honour to the prophet.' The sellers are shouting. The corncobs are fresh. The water chestnuts are fresh from the pond, green and milky. The jamuns are black. Buy the salty batasha. Take the ripe ones, they will be sweet.

The water-bearers bang their bowls. This is for the thirsty ones, in the name of the lord. If you have money then give, if not then at least drink, on the way to the lord.

Ahead, the procession of the flag is going well. It is a stampede of the elite and the common. The clothes are colourful. Hindus and Muslims may be recognised in only one way: the former wear turbans on their head, while the latter wear either saffron turbans or four-cornered caps. Everyone has the same flower garlands around their necks and on their wrists. They fan themselves with khus fans, but are happy getting drenched in the showers. In the middle a large fan hangs on a colourful bamboo support adorned with flowers. Ahead and behind it are members of *akharas*.[15] Umbrellas made of flowers as well.

[15] *Akharas* are the institutions of practitioners of martial arts which contain within them some elements of religious orders.

The tabla and sarangi players play their instruments. The nautch girls, with bells around their ankles, dance. *Nafiri*[16] players sing:

Mora piya gaya hai bides
Mohey chunri kaun ranga de
Bairi saawan aayo ri

My lover has gone *bides*[17]
Who will colour my stole
The tormenting saawan is here

Ahead of them, there are formations of soldiers. The macebearers swing a fan made of peacock feathers. Once in a while they call out: The lord of the world, his highness is approaching.

The fan is offered at the shrine of Qutub Shah. The tabla and dholak play all night long. At the crack of the dawn people bid farewell to the shrine and each other, carrying away souvenirs as they leave.

The next evening the fan for Jogmaya is carried in a similar procession. The celebrations are carried out in a similar manner. The sound of the nafiri rises from the waterfall. Lo, the fan is being lifted now. From the waterfall it starts moving towards the Jogmaya temple. Night has fallen. Decorated in coloured paper, the fan shimmers in the light of the lamps. Ahead of it drums are being beaten. Behind it may be seen the wrestlers; both masters and students demonstrate their skills. *Baank*, *pata*, *binot*,[18] what skills they have. Behind them are the nafiri players. Then the bowl-banging water-bearers. And right at the end, the fan. Shehnai

[16] *Nafiri* is a musical wind instrument similar to Shehnai but smaller.

[17] *Des* refers to the native land, while *bides*, its opposite, literally means foreign land. In folk traditions women narrators use it to refer to their separation from their men folk (seasonal migrants and merchants, etc).

[18] *Baank*, *pata*, *binot* are martial arts. *Baank* is a stick with one end pointed sharp, *Pata* is a fencing game with sticks or gauntlet swords and *Binot* a sparring game, literally means to play but without (*Bina*) use of a shield (*Ot*).

players play sweet tunes as they walk along. People shower flowers from their ledges and balconies. They sprinkle rosewater as well.

Late in the night the procession reaches the temple. Ceremonial sweets are distributed. Hindus and Muslims both accept these and everyone returns home happy. Thus the Phoolwalon ki Sair is concluded. Dilli's fifth commotion is over. But there is still wine left, and the night isn't over yet. Days go by in the hope that somehow new commotions and new carnivals will begin afresh.

11

Much Timepass, Many Games

Kite-flying, pigeon-fancying, quail-fighting, cock-fighting, chess, chausar, banotbaazi, pateybaazi, there were many games in this culture. Many reformers have since said that it was because of its preoccupation with games that the Mughal sultanate lost its own [game]. And these reformers also thought of indulgence in poetry at par with kite-flying, pigeon-fancying and quail-fighting and considered it responsible for the downfall of the sultanate.

But what wonderful games these were; imbued by the people of Dilli with considerable vibrancy and nuance. From the Dheelchi to the ones equal to the height of a man, there were so many varieties of kites and such were their names: Kaleja, Jali, Kulchiri, Sar Khuli, Kandhe Khuli, Pari, Maang Daar, Zulfon Daar, Kul Sara, Do Palka, Do Panna, Do Baaz, Bagla, Al-fan, Gul Zamaan, Chaand Taara, Shakar Paara, Bheriya, Aadha, Adheel, Paunya, Saanp, Ganderidaar, Kuldama, Laldama and Pateel.

Here the day is over, and there the kite-flyers emerge. The famous and the prominent master kite-flyers have taken huge reels of strings, long sticks, spools, kites and *kankawwa*,[1] and are heading north of the Red Fort, towards Saleemgarh. Bahadur Shah Zafar also arrives on his mobile throne. On one side, Mirza

[1] *Kankawwa* is a kite made with paper or a leaf plume.

Yawar Bakht supervises the royal kite-flyers. On the other side the team of Moin-ul-Mulk Nazarat Khan, the royal officer, tugs at the kites. First kite, second kite, third kite. Soon the sky is full of them. Competitive matches begin as well. The masters, from either side, let their kites soar. It appears as if the kites have touched the sky, and the strings, heavily weighed down, are about to kiss the ground. But the riders are ready to prop the strings with their crooked sticks and hold them up. And there you go, one kite is cut loose by another's string. And the crowd erupts with the noise of *woh kata!* (there, it's cut!). And look at the experience of the master; instead of rolling back the remaining string he breaks it off at their end. Where the kite goes, so should the string.

Seeing all this, the emperor is excited. He descends from his mobile throne and makes a gesture. The royal kite-flyer understands perfectly, takes a step forward, makes the emperor wear gloves made from fish skin, and presents him with a human-sized kite. The kite, with a tug, is airborne and keeps soaring until it resembles a star.

The kite-flyers of the city as well as of the fort were a good match. Both were determined and skilled in equal measure. Among the fort's kite-flyers, Prince Yawar Bakht was peerless. Rarely would a competitor be able to cut his kite. But there was one more Prince who had no equal when it came to kite-flying. He was the late emperor Shah Alam's grandson, Fakhruddin Alam, who came to be known as Mirza Fakhru subsequently, and eventually as Mirza Chapati. After leaving the fort, he did not have a fixed address. Though he left his princely comforts behind, he could not give up kite-flying and pigeon-flying, nor could he swear off chess and chausar. In the end, the string and kite became his source of livelihood. Gone were the days when he could act snobby. Now, after cutting the strings of nine kites he would celebrate his victory and make his way downstairs. He was old, lived in a small kite shop, and sold kites and shared tips and tricks of kite-flying with his disciples.

The people of the fort had a unique kite-flying culture. The prominent kite-flyers of the city used to meet every Friday near the Ghata Masjid, situated on the banks of the Yamuna, and fly kites. On the occasion of Shab-e-baraat, Eid and Baqr-Eid one would see much more enthusiasm and excitement. But the biggest display of enthusiasm and excitement would be on the day of Phoolwaalon ki Sair in Mehrauli. What a site it would be with the whole sky dotted with kites!

The sky of Dilli used to be dominated by two things. Kites and pigeons. Here, the passion for pigeon-fancying was equal to, or even surpassed by, the passion for kite-flying. Although pigeons also fulfilled the duty of delivering love notes, Dilli's Farhads and Majnus reposed greater trust in kites. They found it more convenient to send notes via kites. Love notes would be tied close to the kites, which were let loose only when they reached the beloved's house, at which point they were made to crash. There! The love note has been delivered to the desired destination.

Early in the morning, everyone would be on their respective terraces. Bird feed in their hands, eyes on the sky. Pigeons in various hues. Laqa, Sheerazi, Kabuli, Gola, Sabza, Do Palka, Lotan, Phal Sara, Pateet, Babre, Bagh-Baghe, Bamne. Some pigeons eat the grain. Some sit on an umbrella and coo. A bunch of them fly high. While in the air, some perform tricks. Some fly so high that they begin to appear star-like. They return only in the evening. Frankly, it would not be strange if they returned the next day or even a day after. To prepare them to fly long distances, they were trained and fed well.

It is heard that Wajid Ali Shah's coop had 24,000 pigeons. Such was the glory of Bahadur Shah Zafar's pigeons that they would fly right over his entourage and keep him in shade, as if they were not pigeons but clouds. And there you go, now we must mention Mirza Chapati. When he left the fort and was homeless, he kept a cage of pigeons on a pushcart. He would park his pushcart in whichever lane he fancied, and start flying pigeons. He was not limited to flying only pigeons; from time to time he would take a break from the pigeons and fly parrots instead.

Kite-flying and pigeon-fancying were harmless pastimes. In kite-flying competitions, while one kite's string would get cut the other would continue to soar in the sky. In pigeon-flying matches, one's pigeon, at the most, would try to confuse the competitor's pigeon and bring it to its base. But the pheasant-fights and cock-fights would leave the birds bloodied. Both these games were very popular in Lucknow. But were the people of Dilli any less? The master would get to the match ground with his pheasants. The pheasants were tiny, but fought well. Their beaks and claws were as sharp as knives. The masters used to scrape and sharpen the beaks and claws of the birds. The birds would injure each other and the one who either could not get up or ran away was declared the loser.

Along with pheasant there was partridge. Partridges were no less talented. Trained by masters they would also fight pheasants with a lot of gusto. With partridges and pheasants one more bird found its way to the masters. That was the rooster or gamecock. Till now it was only famous for its crowing. With wings puffed up and beak pointed upwards it would crow loudly. He announced his masculinity and remained content. But Dilli's leisure-loving people trained them so well that they used to fight like pheasants. The masters used to challenge one another by saying, 'Master, shall we have a match?' It meant you get your gamecock. I will get mine. Let us see who wins and who loses. As they fought, the gamecocks would begin to lose their senses. They were then disengaged, made to drink water, and once again pitted against each other. The bird that would drop from exhaustion or run away was considered to have lost the match.

This was one category of games. The second kind was the one in which the masters would showcase their talent and prevail over their opponent by using their strength and skills. In this category, banotbaazi and pateybaazi were the two most popular games. Consider arm-wrestling too a part of this category.

These were games but also required talent. Such talent, that while one opponent is wallowing in pride over his strength, the other, though less powerful, beats him using his tricks. This incident from an arm-wrestling match is an example of such virtuosity. Mirza Ali Beg Meer, disciple of the arm-wrestling master Meer, was in his eighties. He was old and on top of that he was sick as well. A wrestler from Meerut arrived to have an arm-wrestling match with him. Mirza Sahab pleaded with him, 'I am an old man, with my feet in the grave. Where is the strength in my arm that I will arm-wrestle?' But the wrestler was adamant on having a match with him. Left with no choice, Mirza Sahab extended his arm, and the arm-wrestling match was on. It went on for a while. Mirza Sahab suddenly used one of his moves called Qimchi. He gave such a twist to the wrestler's wrist that his opponent cried out in pain and collapsed.

If such was the disciple, imagine what the master would have been like? Meer, the arm-wrestler, was famous not without any reason. And he was so famous that the craft he singularly excelled in receded into the background.

And the talent for Banot was extraordinary. All that a banotbaaz required was a handkerchief and a metal coin. After tying the coin in the handkerchief he would charge at an armed adversary. The blow that he would thus deliver to his opponent's wrist would be so powerful that the adversary would drop the weapon he was wielding, whether it be a lathi, a spear or a sword. All he could do then was to run away. Dilli's Banotey were exceptionally good. They would have the sword of the best swordsmen.

And Pateybaazi too was quite popular in Dilli. In the name of a weapon a Pateybaaz would just have a small lathi. He would employ this lathi with such skill that forget about those who confronted him with knives, even swordsmen would begin to sweat.

Banot and Pateybaazi do not involve any display of physical strength. The Banotbaaz and Pateybaaz needed to have mastery over their skills. But in wrestling, both physical strength and skills are equally important. In Jahanabad, wrestling was a common hobby. Even non-wrestlers used to exercise and spar in the wrestling pits. The elite had made arrangements for wrestling pits in their mansions. There was one wrestling pit in Shareef Manzil as well. The youth of this household did not only learn about medicine but also sparred in the wrestling pit.

The third category of games included the best of the games. Chess, Chausar, Pacheesi and Ganjeefa. Chess used to be the favoured game of the Mughals. Emperor Akbar used to like it so much that in Fatehpur Sikri palace he had a floor designed to resemble the chessboard. On this board, instead of pieces, beautiful maids, dressed in colourful clothes would stand exuding style and attitude. When the piece moved from one square to another, they would move accordingly, but with what grace!

Muhammad Shah and Shah Alam used to play chess with the begums in the women's quarters. Bahadur Shah Zafar received this game as a legacy of his ascendants.

Among common people, especially Hindus, Chausar was more popular than chess. Chess had become the game of the kings and the wealthy. Chausar enjoyed popularity among the common people. Chausar and Pacheesi both. The only difference between Chausar and Pacheesi was that tiles were used in the former and shells were used in the latter.

But the biggest and the most colourful game was *Randibaazi*.[2] Or, *Tawaifbaazi*[3] if you please. In Jahanabad, the tawaifs held sway; what respect and glory they enjoyed. During the reign of Muhammad Shah, the tawaifs especially rose through the ranks of

---

[2] *Randi* is a derogatory slang for a prostitute and *baazi* refers to a game or practice. *Randibaazi* refers to frequenting brothels.

[3] Tawaifs were singers/performers who were also often prostitutes. The author's usage here alludes to a hierarchy within the courtesan culture where *tawaifs* commanded more power, respect and money than a lower-ranking *randi*. Although, there were those who considered this mere euphemism.

society. During this time there was a famous tawaif who used to come to gatherings undressed. Urad Begum was her name. In the name of dressing she neither wore big clothes nor small but it was impossible for anyone to tell that she was sitting naked. There were such skilfully drawn flowers and petals all over her body, which resembled the brocade designs then in vogue, that it seemed like she was wearing a brocade dress.

In the ruined and deserted Dilli there were many tawaifs, one better than the other. There were two madams called Dooni and Choni. There was a marriage among the princes. Dooni *jaan*[4] had a performance there. Mirza Chapati, who used to lisp a little, was also in attendance. He interrupted her in the middle of the performance. 'Bai ji, stop for a while. I have a couplet I would like to recite.' He read the couplet thus:

Dhiste Dhiste Ho Dayi Itni Malat
Saat Paise ti Dooni Reh Dayi

The couplet actually went thus:

Ghiste Ghiste Ho Gayi Itni Malat
Saat Paise ki Dooni Reh Gayi

Much grating has turned her to cardboard
Dooni's worth is now reduced to seven paise.

The gathering was crimson with embarrassment. Dooni Jaan arched her eyebrows. Then gathering her wits, she asked for forgiveness and said 'Subhan Allah! Mirza Sahab. I was very sick. I have still not recovered. *Sahab-e-Alam*[5] remembered me. And here I am.' And then she resumed singing.

In the city, Chawri Bazaar was the veritable bazaar of beauty. As the evening arrived, the young and the beautiful began to shimmer in the leisure-houses. How well has Rasikh described this bazaar:

---

[4] *Jaan* is a Persian term of endearment.

[5] *Sahab-e-Alam* literally means Master of the creation.

Chaawri Qaaf Hai Ya Khuld-e-Barin Hai Rasikh
Jamghate Hooron Ke, Pariyon Ke Pare Milte Hain

O, Rasikh! Is Chawri a market or a sublime heaven?
There are gatherings of nymphs and fairies everywhere!

A horde of *hoors* at the leisure-houses and a swarm of onlookers and flirts down the road. Flamboyant and handsome, paan in their mouth, a gajra of jasmine wrapped around their wrist or neck, perfume soaked ball of cotton in their ear. Walking carelessly down the road with their eyes transfixed on the leisure-houses. There are so many who are content to merely look. Then there are those who quickly jump onto the staircase and disappear inside the leisure-house. The scene inside is something else. White sheets are spread on the floor. Large cushions for reclining. Round pillows arranged to rest on. Also the *pechwan,*[6] *khaasdaan*[7] and *ugaldaan.*[8] Chandeliers, hung from the ceiling, shimmer. Delicious smells waft from the cooking pots. Preparations for the evening's performance are underway.

So much about the tawaifs. They had their own influence and culture. And such culture that the elite would send their sons to leisure-houses to learn manners and etiquette. In the culture of the leisure-houses it was also understood that such visiting young men, who have come to receive cultural training, should be strictly monitored. If the madam of the house deemed that the young men were crossing their boundaries then she would send them back home immediately and seek apologies.

So these were the tawaifs. But within the shade of this tawaif culture another creation was blooming. Its description has been presented skilfully by Shahid Ahmed Dehlvi[9]:

---

[6] *Pechwan* is a small hubble.

[7] *Khaasdaan* is a small case to keep paans after they have been prepared.

[8] *Ugaldaan* is a spittoon.

[9] Shahid Ahmed Dehlvi (1906 Delhi-1967 Karachi) was a writer, musician and publisher of the famous literary magazine *Saqi*. This excerpt is from his collection of essays on Dilli called 'Ujra Diyaar' or Desolate Land.

From the side room, dressed in green *peshwaaz*,[10] of fair complexion, a beautiful woman walks in gracefully and stands with both hands folded over her chest. She casts a glance at the gathering and presents the performance respectfully. Oh my, this is Moti *Bhaand*![11] Standing behind her are two sarangi players, one tabla player and one manjeera player, all dressed in bright dresses. Hands caress the tabla. They move across the sarangi strings as well. The tabla player plays the opening piece. As Moti Bhaand presents the *gat*,[12] it seems like a fairy has descended from the inner chambers. As the circular *gat* reaches a crescendo with three salaams, everybody simultaneously exclaims, *Subhan Allah!* Moti Bhaand greets the audience. For an hour she performs difficult kathak compositions. Then she goes on to demonstrate the 16-beat rhythm cycle. In the end she also presents the wonderful *tatkar*.[13] Everybody applauds generously. It is true that Moti Bhaand excels in her talent.

As the applause becomes louder, Moti Bhaand folds her hands and says, 'Sir, it is your generosity and connoisseurship that you are appreciating a slave like this. Otherwise, who am I and what is my status? *Man aanam ke man daanam*.'[14]

In matters of sophistication and etiquette of gathering, it is not only the tawaifs of Dilli, but also the bhaands who were very well-versed. The bhaand devoid of sophistication, who sullied the name of bhaand, is a product of latter days.

---

[10] *Peshwaaz* is a flowing long shirt.

[11] *Bhaand* is the caste name for performers—artists and jesters.

[12] *Gat* literally means 'pace' or gait. Here it refers to the act of performing a narrative.

[13] *Tatkar* are Kathak dance moves in which the feet produce a sound as they strike the ground.

[14] *Man aanam ke man daanam* means ' I know who I am'.

12

Ten Fingers, Ten Skills

Fairs, carts, leisure, sightseeing—everything in its own place, work has its own place. Dilliwallahs were so gifted in work that they took whatever work they engaged in to a level of excellence. Many small and big artisan skills were transformed in their hands to artistry. The skill of *zardozi* [1] is one such example; it had been a tradition for long. The artisans, or rather the artists of Dilli, enhanced it with their innovations. *Kalabattu* [2] was a material used in zardozi. The artisans of Dilli innovated by including a flat metal thread called *mukesh*. This one addition brought such dazzle to zardozi work! Then they scrunched-up the mukesh and created something called *gokhru*. Mukesh paved the way for the work of *salma-sitara* sequin work. The salma-sitara embroidery became so popular that here the princesses of the fort were infatuated by it and there the public and the nobles overindulged it. The wires were beaten a little to flatten them and then threaded into a needle to embroider delicate flowers on stoles. This skill came to be known as *kamdaani* and attained great popularity.

---

[1] *Zardozi* is a kind of embroidery using metal threads, gemstones, etc., on cloth.

[2] *Kalabattu* means metal thread.

Vessel making, mat making, ivory work, stonemasonry, shoemaking—all kinds of crafts reached their zenith in the hands of Dilli craftsmen. In every craft they introduced nuances and made these popular while earning praise for their artistry. And yes, shoemaking! Of course, shoes are worn everywhere, so shoes are made everywhere. But the cobblers of Dilli had to also show their face in the fort. They would think of the delicate feet of the princesses. So they made delicate golden shoes keeping in mind those delicate feet.

The skill of stone masonry of course had to attain glory in this city. The Mughals were fond of building. Stonemasons were in great demand. In this field such skilful persons were born here who made exquisite designs on stone with the help of their mallet and chisel, and carved all kinds of flowers and leaves.

There was another skill whose experts were called *bindherey*. This referred to the skill of beading pearls. Very fine holes were made in pearls, diamonds and other gems. But especially in pearls. We have all heard of the proverb that says that the one that gets beaded is a pearl, otherwise it is a pebble. And truly this is a delicate task. If a pearl cracks while beading it does not remain a pearl, it is rendered a pebble.

The skill of lapidary is similar. The task of setting gemstones in jewellery was not a small one in itself. These artisans were called *jadiya*. And to get jewellery made was not a small task. The jewellers of Dilli used to make all kinds of jewellery for the princesses and while doing so, introduced such finesse in them.

There were some kinds of work that the women adopted and they displayed great skill at it. Women developed great expertise in salma-sitarey and *gota* work and made a name for themselves in it. Women had to be involved in tailoring because the princesses and aristocratic women did not like the idea of men stitching their clothes. After all, how would their sense of decency allow them to get their tops and brassieres stitched by men? This bashfulness gave birth to seamstresses who were called *Mughlani*.

Another skill was that of calligraphy. What great calligraphers were born in Dilli! Calligraphy reached its zenith in their hands and achieved the status of art. Such was its popularity that people would get ornate logos and texts written by the calligraphers and decorate their houses with them. What a calligrapher Syed Muhammad Ameer Rizwi was! Even Bahadur Shah Zafar was a fan of his talent. He was such a great calligrapher and he also used to arm-wrestle. He achieved mastery in calligraphy and attained fame as Mir *Panjakash*.[3] Might and elegance had been united in his fingers. An elegant hand, and an iron fist. In 1857 he was in his 84th year but he was so full of vigour that he jumped into battle and became a target of British bullets.

These were the arts and crafts of the time. There were also those businesses that remained at the level of occupations and could not be called skills. Some of these bid farewell with the changing times. When torches were no longer in use, how could the *Mashaalchi*[4] be saved? The candles and chandeliers in the Diwan Khana and torches in the streets; earlier when the nobles set foot outside at night to attend a gathering the mashaalchi would walk ahead of them. Along with the mashaalchi, the *Hamami*[5] also became a thing of the past. The heat of this place had really troubled the Mughals. They built bath houses to beat this heat, which had given birth to the occupation of hamami.

Another occupation was the one of *Shuhadagiri*.[6] Look at the cruelty of the time that the *shuhade* became loafers and bullies. It was an accepted occupation in Dilli. Not only that, it was a courtly occupation. They were assigned to carry the cots of those special to the emperor. When the dynasty bade farewell, the shuhada

---

[3] *Panjakash* or arm-wrestler.

[4] *Mashaalchi* is the bearer of a *mashaal* or torch.

[5] *Hamami* was the bathkeeper or attendant.

[6] *Shuhada* came to refer to rakes and *shuhadagiri* to debauchery.

were turned destitute and friendless. When the torches were extinguished and the hamams went cold; the mashaalchi bade farewell and the hamami also left. The problem with the shuhada was that when the era of the dynasty departed, they did not make an exit. When the emperor was no more they turned to the houses of the nobles for patronage. They would descend on a gathering the moment they saw any commotion like a wedding, and begin to repeat the same kind of sanctimonious blessings that they used to spout during their services inside the fort. This is exactly what brought disgrace to them.

This was an imperial time. Not only in the palaces, but even in the porches of the villas, doormen could be seen standing. In the palaces even the women's quarters would have women doorkeepers. They would stand with the same pride as the men as they shared the same expertise in sword and spear fighting. With time the women guards were gone altogether. But yes, the creatures called door keepers could still be seen at the villas, mansions and bungalows.

Flowers were in fashion in Dilli, especially in the fort. So the *gulfarosh* [7] and *maalan* were also in business. Well, flowers are still sold. On occasions of marriages and weddings, sehras, garlands and gajras are still bought. The term gulfarosh may no longer be in currency, nevertheless the occupation continues. The maalan continued till much later, but may be seen no longer.

These occupations were just a handful of examples. There were so many others. *Qasai*,[8] *Kunjdey*,[9] *Teli-Tanyoli*,[10] *Baniye*,[11]

---

[7] *Gulfarosh* or flower-seller.

[8] *Qasai* is the caste name for butchers.

[9] *Kunjdey* is the caste name for greengrocers.

[10] *Teli-tanyoli* is the caste name for oil pressers and sellers.

[11] *Baniye* is the caste name for moneylenders.

Baqqal,[12] *Warqsaaz*,[13] *Naanbaee*,[14] *Bhadbhoonje*,[15] Attaar, *Itrfarosh*,[16] *Naai*,[17] *Dhobi*,[18] *Gaddi*,[19] *Halwai*.[20] There were not just *Naai* but also *Naayan*,[21] and Domni, and Saqqe whose bowls would clank in the markets;[22] nobles, especially their women, preferred to call them *bhishti*. It is important here to also mention the *rangrez* [23] because they were experts in dyeing stoles of different sizes. Many of these occupations still survive but the traditions which were associated with them and their role in the culture of the time has all but disappeared. That they were part of the culture is evident in the origin of the idioms mentioning them—*Nai naayan, baans ka nahanna; naai-naai baal kitney, ke jajmaan aaey jaatey hein; dhobi ka kutta, na ghar ka na ghaat ka; kunjri apne beron ko khatta kab bataati hai; teli re teli hai terey sar pe kolhu.*

And Mir went so far as to even go beyond the perfume-maker and bestow a character to the perfume-maker's lad!

Kaifiyatein attar ke laundey mein bohot hein

The perfume-maker's lad has too many attributes

And yes, Dilliwallahs could bear the *khatbuna* [24] but the word *khaat* would fall heavy on their ears. Once a khatbuna appeared

---

[12] *Baqqal* is the caste name for grocers.

[13] *Warqsaaz* is the caste name for metal foil makers. The extremely thin silver foil used for decorative and medicinal value in food was most popular.

[14] *Naanbaee* is the caste name for bakers.

[15] *Bhadbhoonje* is the caste name for the group of people who roast gram and grains.

[16] *Itrfarosh* or perfume sellers.

[17] *Naai* or barber.

[18] *Dhobi* or washerman.

[19] *Gaddi* or milk sellers.

[20] *Halwai* referred to the confectioners or sweet-makers.

[21] *Naayan* or *Naai* woman.

[22] They carried several copper bowls to give people a drink of water and constantly clanked these to gain attention in the market place.

[23] *Rangrez* or dyers.

[24] *Khatbuna* was the weaver (*buna*) of the rope cot (*khaat*).

on Dilli's streets harking 'have your khaats woven'; the residents of the neighbourhood beat him up and warned him saying, 'do not ever come to the neighbourhood of noblemen and utter the word *khaat*. If you have to say it, say '*palang*',[25] say '*chhaparkat*',[26] say '*chaarpai*'.[27]

[25] *Palang* or bed.

[26] *Chhaparkat* is a bedstead with a canopy and curtains.

[27] *Chaarpai* or a rope bed.

13

Colours, Fragrances and Tastes

It is said about Sher Shah that before becoming a king he had the honour of having a meal with Babar. Large cuts of goat leg were served on the table. Sher Shah was anxious about how to do justice with such big pieces of the leg; he drew out his sword, cut one of the pieces into smaller portions and began to eat.

Swords and spears were an integral part of the Mughal culture. Perhaps, at that time, such was the spread of food that doing justice to it required swords. From the time of Babar to Bahadur Shah Zafar the Mughal dining table had undergone tremendous transformation. The table could be recognised as one of the markers of culture. In the early days of any culture the table reflects the simplicity of life. A few dishes, fewer flavours. However, as the culture deepens its artists show their expertise in myriad ways, including the cooks in the kitchen. These were the twilight years of the Mughal Sultanate. Its influence had shrunk and was confined only to the Fort. Yet, Mughal culinary splendour had evolved to a point of perfection and was on vibrant display.

It was no longer the dining spread of Babar where a rustic Pathan had used his sword to cut and eat the pieces of the goat leg. This delectable spread was of the Emperor of India, Zill e-Subhani, Hazrat Bahadur Shah Zafar. It had its rules and etiquettes.

It is early afternoon. Now it is time for *khassa*.[1] The mace-carrier woman calls for the servers, who rush in in hot haste.

A snow-white cloth has been laid with a *chauki*[2] in the middle. A cloth is spread over it too. The chauki is for the king to have khassa. The rest of the space is for the begums, princes and princesses to have their meal.

Dishes are carried in one after the other. They are being served constantly. What a range of dishes; and such variations in each one. Just try to count them. Let us start with the pulao dishes. Yakhni Pulao, Moti Pulao, Nukti Pulao, Noor Mahal Pulao, Kishmish Pulao, Nargisi Pulao, Zamurdi Pulao, Laal Pulao, Muzaafar Pulao, Faalsaai Pulao, Aabi Pulao, Sunehri Pulao, Roopeeli Pulao, Murgh Pulao, Baiza Pulao, Ananaas Pulao, Kofte Pulao, Biryani Pulao, Saalim Bakre ka Pulao, Bonat Pulao, Khichdi, Shola,[3] and Qabooli Zaahiri.

The dishes are in varying colour. Qalia, Dopyaaza, Deer Qorma, Chicken Qorma, Fish, Baingan ka Bharta, Aaloo ka Bharta, Chane ki Daal ka Bharta, Aaloo ka Dulma, Baingan ka Dulma, Karele ka Dulma, Badshah Pasand Karele, Badshah Pasand Daal, Seekh kabab, Shami kabab, Goliyon ke kabab, Teetar ke kabab, Bater ke kabab, Nukti kabab, Khatai kabab, Husaini kabab.

Now come the bread preparations. All kinds of breads. Chapatis, Phulkas, Paranthe, Roghani Roti, Besani Roti, Khameeri Roti, Gao deeda, Gao Zubaan, Kulcha, Ghausi Roti, Badaam ki Roti, Piste ki Roti, Chaawal ki Roti, Gaajar ki Roti, Misri ki Roti, Naan, Naan Punba, Naan Gulzar, Naan Tunki, Sheermal.

Now have a look at the desserts. Mutanjan, Zarda Muzaffar, Kaddoo ki Kheer, Gaajar ki Kheer, Kangni ki Kheer, Yaqooti, Nimish, Rawe ka Halwa, Gaajar ka Halwa, Kaddoo ka Halwa, Malai ka Halwa, Badaam ka Halwa, Piste ka Halwa, Rangtre ka Halwa.

---

[1] *Khassa* or dishes.

[2] *Chauki* is a low wooden seat.

[3] *Shola* is khichdi cooked with meat.

As for the Murabbe: Aam ka Murabba, Seb ka Murabba, Bahi ka Murabba, Taranj ka Murabba, Karele ka Murabba, Rangtare ka Murabba, Lemoo ka Murabba, Ananaas ka Murabba, Garhhal ka Murabba, Kakronde ka Murabba, Baans ka Murabba.

And sweets? Jalebi, Imarti, Barfi, Feni, Qalaqand, Moti Pak, Balushahi, Dar-e-Bahisht, Andarse ki Goliyaan, Halwa Sohan, Halwa Habshi, Halwa Gonde Ka, Motichoor Laddoos, moong, almonds, pistachios, cream, Lozenges made of moong, doda, pistachio, almond, jamun, rangtarey, and phalsey. Sweets made of petha. Pista Maghzi.

These delicious and colourful dishes have been served in large plates, small dishes and saucers. They are resplendent with the scent of musk, saffron and orris. Fine silver paper glitters all over them. Thus, the Mughal spread occupied a unique place in the world of cuisines.

And what were the etiquettes and formalities associated with this spread? Apart from basins for washing hands and rinsing mouths, there are also spouted jugs, soap cases and small boxes of sandal cakes lying alongside. Along with it, the women responsible for the linen are there with kerchiefs: *zaanoo posh*,[4] *dast paak*,[5] *beeni paak*.[6] The king has come and taken his seat on the chauki. On the spread, the queen and the begums are sitting on the right while the princes and the princesses sit on the other side. See, how they eat with such refined manners. If the king picks something lying in front of him and offers it to someone, they stand, accept the gift, take their seat and continue eating.

After the meal, they wash their hands with sandal cakes, rinse their mouths. The emperor retreats to his bedroom, where he sits on the couch and smokes the hukka. The inspector breaks the seal of one of the *suraahis*[7] kept in ice and presents the emperor with

[4] *Zaanoo posh* or napkins.

[5] *Dast paak* or hand-towels.

[6] *Beeni paak* or face towels.

[7] *Suraahi* are earthen pots with long narrow mouths.

the chilled water of Ganga in a silver bowl. On the other side, the begums too have washed their hands and rinsed their mouths. Now they have paan in their mouths, and the pipe of the hukka between their lips. They recline against bolsters as domnis sing melodiously before them.

Babar baeeshkoshke aalam dobaara neest

O Babar, lead a luxurious life as there is no other world.

Babar had only composed the couplet and it was his successors who explained it practically.

These dishes could not be limited to the Fort and trays were regularly sent to the mansions of the rich and nobility, and on special occasions, like Ramzan, they were also sent to the Jama Masjid for Iftaar. So the smell of these colourful dishes also reached the mansions, houses, streets and markets of Dilli. Dilliwallahs were utter gourmands. If not all, they adopted numerous dishes of the Fort. They imbued this food with new tastes. The haleem of the steps of the Jama Masjid, lord be praised! Then some cruel cook started preparing a new dish Nahaari. In the beginning, it was limited only to the working class. But then it became popular among everyone and was considered a gastronomic invention of Dilli. In the days to come there appeared such kababi who created such delicious Seekh kababs that connoisseurs from outside the city would come to their shops and return smacking their lips. They regarded the roasted kabab with great respect.

And sweets. At least about one confectioner it is certain that his sweets would be sought in the Red Fort. He was Ghante Wala Shahi Halwai who had opened a sweet shop at Chandni Chowk. The research by the author of *Aalam-e-Intikhaab Mein Dilli*, Maheshwar Dayal establishes that the founder of the shop was a halwai named Lala Sukhlal. In 1712, he arrived in Dilli from Jaipur. First he hawked his products on the streets. Later he rented a shop in the middle of Chandni Chowk and to give his shop a unique identity hung bells outside his shop, which one of his servants would ring continuously. Though all his sweets were such that whoever ate them returned smacking their lips, the tastiest among them all were the Halwa Sohan Papri Wala and Qalaqand. And yes, Naan Khataai too. These three sweets were especially liked by the people of the Fort.

In these foods, smells and colours held great sway. The food should smell great. And it should be appealing to the eyes. The use of saffron fulfilled both requirements. Whether it was qorma or biryani, zarda mutanjan or sweets, saffron was considered an essential ingredient. Forget food, here even medicines should have an appetising smell. Since everything—food, drinks and medicines—had to be colourful and fragrant, flowers and perfumes were very popular; a Dilliwallah could not even draw a breath without them. Just see the ways and manners of the Dilliwallahs: they get ready and go straight to the Jama Masjid. There, they buy a motibaliya gajra from a gajrawala and wear it on their wrists. From the perfume seller they buy a piece of cotton doused in attar and put it in their ear. Then they get a gilauri from the panwala and keep it pressed in the side of their mouth even as they walk leisurely towards Chawri.

Wherever you go, whatever meeting, drawing room or lounge you step into, the smells of bela, motiya, jasmine and rose will welcome you. If you step into any house, you will see a small unused pitcher kept upon a stand and the string of motiya wrapped around it. In the courtyard there would be a few trees next to the water reservoir. Out of these trees one would invariably be of pomegranate; the red buds of pomegranate create a colourful and attractive sight. Saffron is the colour that is used the most; if this colour does not glimmer in pulao then that would be a *dhobiya*[8] pulao. Every food item or dish has saffron in it. Any sharbat without orris or rose water is not a worthy drink.

---

[8] *Dhobiya* or washed-out.

In Spring, yellow shines brightest among all the colours. From sarees and stoles to turbans, everything is yellow. It happened once that Basant Panchami (an early Spring festival of Hindus) and the birthday of Bahadur Shah Zafar fell on the same day. The entire city of Dilli was vibrant in yellow that day. In such a moment Mir might have seen a rosy-cheeked [beloved] and recited the following couplet:

Basantiqabapar teri mar gayahoon
Kafandijiyo Mir ko zaafraani

I've fallen in love with your yellow garment
Give Mir a saffron shroud.

This was predominantly a culture of the five senses. Numerous articles were available to satiate the five senses and they were considered the necessities of life. All the same, satisfaction of the five senses was not an end in itself. The idea was to acknowledge the five senses and go beyond. The fragrance wafted from the sensual to the spiritual realm of experience and became an aroma of devotion.

At the shrines and mourning houses, colourful girdles; incense sticks burning in the censer; and this smell coupled with the smell of frankincense. Flags, on coffins and shrines are adorned with strings of flower. Now this smell transcends the realm of the sensual and seems to be fetching news from the world beyond.

The fragrance of devotion and the colour of imagination had shaped things in a way that around everything known an aura of unknown could be seen; among the familiar signs a secret appeared to be in hiding. Every ghat could be Nigambodh Ghat. But no. When the creature knew that across from that ghat Brahmaji had dwelt, and that due to the blessings of the river he could recollect the Vedas that he had forgotten, the status of the ghat changed. Similar to Akaas and Kalka temples were other temples. But no. The religious imagination had accorded a unique and different status to these temples. In front of Akaas Mandir two lions of red stone stood on either side. The tradition about Kalka Mandir was that in some forgotten age devas had lived there. Two *rakshasas* [9] tormented them. They appealed to Brahmaji. Brahmaji advised them to beg Maha Mai Parvatiji to rid them of this trouble. The devas did so. Then a goddess appeared from the mouth of Maha Mai, whose name was Koshki. Koshki killed the chief of those demons. But their drops of blood gave birth to many more demons. Then from the brow of Koshki, Kali Devi appeared. She was so huge that one of her lips rested on the mountain while the other reached up to the sky. Now, Koshki went on murdering the demons. Kali Devi was assigned to not let any drop of their blood fall on the ground. So she swallowed the blood of all the demons. Later, Kali Devi made an abode on this hill. And in later days a temple was erected there which is known today as Kalka Mandir.

Now, also read about Jogmaya Temple. It is close to the Iron Pillar of Qutub Sahab Complex. It is said that when Queen Devaki gave birth to Krishna, Vasudevaji lifted him in his arms, took him to Gokul where he left him in the house of Jasoda and returned with her newborn daughter. Kansa thought that Devaki had given birth to a baby girl. He took the baby girl from her mother's lap and threw her on the ground. But she converted into lightning and disappeared. Then she came here and graced the place. And thus this temple came into existence.

Now listen about the iron pillar standing in the compound of Masjid Quwwat-ul-Islam. Hindus believe that it is the same nail that Prithviraj Chauhan had erected on the suggestion of his astrologers to trap Raja Basak who resided deep in the earth. 'If a nail is fixed in his hood he will not be able to slip away from here; and while he is here your rule will be unchallenged and perpetual,'

---

[9] *Rakshas* are demonic beings in Hindu mythology. Historians have opined that the term indicates demonised depiction of forest dwellers who remained outside the caste society.

they said. The nail was firmly fixed in the hood. But the king, naive as he was, had it pulled out to be sure if it was indeed embedded in the hood. After making sure, he had it put back immediately. But it was too late and King Basak had already slithered away by then. The nail remains fixed in the same spot to this day.

On the other hand, the vibrant faith of the Muslims gave birth to many new traditions and changed the narratives associated with many parts of the city. Just listen to the narrative of how the Hauz-e-Shamsi was constructed. Sultan Altamash wanted to excavate a pond. But he could not find a suitable place. One night he dreamt of Hazrat Ali astride a horse. Hazrat Ali instructed Altamash to have the pond constructed in such and such place. In the morning the king narrated his dream to Hazrat Khwaja Bakhtiar Kaki and took him to the place he had seen in the dream. Both of them saw hoof marks there through which water was coming out. So, it was decided to build the reservoir there. It was named Hauz-e-Shamsi.

Located in front of the Tomb of Safdarjang, the shrine of Shah Mardan was built by the begum of Emperor Muhammad Shah, Nawab Qudsia Sahiba-uz-Zamani. It is said that someone gave her a stone that had the footprint of Hazrat Ali. They said that the stone was fixed in the building of that shrine. So, as per common belief, the Shrine of Shah Mardan had the honour of being adorned with the footprint of Hazrat Ali.

Adjacent to the Shrine of Hazrat Nizamuddin Aulia is a *baawli*.[10] About it, too, there is a story. It is said that when the baawli was being built, the Fort of Ghiyasuddin Tughlaq was also being constructed not very far away. Perhaps Sultan Tughlaq harboured a grudge towards this revered Sufi due to what he perceived as his indifferent attitude. He ordered that workers should not go towards the khanqah during the day. Mahboob-e-Ilaahi (the beloved of God) then planned to construct the baawli in the night. The workers who had worked all day would construct

---

[10] *Baawli* is a step-well.

the Shrine in the night by the light of oil lamps. When the Sultan came to know about it, he ordered that oil must not be sold to the shrine. When Mahboob-e-Ilaahi heard this, he said, 'It does not matter at all whether oil is available or not. The water of the baawli will do.' Such was the miracle of the revered saint that the baawli water would turn into oil as soon as it was poured into the lamps.

The story about Jama Masjid is famous and has been mentioned earlier as well. When the construction of the masjid was complete, it was realised that it was not aligned to the West, which was the direction of the Mecca. The administrators were anxious and the emperor dejected. A dervish appeared from nowhere and inquired about the situation. He said it was not a big issue. He stepped towards the mosque and put his back to the Masjid wall. Lo and behold, the masjid was aligned in the desired direction. The dervish disappeared as mysteriously as he had appeared.

In the middle of this town is an old banyan tree known as Badu of Shah Bola. The reason for its name, it is shared, is that in some good time a *majzoob* [11] called Bola Shah had lived in its shade. This banyan tree bore fruit throughout the year. Shah Bola would throw these fruits at passersby. Once, a prince fell ill. The physicians were unable to cure him. He was on the brink of death. Having become utterly hopeless the prince was taken to Shah Bola. Shah Bola asked for oil. He poured it into a bowl and then asked the prince to look at his reflection in the bowl. The prince did so. Shah Bola then drank the oil, lay down in the shade of the banyan tree and closed his eyes. On one side Shah Bola died, and on the other, the prince regained his health.

Thus, this civilization seemed to be travelling from the known to the unknown and from the manifest to the obscure. This was bound to happen. After all, Dilli was not just the capital of kings,it also had the honour of becoming the doorstep of twenty-two Khwajas. Mysticism was an integral part of the city's spirit.

---

[11] *Majzoob* is a synonym for a sufi. It refers to being absorbed (*jazb*) in the thoughts of the divine or God.

14

Doorstep of Twenty-two Khwajas

A variety of dialects and colourful beings existed in Jahanabad. Several modes of life found manifestation here and myriad creatures thrived here. Every aspect was a contrast to the other. Even so they fitted together so perfectly that none stood out. When you looked at any particular colour it seemed as if all of Jahanabad had been painted with it. This was the seat of power, this was the doorstep of twenty-two Khwajas.

The doorstep of twenty-two Khwajas: A diverse range of *walis*[1] made Jahanabad their home. It became a sanctuary for all. Khwaja Bakhtiar Kaki, Hazrat Nizamuddin Aulia, Hazrat Shaikh Nasiruddin Mahmud Chirag Dehlawi. They died a long time ago. But their shrines were so popular that they turned into institutions. Besides them, many *aulia*[2] dwelt here and created sanctuaries for everyone. Every wali had his own style. Sayyid Hasan Rasool Numa had a peg dug into the floor in his dwelling, and tied a rope around his neck the other end of which was attached to the peg. He would circumambulate at regular intervals around the peg and recite the line:

---

[1] *Wali* literally means those who are Allah's close friends.

[2] *Aulia* or patron saint.

Hastam sag-e-Rasul rasan dar gardan-e-maast

I am a dog of the Prophet and around my neck is a rope.

It was said about him that the people he blessed would see the Prophet in their dreams.

Shaikh Nooruddin Yaar-e-Paraan was an elder of excellence. He came here during the age of Ghiyasuddin Balban and stayed near the Yamuna. Another *buzurg*[3] had been living there. He said to the Shaikh, 'You cannot stay here without the Sultan's permission.' The Sultan was in Thatta at that time. It is believed that the elder used his hidden power and communicated with the king in no time. He shared his circumstances and sought the permission to stay near the Yamuna. The king granted his permission, and the Shaikh returned with the royal letter of permission. Those present were surprised by the miracle. Surely, he had flown to Thatta! So, the title 'paraan' (the wings) was suffixed to his name.

The reason Turkman Gate is referred to thus is because Hazrat Shah Turkman Bayabaani is buried there. Due to his aversion to busy cities he was called *Bayabaani*.[4] He wandered in the desert and wilderness. For some reason, he lost his way in the wilderness and arrived in the city, where he passed away. The tomb acquired the status of a shrine and became known as The Shrine of Dada Peer.

There was also Bibi Fatema Shaam, the disciple of Baba Fareed. She is believed to have performed miracles. Dilliwallahs called her Bibi Shaam.

Another elder was Baba Abu Bakr Toosi who was later known as Baba Hande Wale. Another elder came to his shrine and said: 'If I get what I desire I will present this silver jar at your shrine.' His wish was fulfilled and as promised he offered a silver jar to the shrine. There you go, devotees swarmed his shrine. They prayed and

---

[3] *Buzurg* is a reverential way of referring to an elderly person. The word also connotes wisdom. It is often used for a Sufi saint.

[4] The one who dwells in a deserted place or *bayabaan*.

promised to offer silver jars too. Their wishes were fulfilled, and more jars were offered. In a very short span of time innumerable jars were offered to the shrine. So, the shrine was named Hande Wali Dargah or the shrine with jars.

Go on naming the elders and counting the shrines. It will be difficult. Why did someone limit this doorstep to only twenty-two Khwajas, while innumerable aulia and *qalandar* [5] lie in deep slumber in this land?

And those awake are many more. They are awake; some of them immersed in amazement and the other in *jazb*.[6] Some of them have only a loincloth wrapped around their waists while others do not bother to put on anything at all. They smear ash on their bodies and sit stark naked. Various such majzoob and dervishes were encamped in the city. There was Deen Ali Shah who did not have even a string on his body. He did not even have a shelter. Around the *Qadam Shareef* [7] was a dome and he lived there. He used to talk gibberish. But the devotees managed to find profound meaning in his gibberish.

Meer Ahmad used to be in such a heightened state of delirium that he was called mad. He cared not a jot for the world and what it had on offer. He would wander purposelessly and without any aim. At night, he lay down in whichever shop he found empty.

Meer Qutbi was even more radical. Meer Ahmad seemed mad. But he did not deem it necessary to be free from the confinement of garments. Meer Qutbi freed himself from all confinements including that of the dress.

What a majzoob was Shah Abdunnabi! His dinner and lunch consisted of just yogurt and dough balls. He would write

---

[5] *Qalandar* are higher-order ascetics who did not particularly belong to any one Sufi tradition.

[6] *Jazb* is literally, absorbed. The state of being absorbed by the thoughts of God.

[7] *Qadam Shareef* or the revered footprint.

the Qur'an in *Naskh* [8] script. Among the rich of Jahanabad was Bakhshi Bhawani Shankar. He became such a disciple of Shah Abdunnabi that he remained busy in his service day and night.

But Sayyid Askari was quite attuned to the world. Though he was the grandson of Sayyid Hasan Rasool Numa, he was a simple and worldly man. A soldier by profession, he was always busy in his work. But once he visited Alwar. There he met an elder named Maulvi Muhammad Haneef and happened to read the couplet:

Mastum chunan bakun ke nadanam za-be-khudi
Dar arsa-e-khayal ke aamad kadaam-e-raft

Enraptured I have become drunk with divine love
During meditation I do not know where I have come and where I have gone.

That elder looked at him and said, 'go and sit at the grave of your grandfather'. Hearing these words Sayyid Askari lost his senses. He tore his garments, came to Dilli and sat at the tomb of Sayyid Hasan Rasool Numa. His immersion and madness increased so much that he was shackled.

Then there was Baiji. Her name might have been different but she was known thus among Dilliwallahs. Outside the city, she lived under a thatched roof. She would say repeatedly, '*Inna aataina kal-kausar*.'[9] Those seeking a boon or a wish thronged to her. From whatever money they brought, she used to take out 17 kowries, kept them down 17 times and picked them up 17 times, repeating 'inna aataina...' in time with putting the kowries down and picking them up. Then she said to the boon-seekers whatever came to her mind. The respondent would derive some meaning out of her meaningless utterances and return home happy.

---

[8] *Naskh* is a popular Arabic script.

[9] A verse from Quran meaning 'Surely, We have given to you (O Prophet) al-Kauthar (The Qur'an)'.

Quite close to where Baiji lived, was another majzoob who was known as Rasool-e-Shahi, who was the great reformer and scholar, Sayyid Ahmad Khan's grandfather's brother. He had a unique style. He shaved his head, eyebrows, moustaches and beard, wore a loincloth and declared wine-drinking legitimate. There was another elder called Shah Fida Husain. He went to Alwar, took instructions from his peer, Maulvi Mohammad Haneef, and wrote academic books. Then on the commandment of his spiritual guide he threw all these books into a well. After that he returned to Dilli clean-shaven. His only garment was a loincloth; he had smeared ash all over his body. He remained alone in a room for 40 years. When he felt like sleeping he would place a brick under his head and go to sleep.

Going by this description it would appear that Jahanabad was in the first place an abode of Sufis and majzoobs. But just have a look at the poets sitting in their favourite haunts. It would seem as if the city is in fact populated only by poets. Just turn away from this alley and peep into the street of the *hakims*[10] and you will think for a moment that this city is, in fact, more an abode of doctors and hakims. And then seeing the *ulema*,[11] you will feel that in the first place this city is their home.

The elite, the scholars, the physicians and the poets—whomever you look at, they would seem to be the sole members of society, and Jahanabad thrives because of them. The most prominent among them were the physicians. Indeed, their role was much more than that of a physician. Their clinic was a sanctuary for the sick but also the centre of social life. Physicians who had access to the Red Fort would be known as the royal physicians. Hakim Ahsanullah Khan was fair-complexioned, round-faced, sported a white beard and always dressed in white. Apart from medicine he was also a history enthusiast. He was fond of poetry and literature too, and had a deep interest in stories. He persuaded Zaheer

---

[10] *Hakim* or physician.

[11] *Ulema* or scholars. Plural of *Alim*, the seeker of *ilm* or knowledge.

Dehlavi to write a story known today as 'The Story of Mumtaz'. He was Emperor Bahadur Shah Zafar's special physician. But he had not confined himself just to the emperor's treatment. He held sway in all government matters. It is as though he, besides being a physician, had become a minister and counsellor to the king as well. Several titles were conferred on him: Ihteram-ud-Daulah, (the honour of the kingdom) Umdat-ul-Hukama (Gem among hakims), Motamad-ul-Malik (the trustee of the king), Haziq-uz-Zaman (the expert of the time), and Hakim Muhammad Ahsanullah Khan Bahadur Thabit Jang.

Hakim Mahmood Khan on the other hand was far removed from the court. But his clinic itself was like a court. He was the guardian of the legacy of the Sharifi clan. Hakim Sharif Khan who had had an excellent practice in the city long ago had passed away. His son Sadiq Ali Khan was not an insignificant physician either. He was witness to the age of Akbar Shah II and how the changes it brought pushed him away from the court, closer to the public. Now, it was the time of Bahadur Shah Zafar and the son of Hakim Sadiq Ali Khan, Hakim Mahmood was carrying on his family legacy. Away from the Fort and unconcerned about regal favours. But his treatment was famous among the common people. He had a unique fashion; he wore the same garment in all seasons: winter, summer and during the rains. He would wear a *do palli topi*[12] and a muslin *angrakha*.[13] Every day, he went, riding a horse, to the tomb of Sayyid Hasan Rasool Numa and read the Fateha there. In the evening he went out on a phaeton for a leisurely ride. He gave the same attention to both the rich and the poor while administering his treatment. What an excellent physician he was! Cheap prescription, precious treatment. His diagnosis was unmatched. A patient came wailing with a stomachache. The Hakim felt his

[12] A type of cap.

[13] *Angrakha* refers to a double-breasted long shirt tied with buttons or long ornamental strings. Ang can mean the body or a body part, rakha can mean a keeper or protector.

pulse and advised him to eat grams. The patient chewed grams and the stomachache disappeared. Someone asked the physician how could the stomachache be cured by eating gram. They remarked that the ache should in fact have intensified. The physician said, 'From the oiliness of his palm and smell of fat I knew that he had had cold water after eating biryani. So, the treatment was that he should be made to eat gram that would absorb the oiliness.'

A revered and aged gentleman came to him complaining of fever. The hakim wrote the prescription and said it would make him sweat which will cause the fever to abate. The patient used the prescription but it did not cause sweating nor did the fever abate. The hakim modified the prescription. Yet, it did not cause sweating nor did the fever abate. The gentleman came to the clinic with his complaint again. The hakim stared at him with anger and thundered at the gentleman saying that he was an utter fool. Hearing this, the self-respecting gentleman sweated profusely. Then the hakim asked the gentleman softly not to mind his language. 'This was your treatment. Now that you have perspired, God willing, the fever will go away.' Indeed, the fever abated.

And there were also such hakims who wrote more ghazals than medical prescriptions. Now it is up to us whether we consider them hakim first or poet. Momin Khan was undoubtedly a physician but in his time he was known more as a poet than a physician. He also held knowledge of astrology and divination. Such was his interest in this field that had he not been a poet he would definitely have been an astrologer. Once while sitting in the clinic he looked at a lizard stuck to one of the walls, and thought to himself, 'she is waiting for her partner; he'll come from the north.'

While he was uttering these words a Pathan appeared carrying a bale of cloth. He opened the bundle and laid out the cloth so that Hakim Sahab could take a look at it and buy something. When he opened a particular bale a lizard leapt out of it and hurried straight to the lizard which had been waiting on the wall for so long. Then both the lizards moved swiftly towards the roof and disappeared.

Hakim Aanamajaan Aish too was a physician and a poet. Though he was a royal physician, he would spend less time in the Fort and would hover near the Fort walls more. The reason was that along the wall a majzoob had encamped and Hakim Sahab was his disciple. Aanamajaan Aish was a poet and would play practical jokes too. In a well-attended mushaira he read the following quartet addressing Ghalib:

Agar apna kaha tum aap hi samjhey to kya samjhey
Maza kehne ka jab hai ek kahey aur dusra samjhey
Kalaam-e-Mir samjhey aur Zabaan-e-Mirza samjhey
Magar inka kaha ya aap samjhein ya khuda samjhey

What of it, if you speak and are the only one who understands
The joy of speaking is that one says and the other understands
We understood the words of Mir[14] and the language of Mirza[15]
But what this one said, only he himself and God understands.

He was such a great poet that he compiled 12 thick diwans. But he kept them hidden. As he lay dying he made a will to his son, 'Don't have it published, nor show it to anyone or I shall complain against you on judgement day.'

There are so many names when it comes to the poets of the city that we cannot possibly count them. It seemed that the city belonged only to poets. And poets of such calibre, like Mir Taqi Mir! The greater the poet the more conceited he would be. Someone asked Mir once, 'Mir Sahab, who all are the poets of the contemporary times?' He replied, 'Sauda is one, the other is this humble man.' He stopped and then resumed, 'half—Khwaja Mir Dard.' Someone mentioned Mir Soz. He crossed his brows and said, 'Oh, so Mir Soz Sahab is also a poet?' Then he softened a little and said, 'Well, okay, let us say he is quarter of a poet.' Thus, he wrapped up his whole age in just quarter to three poets.

---

[14] Mir Taqi Mir.

[15] Mirza Muhammad Rafi Sauda.

Mir was unique in ghazal, and Sauda peerless in *qaseeda*[16] and *huju.*[17] The poetry of one led you to exclaim 'Ah!' and that of the other 'Wah!' And if Sauda's ode is 'wah!' then his satire is 'wah, wah!' As soon as Sauda became angry with someone he called for his servant, Ghuncha, and said, 'Ghuncha, just bring my writing case.' Ghuncha brought forth the case. Janaab Sauda started:

Let us begin, my pen, with the name of Allah.

He wrote such a bite that the rival would have to hide his face in public. But that he did not only write satire only his contemporaries knew. While crossing an intersection once he saw a female innkeeper and her young daughter who always got into arguments. One day he wrote in her honour thus:

Ladki wo jo ladkiyon mein kheley
Na ke laundon mein jaa ke dand peley

A girl is that who, among girls, plays
Not the one who with boys, her strength displays.

This *Huju*, when disentangled from the matters of individuals and took up themes of society, became *Shahr Aashob.*[18] A *Huju* was used to expose individuals. *Shehr-e-Ashob* seemed to expose the entire society.

As for Mir Dard, undoubtedly in the view of Mir he might only be half a poet, but he was a great buzurg. He had consistent manners and was content with his condition. When the conditions at Dilli became abysmal, the great and proud poets left Dilli for Lucknow. But he remained at his place.

And Mir Soz. Mir called him a quarter of a poet. But Maulana Hussain Azad has called him the Shaikh Sadi of Urdu poetry. He avoided simile, metaphor and Persian techniques. He instead took to a simple narrative style. Then, along with poetry he adapted

---

[16] *Qaseeda* or an encomium ode.

[17] *Huju* means lampooning.

[18] *Shehr Aashob* is a social commentary on the state of affairs in the city.

such a method of recitation, which doubled the joy of poetry. He once read this couplet in a gathering:

Gaye ghar se jo ham apne sawerey
Salaamullah Khan Sahab ke derey
Wahan dekhe kayi tifl-e-pari-roo
Are re re, Are re re, Are re re

In the morning we left our place,
Reached Salamullah Khan's base,
There we saw numerous fairy-faced children,
Are re re, Are re re, Are re re

While reading the fourth line he fell down. People thought he had died.

Among the poets there were Mirs and Mirzas. We have already mentioned Mirza Sauda. But in that very time there was another poet Mirza Jaan-e-Janan Mazhar. Father: Mirza Jaan. Son: Jaan-e-Jaanan. Title: Mazhar. He was fond of both poetry and mysticism. He swept the floors of madrasas and khanqahs. And this led him to be considered a saintly elder. Among his disciples were Muslims as well as Hindus. He was a thorough aesthete. Rather, aestheticism was his second nature. Even during his infancy, he hurried to rest in the laps of the beautiful and leapt out of the laps of those he did not find attractive.

One of his disciples was Mir Abdul Hai Taban. He was a great poet and such an exquisitely graceful young man that he was called Yusuf[19] the Second. He was always dressed in black. His fair complexion went well with the colour. And on top of that, his poetry went thus:

Jab paan kha ke pyara gulshan mein jaa hansa hai
Be ikhteyar kaliyan tab khilkhilaein hein

---

[19] Yusuf, a prophet, has been mentioned in the Quran as having been so beautiful that people would cut their fingers looking at him and not realise it.

After eating paan when the beloved went to the garden and laughed,
the buds giggled uncontrollably too.

But this handsome poet, while in full bloom, waved goodbye to his legions of fans and left them with the scar of separation.

And what happened with Mirza Mazhar Jaan-e-Jaanan? He was a mystical man. He described his faith and *maslak* [20] thus:

Hoon to sunni par Ali ka sadq-e-dil se hun ghulaam
Khwah Irani kaho tum khwah turani mujhey

Though I am Sunni, I am a servant of Ali all through
Irani or Turani, call me what will you

The end of that mystical poet was that on the seventh night of Muharram when someone came to him pretending to be his disciple and shot him with a gun, the bullet went through his chest. His own couplet came to his mouth:

Bana kar din khush rasm-e-najun-o-khak-e-khaltaidan
Khuda rehmat kundaein aashiqaane paak tanyat ra

They have invented a good custom; to be soaked in blood
May God have mercy upon these lovers of purity.

Reading this couplet he departed from this world. He was buried in his very house which later became a khanqah.

When this generation of poets left the world after such pomp and show, another generation of poets rushed in to fill the vacuum. These poets had their own elegance and manners. The writ of Ustad Zauq ran large in the Fort. Outside the Fort, Ghalib had great influence. Momin Khan had his own splendour; his ghazals had their own aura.

Then Nawab Mustafa Khan Shefta, Mufti Sadruddin Aazurda, Imam Bakhsh Sahbai. What great poets and what excellent scholars who created and occupied their own niches!

---

[20] Maslak (literally, a way) refers here to Islamic schools of thought.

15

Dandy, Novel, Awesome

Half the head is shaven. And such is the state of the other half that hair almost reaches the ear. Some have left their hair loose. While others have braided it into a plait and put it across their chests. Some have shaved half of their moustache and the other half is so long you can't find its end. The trousers are loose but one leg is short and knee-length, while the other is so long that it is being dragged along the ground. They carry double-edged swords or heavy maces like Hanumanji. All is well as they walk around looking strange. But dare anyone raise a finger at them! Forget the finger, even their head would not remain intact. O lord, what species is this:

Anokhi wazi hai, saarey zamaaney se niraley hein
Ye aashiq kaun si basti ke yarab rehney waaley hein

Novel situation it is, novel even more is their way
These lovers, O lord, which place do they stay

The place is the one about which Mir cautioned:

Pagdi apni sambhaaliyega Mir
Aur basti nahin, ye Dilli hai

Do take care of your turban, Mir
This is no ordinary place, Dilli it is

And these people are unique; they are nothing like the rest of the world. If they are sighted anywhere other than Dilli, then understand that it has to be Lucknow. Hear attentively how the youth there dress.

> Wearing sharp angrakhas with many folds. Pointed caps on their head, they are prancing around with *dhaatas*[1] tied around the waist. A pair of holsters is tied to their waist, each with an imported pistol. *Qarabchah* [1 2], knife, dagger, scimitar, musketoons[3]—armed with weapons they look like gunslingers.[4]

Who on earth were these people? What were their antecedents? Maulana Abdul Haleem Sharar opines that 'in Dilli's court people from Qandahar routinely came and joined the army in numbers. Since these people were considered brave, therefore a lot of their manners, dressing style, habits, and characteristic traditions are found amongst local ordinary soldiers. And it is because of their blessing and company that Dilli's *Baankey* [5] began wearing loose trousers with a lot of folds. In the last era of Dilli their manners and the bravery of the dandies came to be liked so much that emulating them the elite youth abandoned the usual high fashion and adopted fashions in their likeness. So much so that the elite went around like the Baankey.'

Anyway, whoever they were, they had their own sense of style. Ready to die for honour, benevolent towards the poor and the deprived, giving support to those who had none, lending a

---

[1] *Dhaata* is a cloth band tied across the waist as a belt.

[2] *Qarabchah* refers to a kind of gun. Derived from *Qarabeen*, a common noun for guns in Urdu, derived from the English 'carabineer', or a cavalry soldier whose principal weapon was a carbine.

[3] Musketoon is a short-barrelled version of the musket.

[4] Although Intizar Husain does not reference this as such in the original, this quote, like the one in the next paragraph, appears to be from the writings of Abdul Haleem Sharar (1846-1903). Sharar was a journalist, chronicler and novelist from Lucknow. He is best known for his work 'Guzishta Lakhnau'.

[5] *Baankey* means Dandy.

hand to the helpless. Fiercely true to their words, once they had promised something they would fulfil it even if it meant that they would risk losing their life doing so. That is why they were trusted. Whether it was their own need or for someone poor and needy they could borrow thousands against a guarantee of just one strand of hair from their moustache. And for the moneylender the guarantee of that one strand of moustache-hair was greater than the valuable guarantees of the rich. A petty criminal once saw a Baanka borrowing money from the lender by pawning a hair of his moustache and thought it was a great way of making some money. After a few days he dressed up like a Baanka and approached a moneylender. He plucked out a strand of hair from his moustache and offered it. Said, keep this and lend me some money. The moneylender looked at him with suspicion. Then he looked at the strand carefully and said it was not quite all right. The criminal immediately plucked out another strand of hair and said, here, this one should be good. When the moneylender still appeared unconvinced, the criminal plucked out several strands and laid them out in front of him and said, take whichever you think is fine and give me some money.

The moneylender then said, now I know you are not a Baanka. If you really were one then you would have taken out your sword the first time I refused you and severed my head.

Dandies flourished during the reign of Muhammad Shah Rangeeley. And this was the time when the sultanate was in a state of disarray. As if the rule of law had been deferred. There was no discipline. The nobles found it difficult to protect their honour. In such circumstances the dandies played their role well. In difficult times they used to help the nobility. And to defend the honour of the ladies they would endanger their own lives.

In one locality a few criminals had made a habit of waylaying palanquins passing through the area. They used to take away the jewellery of the noblewomen riding in the palanaquin. Sometimes they would kidnap the ones wearing the jewellery as well. Three brothers had become particularly notorious in this line of work. Hardened criminals, all three. Dare anyone say anything to them. Upon hearing of their exploits, one Baanka decided to take them on. One day the Baanka dressed up as a woman, put on jewellery, and took some weapons along as well. He sat in a palanquin and instructed it to be taken through the same neighbourhood. The palanquin bearers were scared. Partly because of the bullying and partly due to the lure of money, they finally agreed to go.

As the palanquin passed through their neighbourhood, the criminals saw a bejewelled hand dangling out. Immediately they attacked the palanquin. Baanka leapt out of the palanquin and finished the trio with his sword in no time.

The residents appreciated his effort. The news of his heroics reached Muhammad Shah Rangeeley too. The Emperor summoned him. Baanke Miyan reached the court in the same dress he had worn while slaying the criminals. The Emperor bestowed him with rewards and accolades and said, now get rid of this feminine dress. Baanke Miyan replied, do pardon my insolence but from now on I'll only wear this dress. So, Baanke Miyan began to dress as a woman. People started addressing him as 'begum'. And thereafter Baanke Miyan came to be known as Baanke Begum.

When Nadir Shah started his military campaign towards Dilli and the royal army was on the verge of defeat, the emperor recalled Begum. He was surprised that in times of such crisis for the Empire, the Begum was absent. The emperor was then informed that Baanke Begum had lost his life while fighting in the battle. The news made him extremely sad.

Begum had to be in the battle. Baankey were really fond of the sword. They really had no use for shields. Their principle was to attack the enemy head on. To use a shield was against their masculine honour.

Now, listen to the story of a Baanka from Lucknow. His name was Jahangir Beg. This was in the time of Nawab Sa'adat Ali Khan.

The news of Baanka's exploits reached him and Baanke's father was summoned to register a complaint.

The father returned and told the wife about the complaint, and scolded his son a lot. He was angry that his good-for-nothing son has brought him dishonour. And he repeated the taunt of the enraged Nawab Sa'adat Ali Khan: 'Tell your son that he should not be very proud of being a Baanka. I'll have his nose cut.'

The upset Baanka took his sword out and in one swift move cut his own nose. He picked up the severed nose saying: 'Father, Nawab Sahab only threatened you. I cut my nose myself. Here it is.' And lobbed it towards his father.

From that day onwards he became famous as Baanke Naktey.[6]

Thus was the tradition of the Baankas.

[6] *Naktey* or severed nose.

16

Djinns and Fairies, Pir[1] and Faqir[2]

It's been six days since the birth of the child. The festivities of chhatti are underway as the *dholak*[3] is played and congratulatory songs are sung.

Naurang jodey waaliyaan, meri jachha raaniyan
Soha joda pehen suhagan moti bhari maang
Naurang jodey waaliya…

My dear new mothers, wearing newly coloured suits
Married woman wearing nice befitting suit, pearls adorning her hair
Wearing newly coloured suit …

The day has passed. It is now the night of the chhatti. The new mother will observe the ritual of gazing at the stars. The new mother and the infant are both dressed for the occasion. The new mother comes to the courtyard with the baby in her arms. She stands on the wooden cot with much pride because the Quran has been placed on her head and she has the infant in her arms. On her left and to her right two women stand with uncovered

---

[1] A *pir* is a a sage or guide.

[2] A *faqir* is a beggar or mendicant.

[3] *Dholak* is a small cylindrical drum with two playing surfaces. It is placed horizontally on a surface and beaten with the palm of the hands.

swords in their hands. The midwife, carrying a four-sided dough lamp, walks forward till she is in front of the cot. Now she stands at a slight distance. The new mother raises her eyes to the sky and counts seven stars. The women standing by her make an arch over her head by making the tips of the swords touch. What does it mean? It signifies that now no djinns or fairies would be able to pass overhead. She is under the protective shadow of the swords. The shadow of the djinns or fairies cannot fall upon her.

You can imagine from this ritual how popular references to djinns and fairies were in this culture. All kinds of efforts were made to avoid falling under their influence. Their shadow would still keep chasing one. No one could foresee when a djinn might take hold of someone or when a fairy might cast her shadow. Mir's[4] childhood passed by peacefully. But in his later years his mind started acting up and he began to see the face of a fairy in the moon.

Nazar aai ek shakal mehtaab mein
Kami aai jis se khor-o-khwab mein

Sighted a face in the moon
This has undermined both speech and sleep

References to djinns prevailed as well. It was not necessary that djinns should always cause trouble. There were good djinns too. One Mughal lady, who was very proficient in tailoring, told her tale thus:

> Oh dear, I'd be damned if I knew who all had come to take me. They said there is a wedding in our family. The bride's dresses are to be stitched. We have brought a palanquin. Come with us. I am such a simpleton I did not even ask them, Brother, who are you?

---

[4] Mir Taqi Mir (1722-1810) who was a contemporary of Sauda was called *Khuda-e-sukhan* (literally, god of poetry). He was a court poet most of his life in Dilli and Lucknow. He wrote ghazals on the theme of love but is also famous for his scathing comment differentiating between the poetry of 'love' and the poetry of chuma-chati (kissing and petting).

Where are you from? Without asking anything I went and sat in the palanquin. Well, I sat but after that I became very suspicious of who they were and where they would take me. When I peered out through the curtains I could only see a deep jungle. My heart gave a jolt. Hundreds of suspicions came to me. And then when I happened to glance at the feet of the *kahaar*,[5] I nearly died! Oh dear, they had their feet backwards—ankle in front and toes to the back. They were wretched, godforsaken djinns. My heart started thudding. Then the palanquin entered a gate. Hey, it was not a house, it was a palace! Reams of silk were placed in front of me. The bride's dresses have to be made ready. But I have to say what is right. They never troubled me a bit. They were very courteous djinns. When I was ready to leave, they gave me clothes, gifts and gold coins. And sent me back in the same palanquin in which I had been brought there. I had barely alighted from the palanquin and it vanished. The kahaar had also evaporated into thin air. O Allah! Did the sky swallow them or had the earth eaten them up?

This talk of djinns and fairies was more popular among women. The fairies had their own names. Lal pari,[6] zard pari, sabz pari, siyah pari, aasmaan pari, dariya pari, noor pari. The ladies used to believe that Allah had sent them from heaven to serve Bibi Fatima,[7] and to amuse her by playing with her.

Some special djinns also had names and became quite famous among women. These were Shah Dariya, Shah Sikandar, Zain Khan, Sadre Jahan, Nanhe Miyan, Chehal Tan. But Sheikh Saddu was the most famous of them all. Sauda's parodies talk of him. Rangeen[8] has also referred to him:

Kisi ko ji se hai ikhlaas Sheikh Saddu se
Kahe hai aap ko Nanhe Miyan ki koi haram
Some have heartfelt affection for Sheikh Saddu

---

[5] *Kahaar* or palanquin bearers.

[6] *Pari* or fairy.

[7] Fatima is Prophet Muhammad's daughter, of whom he was very fond.

[8] Rangeen refers to Rangeen Saadat Yar Khan, a poet from Lucknow.

Some call themselves servants of Nanhe Miyan

Apparently, Saddu and Nanhe Miyan's fame had spread from Dilli till Lucknow.

But these djinns were more ghosts and ghouls, and less djinns. Sauda, however, got them to do a little more:

Zahik ki ehliya ne dhol apney ghar dharaaya
Tab Sheikh Saddu us par... khaa ke aaya

When Zahik's wife placed a dhol in her house (to start singing)
Sheikh Saddu came upon her having eaten...

References to Sadre Jahan, Dariya Khan, Nanhe Miyan, and Zain Khan can be found in the same lampooning poem. But here they are mentioned in a sexual context in quite a funny manner signifying that these spirits were wicked.

Along with djinns and fairies, ghosts and ghouls, witches and *pichchhal pai*[9] were also popular. For this reason, there were also a large number of religious scholars, pirs and faqirs. You could get treated if you were possessed by djinns, or if you wanted some black magic rituals performed. The *jotishi*,[10] *najoomi*[11] *and raml*[12] were also much in demand.

A woman sitting at home heard a voice say, 'Send! It will be beneficent to you.' She understood that it was a faqir. She answered him, '*Saaein*,[13] we just have enough.'

'She claims to only have enough,' the faqir hollered from the door, 'seven and a half aanaas are kept under the pillow. Lying to faqirs!'

---

[9] *Pichchhal pai* is a witch with her feet turned backwards.

[10] *Jotishi* or Jyotishi refers to the astrologer. Jyotish is an Indian system of astrology.

[11] *Najoomi* or astrologer. *Nujoom* is Arabic for 'stars'.

[12] *Raml* is an Arabic system of predicting the future with the help of dice.

[13] *Saaein* is an honorific often used to address pirs in North India.

The woman's face drained of all colour from shock. She thought that certainly this is some faqir of high standing. She had received seven and a half aanaas for stitching only today, which she had kept under the pillow. She took one aanaa from under the pillow, went to the door and placing it in the faqir's palm, apologised. She explained, 'My husband has gone out of town on a job and there is difficulty at home; I shall not be able to serve you more. I am alone at home. I am here with my daughter.'

On hearing this, the faqir thought for a bit and put his hand in his bag and took out a dried root of some tree. He broke it in two, recited something and then blew over them. Then he said, 'Tonight take one piece of the root, wrap it in cloth and tie it on your arm, do the same to the other and tie it to your daughter's arm. All poverty will leave you.'

Listen ahead to Firaq Dehlavi, 'At midnight, she was woken up by a sound: "What should the poor root do, it is tied in *tanbol*."[14] This sound came repeatedly after every little while and it can be presumed that in the silence of the night it travelled far. "What should the poor root do, it is tied in tanbol." The sound did not resemble a human voice. Instead the extraordinary sound seemed to be that of a stone, or the earth, or a piece of wood. It was terrible. It was frightening. Umrao Begum and her daughter kept hearing these words and their hearts sank. They sat on the bed and shivered. The sound kept coming every now and then. After an hour, Umrao Begum understood that it was the sound of the roots which she had tied in the tanbol tree and then forgotten about them; she had not tied them on her own and her daughter's arms. "This root is magical. God knows what would have been its effect had I tied it." She kept crying and kept praying that "God, the heir of the house is also not at home. There are also no relatives here. Let us see what happens."

Dawn came. The sound stopped. Umrao Begum steeled her heart and got up. She came out of the room, performed ablutions,

---

[14] *Tanbol* is Arabic and Persian for betel vine (paan).

and offered her morning prayers. She had not even got up from the *janamaaz*[15] when many of her neighbours came to her door and clanked the latch. When she went to the door the neighbours asked her, 'Bibi Umrao Begum, a sound kept coming from your house from midnight until morning, "What should the poor root do, it is tied in tanbol". What is the matter?'

Umrao Begum narrated the entire incident and said, 'I'll go into the room, please come in and have a look at the root.'

She went into seclusion. The neighbours came into the house and saw the root tied to the tanbol tree. One of the elders among the neighbours said, 'I have known this *jogi* [16] for the last 50 years. He lives near the palace of Bhuri Bhatiyari. He's a great magician. Had Umrao Begum tied the root on her own arm or the girl's arm, they would have been lured to the jogi in a hysterical state.'

A few strongmen then went to the Bhuri Bhatiyari palace, having understood the location from the elderly neighbour, and gave the jogi a good hiding.

These were remarkable people. They were quite indulgent by their very nature. A fondness for fine things was observed like a faith or religion. This faith gave birth to so many superstitions, and good and bad omens. All kinds of rituals had therefore come into existence. If Sheikh Saddu possessed a woman then dispossession was extremely difficult. Sessions would have to be organised to achieve this. This meant women singing together at night. Then a goat would be sacrificed. Only then Sheikh Saddu would make a move. But Didaar Pir was a good spirit. *Koonda* [17] would be organised in his name. Didaar Pir was a pir only of women. They believed that Didaar Pir was the pir who enabled meetings by ensuring that travellers returned home safely. So the ritual

[15] *Janamaaz* is the mat on which Namaz is offered.

[16] *Jogis* were ascetics and musicians, who were also famed as charmers.

[17] *Koonda* is a large, round and shallow earthen bowl, which is used in ritual cooking. The ritual cooking and feast is thus named after it.

associated with travel was a rupee in the name of Imam Zaamin wrapped in cloth and tied on the right arm of the traveller. A mark would be made on his forehead with some curd. A lamp would be filled with mustard oil and kept burning. The traveller would see his reflection in the oil, and put in a few grains of Urad lentil. This oil would then be given away to the sweeper-woman. The *taka* [18] for charity would be distributed among the poor. Then koonda would be organised in the name of Didaar Pir. This involved prayers with offerings of jalebi, zarda or shakrana.

Along with pirs and faqirs, jotishi and najumi were also much sought after. Whether it was His Excellency, the Emperor or the common people, jyotishi and najumi were in demand everywhere. And this was not a new trend. This had been the way of this city for centuries. The Hindu kings never took even a single step without the counsel of jyotishi. Whatever they said was a line carved in stone. Whoever hesitated in believing them incurred a loss. What had happened to Prithviraj Chauhan? First he believed the astrologers so much that he had the nail hammered in exactly where they had indicated, but later he was stricken with disbelief. This proved to be fatal. The same happened to Bahadur Shah Zafar. The najumi had warned him that night time is not auspicious for him to be crowned emperor. But he was in such haste to sit on the throne! Ultimately, the najumi were proved right. So bad omens kept occurring, and in 1857 such catastrophe befell the city that neither the throne remained nor the crown.

[18] *Taka* was a unit of money. Hundred taka made a rupee.

17

How Things Changed in Just Two Days

Dilli had started to breathe easy after a long time. Following the death of Aurangzeb it seemed as if Dilli, instead of being Dilli, was more a favourite target for misfortunes. The calamities had found their mark. All the adventurers, in a fit of excitement, rushed straight to Dilli and destroyed it. There was Nadirgiri (the looting of Dilli by Nadir Shah), then the Maratha roistering. And the list goes on. The bargain with the English might have been costly, but it allowed Dilli and its ruler to heave a sigh of relief. Dilliwallahs remembered the time that ensued as a time of peace. Days of contentment returned to the city and Dilliwallahs forgot their hardships once again. How quickly the splendour of Dilli had returned! From Chandni Chowk to Chawri Chowk, Jama Masjid and Yamuna Bridge, everywhere tourists were flooding in; there was a crowd of dandies everywhere. Then poetry resumed and reached its full bloom with mushairas, and storytelling gatherings were held frequently as well. Some others, not interested in these, laid out their chessboards and others busied themselves in playing cards. Besides, a gathering of singing and literature was not uncommon. Who could have imagined it was the last spring of Jahanabad?

But Ghalib, while writing to one of his friends, made a strange comment about the mushairas of the Fort. 'I sometimes go to this gathering, sometimes I don't. And this company itself is just for a few days. It is not going to last long. Who knows in the coming days they will be past.'

In fact, the atmosphere was beset with unease. The residents of Dilli had witnessed so many revolutions that it had sharpened their senses. Their intuition said that something was imminent. They had always been believers in omens. They had faith that the signs appearing on the earth or in the sky augured omens, both good as well as bad. But now they could see nothing but bad omens. It was during those days that somewhere in Dilli appeared a comet in the sky. The pounding hearts of Dilliwalas were audible even to bare ears. There were hundreds of apprehensions. And Ghalib wrote to a friend,

> Now it is about time that I must write about that comet. When the mode of age is that of destruction, only then such shapes appear on the surface of the sky. In which sign of zodiac it appears, its class and minutes are seen; thousands of tactics are used to draw just a conclusion. In Shahjahanabad it would appear on the western horizon of the city at sunset. Since the sun was in the first sign during those days it was understood that it is in the scorpion shape. The status of the stage and the minutes was unknown. This star had been at the centre of people's attention for many days. Now it has been ten or twelve days since it was last seen.
>
> I know just that these shapes are of divine wrath and evidence of the country's destruction—conjunction of two inauspicious planets, the solar eclipse, then moon eclipse, and then this inauspicious shape. We seek refuge with Allah.

The *murshid* [1] of Hakim Aagha Jaan Aish, Shah Bhore had encamped under the fort wall, and breathed his last there. Now a majzoob who was encamped near the tomb had begun to behave strangely. A heap of empty plates was lying near him. He repeatedly laid them one over the other. When finished, he pushed

---

[1] *Murshid* or spiritual guide.

them down with his hands crying, 'There! Demolished the Red Fort, destroyed.'

Zaheer Dehlavi was witness to another occurence, which he narrated thus,

> One day when I was sitting in a bookstore scanning books, a buzurg arrived—plump, tall, corpulent, long-bearded, with a dark, spotty beard, about 60 years old, wearing a loose narrow-sleeved *achkan*,[2] *sharai pyjamas*,[3] and a round cap, stick in hand, and prayer beads around his neck. He asked for a Quran and started reciting it. He had recited not more than a small part when he was overcome with jazb. His eyes turned red, his face too reddened, the veins in his neck bulged, and in that state of anger and wrath he waved his hands towards the market and said, 'Here, here, there he killed, there he killed. There he hanged, there he hanged. Wow! What a show. One goes on killing the other. One goes on hanging the other. The rest remain silent spectators. And Janaab Barbatan[4] is entertaining himself.' Having said all this, Hafiz Sahab himself said, 'Be quiet. Who has allowed you to expose the secrets of Allah?' He lowered his head and again became busy in recitation. Having completed another *rukoo*,[5] he underwent the same condition, and again he repeated the same words.

For the third time it happened so. But after that the buzurg went silent. He kissed the holy Qur'an and in a gesture of extreme reverence touched it with his eyes, put it over his head and then handed it over to Zaheer Dehlavi saying, 'What are you doing round here in the city? Go on a walk in the principality.[6] And a

[2] *Achkan* is a tight long coat buttoned down till the bottom in front.

[3] *Sharai* means as prescribed in Islamic law. A *sharai pyjama* for men ends above the ankles.

[4] We could find no reference to this name despite our best efforts.

[5] *Rukoo* is one set of actions accompanied by the recitation of verses from the Quran, that are repeated to form the full namaaz or salaat prayer.

[6] Principality is the territory over which a ruler holds sway.

demand with it: "Dear, bring me fried bread and cooked potherb of fenugreek.'"

Thereafter, he went away. The identity of the buzurg remained unknown. He disappeared, never to be seen again.

A mushaira was held in the Fort. A majzoob poet happened to arrive there. When he found the mushaira was to begin some time later, he started reading out his composition. He started with a ghazal, the refrain of which was '*kuchh bhee naheen*' (nothing at all). The last couplet of the ghazal went thus:

Shama bhi, gul bhi hai, bulbul bhi hai, parwana bhi
Raat ki raat ye sab kuchh hai, sehar kuchh bhi nahin

The lamp, the flower, the nightingale and also the moth
All these are here for the night, for dawn—nothing at all

He saluted the attendees and went out saying, '*kuchh bhee naheen, kuchh bhee naheen*'. A dervish-type man who was reciting the holy Qur'an suddenly stopped and started crying, 'Killed the cruels, killed.'

A stranger arrived in the city. He handed a palm-sized *chapati*[7] of two *tolas*[8] to a gentleman and instructed him to have similar chapatis cooked and then sent to the next village. The gentleman could not understand what type of chapati it was and what the reason was to send such chapatis to the neighbouring village. The gentleman mentioned it to someone else. The other conveyed it to the third one. The third to the fourth. So, the news spread all over the city and created a sensation. It never became known who that stranger was and where he went. But the people who knew the news a little, stood warned. And there were rumours everywhere which got increasing credibility, more so after a big advertisement was seen stuck on the wall of Jama Masjid. The advertisement had a shield and a sword on it and it suggested that Iran was

---

[7] *Chapati* or flat bread.

[8] *Tola* is a unit of weight. A tola is equal to 10 grams.

willing to arrive to free Muslims from the English. Immediately thereafter a rumour found heedful ears that the Iranian army was actively marching via *Darra*[9] Bolan and that Russia was sending a reinforcement for it.

Meanwhile the month of Ramzan started. It was the fourteenth day of Ramzan. In accordance with the tradition, the mace-carriers came out of the Fort at sunset carrying *iftaari*[10] trays to the Jama Masjid. All of a sudden a flock of eagles appeared in the sky. They pounced upon the trays and made them fall down. The iftaari lay scattered on the ground.

It was such an immensely bad omen, it left every listener amazed. The pious women spread their scarves[11] and started making prayers: O Allah, let the Red Fort remain safe and protect our Sahab-e-Aalam.[12]

But safety and protection were elusive now. This accident made a woman recall what she had witnessed the previous night, 'O *Bi*[13], it was but yesterday that I came out in the yard after having the pre-dawn meal and looked up. O Bi, sure enough. The whole sky was becoming red like meat. I was aghast.'

The woman who was listening heaved a sigh in despair and said, 'Bibi, these signs are not good. Every day there is a bad omen. May Allah keep Dilli under His protection.'

But amidst the bad omens sometimes there were good ones too. A water-carrier had a strange dream, rather a good tiding for Dilliwallahs. He narrated that as he was standing at the Chowk of Jama Masjid offering water to the thirsty his ears heard the sound of azaan.[14]

---

[9] *Darra* or Pass.

[10] *Iftaari* is the food eaten to break the Ramzan fast.

[11] Gesture of asking for supplication.

[12] *Sahab-e-Aalam* or Sire of the world.

[13] *Bi* is short for *bibi*, a term for addressing women, an endearment.

[14] *Azaan* is the call for prayer.

I hurried to the mosque, offered prayer and returned soon. As I was coming down the stairs I heard someone calling, 'I am thirsty. Is there any slave of Allah who will give me a draught of water?' I turned and look around. The stairs were empty. No one was there to be seen. I was amazed, 'O God, who was it asking for water?' Suddenly my eyes rested on the tomb of Hazrat Sarmad Shaheed. Behold. There was a light coming out from the middle. Some strange power attracted me to that place. Now, right before my eyes there was a hand coming out of the grave holding a glittering silver bowl. I opened the mouth of my water-skin and poured water into it. The hand along with the bowl disappeared. In a moment the hand again comes out of the grave holding the bowl. The bowl is empty as if someone has drunk the water. But it has two gold coins in it. I take the coins. But I thought, 'I am a poor man. If I go in the market with the gold coins the shopkeepers will raise hundreds of doubts.' Suddenly my ears heard someone saying, 'By means of these gold coins you will go to the king. Say to the king that I forgive my blood. Govern with justice. Avoid shedding blood of the innocents'.

What a pleasant dream it was and how virtuous the glad tidings! Hazrat Sarmad Shaheed had guaranteed that the Sultanate would remain. On the other hand, a prophecy of Shah Nematullah Wali was the point of public discussion. The prophecy was that English rule would remain only for a hundred years. Thereafter it was to end. And ever since the Battle of Plassey a hundred years were just coming to an end.

Amidst these prophecies and rumours, the month of Ramzan commenced. However (as narrated before) on the very first day of Ramzan an accident took place that augured a bad omen: the trays of iftaari which were sent to the Jama Masjid were scattered on the ground by the pouncing eagles. The fasting Bibi looked at the sky at the time of *suhoor* [15] and saw that it had turned red like a piece of meat. Amidst such restlessness and anxiety the fourteenth day

[15] *Suhoor* is the time to take the pre-dawn meal in the month of Ramzan.

of Ramzan came and passed. Today, it was the blessed morning of the sixteenth day of Ramzan. The morning of Jahanabad, *Subhan Allah.*[16] And then came a morning in the middle of May. Ten days have passed in this month. First the sun's rays got intensified and now if you step outside the house you will be drenched in sweat immediately. But the mornings are still pleasant. Value them. And the tourists of Dilli do value them as it is in the morning that they hurry to the sandy banks of the Yamuna. Crowds of tourists bathe at this time on the *ghat.*[17] Rows of moon-like faces wrapped in sarees head to the ghat. But this is the morning of Ramzan, there will be few tourists, as they are sleeping after having their pre-dawn meal. They are not going to wake up so early. So it is only the Hindu priest men and priest women who are going to the ghat.

In the Red Fort too people are yet to awake; the princes and princesses are all sleeping. They have gone back to sleep after having the pre-dawn meal. How will they rise so early? After the meal, deeper sleep overcomes you. They have been sleeping too soundly. They are not going to rise very soon. But *Zill-e-Subhani*[18] Bahadur Shah Zafar is awake. Having had his pre-dawn meal he sits in the casement reading his *wazeefa.*[19] This is an octagonal tower. Under it 200 arms carriers stand respectfully wearing greying turbans and girdles. Here on the Matia Mahal Road in front of the magnificent gate of Badi Haweli (the big mansion) a phaeton is ready. This belongs to the *Sadr us-Sudoor* [20] Mufti Sadruddin Aazurda. The city has just one phaeton and it is seen only at this mansion. The two-horse phaeton moves at a swift pace. On its arrival at Kashmiri Gate the eastern watchman, as per

---

[16] *Subhan Allah* or Allah be praised.

[17] *Ghat* or Riverside, usually with steps constructed to lead to the river.

[18] *Zill-e-Subhani* or The shadow of God. Title to refer to the sovereign, the king.

[19] *Wazeefa* or incantation.

[20] *Sadr us-Sudoor* or the Chief of chiefs. *Sadr* or *Sadar* means chief. *Sudoor* is plural of *Sadr.*

British rules, salutes the Sadr us-Sudoor with gun and bayonet. The Mufti goes past to the *Kachehri*[21] and the court starts as usual.

It is an English court. Bahadur Shah Zafar too is about to set off for court and the *Takht e-Rawaan*[22] is ready with its golden *howdah.*[23] As he reaches up, his eyes go to the Yamuna Bridge and he stops suddenly. He can see across the river that there are flames reaching up to the sky. Immediately, cavalry men are instructed to rush there. In a moment they return with the news that troops had invaded Dilli, killed the admiral, set his bungalow on fire and are now bent upon plundering. The order was passed: demolish the bridge, pull the boats back, fill the fort gate, let the garrison protect the fort completely, shut the gates of the city walls. Here the orders were being passed and there the army of mutineers that had set off from Meerut came past the boats' bridge to the casement. They told the king about their mutiny and requested him to lead it. The king was hesitant in assuming this thorny leadership.

Disappointed, the mutineers march towards the Raj Ghat Gate but find it closed. On one hand Hindu men and women are insisting upon going to the ghat for their ritual ablutions and on the other the mutineers are knocking on the door to enter the city. But the watchmen of the gate remained unmoved. Then how did the gate open? Everyone hazards a different guess. But the reason cited by those having faith in heavenly assistance found a place in the hearts of Dilliwallahs. They said that two green-liveried horsemen appeared from an unknown direction and threw open the gate. Opening the gate was like demolishing the river's embankment. The mutineer horsemen entered the city and a scene like that of Doomsday prevailed.

Mufti Sadruddin was hearing cases at that moment. Suddenly a blast shook the earth. A stampede ensued in the court. But Mufti

---

[21] *Kachehri* or Court.

[22] *Takht e-Rawaan* is a mobile throne.

[23] *Howdah* is the covered seat atop an elephant.

Sahab remained firmly in his seat. Then the reader came and told him, 'Huzoor, there has been mutiny.'

'What? What mutiny?'

The local army took to mutiny in Meerut and killed the English. That very army has advanced into Dilli. They are murdering the English and have set the gunpowder factory at Kashmiri Gate on fire; there is calamity in the city. The phaeton is ready for you.'

The Mufti uttered, '*Inna lillahi wa inna ilaihi raajeoon*'[24] and stood up. But now his prestigious post was of no value. The sentry at the Kashmiri Gate who had saluted him some time ago looks at him brazenly. What salute? Now, he does not even talk politely. The court reader asks him to open the gate for the *Sadr us-Sudoor* but he refuses to do so. Somehow or the other the reader persuades him to open the gate for a moment. The phaeton of the Mufti rushes back to his mansion but now even the days of the mansion are numbered.

And that huge mansion, the Red Fort—the Qila Mualla, according to Dilliwallahs—has now lost its status. The commandments of *Zill e-Subhani* about the Fort are completely ignored. The garrison is overpowered. The gate has been opened and the mutineers flood in. Now eastern soldiers are roaming about in the Red Fort. Everything is altered. Regal elegance, royal etiquette, appellations adorned with Urdu e-Mualla (the eloquent and authentic Urdu spoken in Dilli's royal encampment), titles, all have come to an end. Now Zill e-Subhani Sahab Aalam Shahanshah Hazrat Bahadur Shah Zafar is only '*budhau*'.[25] And Ihteramud Daula Umdatul Hukama, Haziquz Zaman, Muatamadul Malik Hakim Muhammad Ahsanullah Khan Bahadur was cut short to '*bhaiyyan*'.[26] In this condition, Bahadur Shah Zafar said, 'My two

---

[24] Verse of Quran translated as 'Surely, we belong to Allah and to him we have to return'. Often recited on hearing the news of someone's death.

[25] *Budhau* is a jocular and disrespectful reference to an old person.

[26] Bhaiyyan or Brother (Informal, slightly disdainful).

unfortunate ears have been reduced to spittoons, in which the easterners are spitting by constantly saying *budhau, budhau*.'

Zaheer Dehlavi was the Inspector of *Maahi-e-maratib*[27] at this time. He was ordered to immediately reach the Fort, and he did so. Outside the Fort he saw the torn pages of English books fluttering about. At some distance from the gate an intoxicated malang (unorthodox mendicant) was sitting naked. He held a tattered English shoe. He assembled the pages that were strewn about and then hit them with the shoe. On stepping inside the Fort Zaheer Dehlavi saw Mahboob Ali Khan *Khwaja Sira*[28] sitting silently inside the *Diwan e-Khaas* resting against a pillar. In front of him Hakim Ahsanullah Khan sat dumbstruck resting against another column. Other courtiers were sitting in two rows. In the middle, the tailor was sewing shrouds. Zaheer Dehlavi was amazed at this scene and wondered whose shroud was being sewn. He asked the man next to him softly, but Hakim Sahab overheard him. He said loudly, 'The fact is that the mutineers have assassinated Sahab Resident Bahadur. Huzur (the King) is anxious over his death. On his order it is arranged to bury him. Seven more people have been killed. Their corpses are lying outside the Fort gate.'

While this conversation was going on, some mutineer horse riders descended from their horses and entered the *Diwan e-Khas*. They wore *kurtas* of *lattha*[29] and loose skirt-like pyjamas. On their heads were wrapped *angochha*[30] and their bald heads were exposed. They carried guns, pistols and carbines. Hurriedly they looted the

---

[27] *Maahi-e-maratib*, or 'Order of Fish', was an honour bestowed by the Mughal Emperors. This fish insignia, given only to very high-ranking nobles, was a figure of a gaping fish head with a streamer behind it. It was mounted on a staff and carried by a camel or elephant rider ahead of all important processions of the awarded nobleman.

[28] *Khwaja Sira* were the eunuch attendants in the royal women's quarters.

[29] *Lattha* or a coarse white fabric.

[30] *Angochha* is a cotton hand-towel, often worn casually around the neck or wrapped around the head by people in North India.

rolls of cloth for shrouds, tore them into pieces and wrapped them over their heads. One of them put a pistol on Mahboob Ali Khan's potbelly.

Such was the scene in the Fort. Out there the mutineer horse riders were roaming freely. They were out to murder. Dilli was once more drenched in blood. The only difference this time was that the English were butchered indiscriminately. The Dilliwallahs were safe. But this was only the beginning. Let's see which way the wind blows. Dilliwallahs were yet to witness much more. Jahanabad's game will not be folded up this easily.

Ibtidaa e-ishq hai rota hai kya
Aage aage dekhiye hota hai kya

It is just the beginning of love, why weep
Keep looking ahead; see what is yet to happen

18

After Eleventh May

Jahanabad's topography was now transformed. A particular wind blew and the colour of the city became unrecognisable. The days of safety were a thing of the past. Peace and tranquility was a distant dream. The razzle-dazzle of Chandni Chowk had vanished and the Jama Masjid Chowk was no longer teeming with people. Mushairas have stopped, and the gatherings of storytellers are suspended. What poetry and what of storytelling? It seemed as if everything had come to an end. The fort was no more the same fort and the streets were no longer the same streets. The tourists, fops and dandies of Dilli had vanished. A different creature was moving about without let and hindrance in the city. First, the eastern sentries led an assault, and then General Bakht Khan advanced like a ravaging storm from Bareli and did not stop till he had reached Dilli. The English cavalries came rampaging next and stationed themselves in the hills outside the city. Behold, cannons are firing from both the sides!

But what was Bahadur Shah Zafar doing? Earlier the English had handicapped him. The splendour of the Mughal Sultanate had ceased to be. In Zafar merely a lamp flickered. But now the mutineers had beaten and ousted the English, and were requesting the emperor to really become the King of India and assume leadership of the mutiny. The mutineers, not only the rebels of

Meerut but all those who were rebelling in different parts of India, were looking for a leader. They looked all over before their sight was raised towards Dilli and became focused on Bahadur Shah Zafar. However little and residual the status of the Mughal emperor might have been, it was only he who could assume a central status. The mutineers were in pursuit of a leader. And while Bahadur Shah Zafar was visited by the consideration of regaining the lost Mughal grandeur, the thought was also frightening for him. He hesitated at first. Then what did this king decide?

We have two pictures of that king. One is based on the narrations presented after the apocalypse by biographers who belonged to Dilli and who had faith in English blessings. The other picture is presented by later historians who refused to call the mutiny 'treachery' and insisted on referring to it as a freedom struggle. Their statements presented a different picture. The Nawabs and the kings who had declared freedom started sending offerings to the Emperor of India and the Emperor happily accepted the offerings with grandeur and dignity. When Bakht Khan arrived in Dilli, he (Zafar) welcomed him. He offered him a shield and a sword and entrusted to him the army's command.

Right now I have two books before me. One of them is *Dastan e-Ghadar* ('Story of the Mutiny') by Zaheer Dehlavi. Zaheer Dehlavi had been associated with the Fort as the commander of the maahi e-maratib. He bore witness to incidents in Dilli and the Fort ever since the mutineers arrived and till the fall. He narrated these and he has his own point of view. In his narrations, it seems as if Bahadur Shah Zafar's condition was one of landing in the fire from the frying pan. He escaped the clutches of the English only to be surrounded by the mutineers. He did whatever he had to because he was compelled to do so. He was leading the mutiny but,

Dast-e-tah-e-sang aamdapayman-e-wafa hai

Pact of loyalty has been forged with a hand of rock

Bakht was undisciplined and unaware of royal etiquette. But what was the emperor to do. He was forced to bestow all power on him.

I have another book in front of me, *Cry for Freedom*; this is a collection of documents about the 1857 war which Salimuddin Quraishi[1] has unearthed from among the heap of documents in the India Office, which means documents have been given priority over presumptions.

According to some documents, it was not even the case that Dilliwallahs were caught unawares. Murmurings had been going on for a long time. The poster stuck on the wall of Jama Masjid mentioned earlier was not just there, but in every street and on every wall. And there was a man who accepted responsibility for that advertisement. He said his name was Muhammad Sadiq Khan and he claimed that as many as 900 Iranian soldiers had entered India. Among them 500 were wandering in Dilli in disguise. He said that he too had arrived in Dilli for this purpose on 2 March, a month and a few days before 11 May. He also claimed to have been receiving information from all nooks and corners of India and that he sent all these pieces of information in writing to the Emperor of Iran. *Sadiq-ul-Akhbar*[2] commented on this poster in its 19 March 1857 edition. What a comment it was! First it criticised it, upbraided Muhammad Sadiq for coming to Dilli. Then it ridiculed the idea that the Emperor of Iran would occupy India and questioned if our Hindu brethren would like it. It added,

---

[1] Salimuddin Quraishi (or Salim al-din Quraishi) was in charge of the Oriental Section at the British and India Office Library, London. His *Cry for Freedom: Proclamations of Muslim Revolutionaries in 1857* was published originally by University of Michigan Press and reprinted by Sang-e-meel Publishers, Lahore in 1997.

[2] *Sadiq-ul-Akhbar* was a weekly journal, edited and published by Saiyad Jamiluddin Khan from Dilli. Along with *Dehli Urdu Akhbar*, it was held responsible along with the fort for 'fomenting trouble' by the English prosecutor in the Ghadar trial. Many Indian publications including *Sadiq-ul-Akhbar* were closed down for sympathising with rebels and their editors executed or imprisoned. Jamiluddin Khan was jailed for three years.

yes, if the Emperor of Iran, following in the footsteps of Shah Abbas Safwi, helped our Emperor get back his throne, then there would be an element of happiness in it for our Hindu brethren. Then it added more. It wrote that if it so happens, it should not be surprising as it was Timur who had bestowed the Iranians with the bounty of sovereignty. And it was this feeling that had persuaded Shah Abbas to help Humayun.

Leave aside whether the Emperor of Iran had taken such a step or had just intended it. Muslims of the subcontinent had been sanguine about Muslim countries ever since the beginning. Many a times they had hoped for assistance from them. Sometimes from Iran, sometimes from Afghanistan or from Turkey. It was very possible that this rumour had no basis, instead it was indicative of the wishes of the governed and about the fact that the hearts of Dilliwallahs were simmering. They had sensed that some trouble was going to take place with the English. They were hopeful about the future, but also apprehensive. Hundreds of apprehensions and worries had surrounded them—bad omens, good and bad dreams, suppositions, prophecies, clear and vague indications. If all this was going on, was Bahadur Shah Zafar unaware of it all? But the announcement by the royal army, a document pertaining to which has been discovered at the India Office by Salim Quraishi, speaks otherwise.

This document is an announcement by the 'Royal Army of Dilli' to Indians. Evidently when the English occupied the Red Fort in September 1857, they found this among other documents and it was then sent to the India Office. The announcement was in Urdu. It was translated into English and then studied deeply.

In a way this announcement makes the mutiny evident. It lists the atrocities and cruelties by the English which had led to the mutiny being unleashed. It also mentions the dream of the water-carrier. It said that the gold coins which he had received in the dream were in his hand to be used when he woke up. When he went to the market with them he did get questioned. He was asked where he got the coins. He told his questioners that they were bestowed upon him by the emperor. The royal men caught him and produced him before the emperor. Bahadur Shah Zafar saw his abysmal condition and said indeed he had given him the coins. But thereafter the water-carrier was made to stay in the Fort. He was asked in isolation what the matter was. Where had he in fact got the coins? The water-carrier narrated his dream and also repeated the edification that he had received for the emperor. Upon this the emperor heaved a sigh of resignation and said, 'I am weak and feeble. I have one foot in the grave. But this omen is good. Let us wait to see what appears from behind the curtains of the unseen.'

And what appeared from behind the curtains of the unseen did so in the mixed atmosphere of expectation and disappointment. The case with Bahadur Shah Zafar was such—many expectations and amidst them little hope. In the beginning, there was hesitation. Slowly as hope came alive, he might have begun to trust that the mutineers would succeed: now that I have been crowned the leader of the mutiny I should do it trusting Allah and see what appears from the unseen. Thus the stale curry was brought to boil. The Emperor tried to manage and order the mutiny. He handed over the command of the army to his sons, appointing Mirza Mughal Commander-in-Chief. But it turned out that Mirza Mughal was a Mughal only in name. Had this Mughal ever witnessed a battlefield he would have known what a war meant and what a Commander-in-Chief was supposed to do. But in fact, he had not.

Mirza Mughal could not enforce any discipline on the battlefield. Bahadur Shah Zafar took many steps on the civilian front which led to an improvement in the situation. A serious problem arose when a religious scholar known as Maulvi Muhammad Saeed raised the slogan for jihad, and he went and hoisted the flag of jihad in the Jama Masjid. Bahadur Shah Zafar immediately had this flag removed and declared that both Hindus and Muslims were equal. It was his efforts on Eid-e-Qurbani that prevented cow sacrifice from happening in the city. And now General Bakht Khan too had arrived from Bareli with his infantry regiment.

Bakht Khan arrived in Dilli on 1 July. He had been associated with the English army. The Bareli Brigade, a detachment of the British infantry, had achieved many memorable feats under his command and bagged many medals. Emperor Zafar offered him a sword and shield and appointed him supervisor of the army's affairs. But Mirza Mughal remained as he was. And how could this Mughal prince bear that a Rohilla chief from Bareli would interfere with his affairs. A diarchy emerged at the war front. And from here a series of conspiracies began to be hatched, further exacerbating the prevalent atmosphere of intrigue at the Fort. All the same, Bakht Khan's arrival did bring a new wave of excitement. The people of the city, too, felt encouraged. The religious leaders of the city gathered and issued a fatwa advising people to lay down their lives and properties if need be.

At the same time, however, the strength of the English army, too, had increased considerably. Brigadier Nicolson had arrived unexpectedly armed with military equipment. The time of a decisive fight was nigh.

When Bakht Khan arrived, another jewel too emerged on the scene. He was a European war expert. Prior to the mutiny he had been Sergeant Major in the English army and was stationed in Bareli. Now he was a companion of Bakht Khan and was fighting against the English. PJO Taylor has left a detailed account about him in his book *A Star Shall Fall.*[3] According to Taylor, Emperor Zafar had also assigned him the key post of second in rank to Bakht Khan. When the English army assaulted the city, a fierce battle took place at Kashmiri Gate and he fought desperately.

---

[3] Major PJO Taylor came to India in 1943 to join the Maratha Infantry. He also fought in World War II and subsequently wrote columns and books on India, especially the mutiny. *A Star Shall Fall* was published in 1993. The title refers to a slogan or war cry '*sitara gir padega*' popular among mutineer soldiers.

Ultimately the moment arrived whose signs had already started appearing. In the Fort consultations were in progress. Hakim Ahsanullah Khan and Mirza Ilahi Baksh, father-in-law of the emperor's son, advised the emperor to bid adieu to the war and leave the Fort. On behalf of the English they assured him that he will be spared death and pardoned with honour. And ultimately, they succeeded in their mission.

Behold, it is time to leave the Fort. The British army has already entered the city through Kashmiri Gate. The city is witnessing a calamity. The battle is fierce and bloody. A handful of people were gathered in the Jama Masjid. Seeing the British army marching towards the Masjid, they drew their swords. A furious fight took place. There were corpses everywhere. Now, people came out in the streets and neighbourhood compounds ready to die. If one could not get a sword, he took a *lathi*[4] and ventured out. Those to whom even a lathi was not available, took a *phukni*[5] from the kitchen and went on their way. Fighting ensued in every street. Those lacking courage fled leaving behind their houses. People had to leave sooner or later as it was clear that the English had turned bloodthirsty. They were hell bent on revenge. The unarmed were their targets. Women and children pleaded for life but in vain. In such a situation there was no option left but to leave the city if you could. Dilli was emptying out. The game of Jahanabad was being folded up. The city gates were open for the time being. The people were free to leave if they could.

In the meantime, there is anarchy in the Red Fort. The Fort is no more a place of safety for the princes and the princesses. Even its walls seem ready to swallow them. Everyone is fleeing. Now they seem to have no protectors. The erstwhile leader is in fatal danger himself. The Emperor of India Bahadur Shah Zafar is not

[4] *Lathi* is a thick and long piece of bamboo used as a staff or mace.

[5] *Phukni* is a metal pipe used to blow air into an earthen stove to supply oxygen and help the fire burn better.

an emperor of anywhere anymore. He took Begum Zeenat Mahal and the minor prince Jawan Bakht and left. No elephant rides; no golden canopied seat. Neither palki nor nalki. Mobile thrones and announcing kettle-drums, no more. He only wishes to somehow escape stealthily. The Red Fort is emptying out. After nearly 200 years it bears witness as its inhabitants leave anxious and in trouble. Bahadur Shah Zafar salutes the Red Fort for the last time,

Damdamon men dam nahin ab khair maango jaan ki
Ay Zafar bas ho chuki shamsheer Hindustan ki

The mighty forts have lost their might, now pray for your life
O Zafar, the sword of India is a thing of the past

Now he heads towards Humayun's Tomb.

For the last time Bakht Khan pleaded to him at the Tomb that even now everything was not lost. Only Dilli had been lost while all of India was still not taken. There were pitched battles happening at numerous fronts in various places. He requested the emperor to leave with his army, that they would pitch camp somewhere suitable, that all of India was looking at the emperor with expectation.

But Bahadur Shah Zafar Ji had lost courage. He sought to excuse himself on account of his old age. Bakht Khan came out biting his lip in frustration and stamping his feet in anger, and led his troops in some unknown direction.

Here, after bidding farewell to its inhabitants the Red Fort stands deserted. An empty house is occupied only by ghosts. Bahadur Shah Zafar came out of the Fort on 19 September. On 20 September the British occupied Dilli and General Wilson entered the Fort with pomp and show. The Diwan-e-Khas was now his headquarters.

Bahadur Shah Zafar had considered Humayun's Tomb a safe place. But there was no safe place in Dilli at this time. Captain Hudson sought permission from General Wilson and hurried to Humayaun's Tomb. Maulvi Rajab Ali went inside to Bahadur Shah and explained the entire scenario to him. He assured him on behalf of the British and got him to agree to whatever he proposed. And behold, Bahadur Shah Zafar came outside and surrendered to Hudson. Zeenat Mahal and Jawan Bakht were with him. And they were taken back to the Red Fort.

Lucky were those Mughal children who trusted their own judgement and went their way. They would be insulted much, suffer much. But at least their lives would be safe. The three unlucky princes Mirza Mughal, Khizar Sultan and Mirza Abu Bakr, had followed the emperor and stayed at Humayun's Tomb. Perhaps they thought their lives would be safe if they stayed by the emperor's side. Now it dawned upon them that they had, in fact, been dragged there by their death. Hudson was murderous. He spared Bahadur Shah Zafar only due to the General Wilson's instruction to bring him alive. There was no such instruction regarding the princes.

Hudson hurried to Humayun's tomb. Maulvi Rajab displayed his talent of persuasion once again and ensnared the princes making them believe whatever he was saying. A message was conveyed from inside the tomb that the princes were ready to surrender. Upon this, Hudson sent 10 men in. See the three princes are riding out on the *rath,*[6] five guards on their right and as many on the left. Immediately on coming out they enquired if they would be assured protection. Hudson sharply answered, 'Absolutely not!'

First Hudson ordered the crowd gathering there to lay down their arms. Then he ordered the princes to take off their clothes. Then he took his rifle and shot them dead one after the other. He ordered his soldiers to take the corpses to the spot in the city where the mutineers had killed 49 Europeans, and heap them there. Then he boasted that he had cleansed the Timur dynasty.

In the meantime, the defeated Bahadur Shah Zafar ultimately reached the Red Fort. But the entire scene there had changed in

---

[6] *Rath* is a four-wheeled carriage driven by bullocks.

the two days that he had been gone. The Red Fort was not the same Red Fort, nor was Bahadur Shah Zafar the same Shah Bahadur Shah Zafar. It was a strange flip of fortune. The place which, just a few days ago, was a place for Mughal princes and princesses to strut around was now a place where the English went charging. Many English officers had turned up there with their families. Plunder was imminent. Royal dresses, jewellery, diamonds and gems were all bounty for the rivals. The heir of the Mughal throne and the Shahjahani Fort was sitting imprisoned in a destroyed corner. What was his condition? Let it be narrated by those who were responsible for bringing such an abysmal condition upon Zafar. Who else would dare to sneak a look at the Red Fort? Now, there was a profusion of the English there. It was they who became the eyewitness of the dethroned king.

It was decided that the life of the dethroned king would be spared and that he would be shown regard as per his status. The first condition was fulfilled but the second was not given even the slightest importance. He might have been a king. Now he was a prisoner of the English. Among those who saw him in this state, two eyewitnesses are considered trustworthy. One of them was Richard Temple and the other, the correspondent of the *London Times,* Russell. Richard Temple met the emperor regarding the case that was being brought against him. Russell met him as a newspaper correspondent. First hear whatever Russell narrates:

> At the place where we were standing, there was a narrow and dark pathway which seemed to be leading to an open yard. Ahead of it there was a cell that was darker than even that place. Here, there was squatting a weak and ill looking old man. He had a dirty muslin *kurta*[7] on. A small cap covered his head. The feet were bare. We had arrived at a wrong time. In fact, the dethroned king was sick. He was about to vomit. Due to the exertion to vomit in the brass trough he had almost doubled over.

[7] *Kurta* is a long shirt.

> Only after some time did his nausea cease. Still he was breathing falteringly. He used hand signals to reply to us. Simultaneously he would mutter something.

In what state did Sir Richard Temple see him? Take a look at this too:

> I had also to meet the dethroned king. It was a strange sight that the aged man was sitting in a darkened cell of his own palace. Sharp features, arched brows, thin waist, ill looking yellow skin tone, a defeated look on the face. Rosary beads moving in his thin delicate fingers. In between he mutters to himself. Speech that one cannot follow. All in all it made for a strange image, such that if a spectator was acquainted even a little with the history of Asia he could not avoid being affected. This person, who was sitting here in this state was the last symbol of Mughal grandeur—the descendent of the kings who had ruled the landmass with the world's second largest population for 200 centuries. And although this Emperor had a status which was only that of a shadow of the past emperors he had been treated with regal honour. He was now to be presented in the courts of the judges whose forefathers had petitioned his royal ancestors for favour and protection.

This was the condition of the Emperor. As for the condition of his city, do not even ask. Dilli was facing the apocalypse. The valiant who had arrived here with a determination to free India and the intent to restore the Mughal Empire dispersed after they had fought to their capacity. Now it was just the citizens of Dilli and the enraged English. The fire of revenge was raging in English hearts. Those from whom they had to extract revenge had given them a slip and left. The weak always get it in the neck. The common citizens who had had nothing to do with the mutiny were now being killed indiscriminately. Listen to the rest in Ghalib's words:

Jab ke faal-e-maireed hai aaj, har salahshor Inglistaan ka
ghar se bazaar mein nikalte hue, zehra hota hai aab insaan ka

chauk jisko kahin wo maqtil hai, ghar bana hai namoona zindan ka
shehr dilli ka zarra zarra-e-khaak, tishna-e-khoon hai har musalmaan ka
koi waan se naa aa sakey yaan tak, aadmi waan na jaa sakey yaan ka

Now that each soldier of England is an emperor himself
People are mortally scared to go out of the houses to the bazaar
The Chowk is the execution ground, the houses are modelled on dungeons
Each speck of dust of the city of Dilli is thirsty for the blood of all Muslims
Neither can anyone come here from there, and people from here
cannot go there.

As for Ghalib, the fact that he was close to the Sharif family saved him. This family had old relations with the Patiala King. And Raja Patiala shared good relations with the English. When the English vented their wrath on Dilli the officers of the state arrived at Kucha Ballimaran to protect Shareef Manzil. Thus, the people of the entire street could remain alive. And Ghalib's house was adjacent to the Manzil. 'After the conquest, the soldiers of the king arrived here. And this street remained safe. Or I would have been no more in the city.'

Well, his life was safe. But how? Listen in Ghalib's own words, as the sufferer has a more realistic explanation.

> I remain sitting in my home; cannot go outside the door. Not to speak of riding and going anywhere. Can anyone not come to me? But who is in the city? Every house is childless. The criminals have been acquiring dominance in politics. Army administration has been in place regularly since 11 May until today, Saturday, 5 December 1857. Do not know what the city has been going through.
>
> Each breath I take is a boon. I am still alive with my family. Anything may happen in the future. The pen is in my hand and I wish to write so much, but I cannot write anything. If it is destined that we get together, we will meet. Or else *Inna lillahi wa inna ilaihi rajeoon*.

But at the time the entire city required reciting *Inna lillahi wa inna ilaihi rajeoon*. For so many days this cruelty kept the trade of death active in Dilli. The British fire of revenge kept raging. So many people were killed. A large number of people fled the city for their lives and honour. Then there was quiet. And in the words of Ghalib, 'A city in ruins with neither a man in sight nor mankind.'

When Russell of *London Times* arrived in this city lying in ruins he witnessed a strange sight:

> All of a sudden I found myself on the ruined and destroyed roads of the deserted city where every house had scars of either cannons and bullets of guns or something else that indicated large-scale plunder. It reminded me of the sight of the city of Sebastopol after the defeat of Malakoff. When our vehicle was running under the lofty city-walls, the roads were deserted except for hungry donkeys and stubborn crows.

And the author of the *History of the Indian Mutiny,* Charles Ball has described the ruins in the following words:

> The citadel of the Mughals was now little better than a hideous ruin and a heap of rubble. The houses and streets were deserted. No man could be seen defending it. The shattered gates and once defiant minarets were now desolate and destroyed. The sweepers were collecting dead bodies of thousands of people who had given up their lives for the restitution of the Mughal throne, and burying them in pits. And now there was no one left in the entire city who could even squeak against the victors.

19

Where Have Those People Gone?

'Sahab, are you aware what has happened here? What took place? That was a life in which you and I were friends. There was love between us. We composed poetry and compiled poetry books. There was an elder at that time. He was our fast friend. His name was Munshi Nabi Bakhsh and his pen-name, Haqeer. Neither does that time exist anymore, nor those people, nowhere those get-togethers and that cheerfulness.

After some time passed we got a second life, although this new birth could not be compared to the first. Anyway, I sent a letter to Munshiji. Its reply arrived. One letter to you, as you too are named Munshi Har Gopal and your pen-name is Tafta. The city where I live is called Dilli and my *muhalla* [1] is called Muhalla of the Balli Maaron [2] But in this life, I have no friends.

By Allah, you cannot find a Muslim in this city if you went looking for one, whether poor, or rich, or people of words. If at all there are some, they are from the outside. Hindus, though, are now somewhat settled.'

Ghalib has spoken rightly. That life was quite different and the world then was something else. Its name was Jahanabad. In

[1] *Muhalla* means neighbourhood.

[2] *Balli* literally means a pole. *Balli Maaron* refers to oarsmen.

the illogical doomsday that world was completely ruined. Now when the uproar has slowed down a bit, the whole scene was changed. Where have those people gone? What happened to those friendships, the love, and the companionship? The city which had all these was destroyed. Cities take time to get settled and decline slowly. This is the process usually seen. But this city started with a celebration and got blown apart with an explosion. Jahanabad started with the inauguration of the Red Fort in 1648 AD and in 1857 AD when the last Mughal emperor was waving goodbye to the Fort, Jahanabad drew its last breath amidst blood and carnage.

When the strength of the storm stopped, Ghalib opened his eyes to find what was lost and what remained. He found that 'hundreds of dear ones had left this world, hundreds had disappeared untraced such that nothing is known about their life or death. Perhaps two or four are alive but God knows their whereabouts.' Slowly he could know about three of these 2–4 persons among them. 'In Meerut, Mustafa Khan; in Sultanji, Maulvi Sadruddeen Khan; in Ballimaran, a dog known to the world as Asad; the trio rejected, dejected and stressed.'

Nawab Mustafa Khan Shefta and Sadruddin Azurda were both found guilty. Shefta was sentenced to seven years of imprisonment but later he was pardoned and released. The orders however were only for his release. 'No orders were passed yet about the estate of Jahangirabad, properties of Dilli and the pension. Having no recourse, he is staying in the house of a friend in Meerut after his release.'

The crime of Mufti Sadruddin was evident. He had signed the jihad fatwa. He paid for it. Ghalib writes:

> Hazrat Maulvi Sadruddin Sahab was kept in custody for many days. His case was presented in the court and the hearings were conducted, ultimately decreeing pardon of his life. Employment stopped, properties were seized. He was compelled to go to Lahore in a bad and devastated condition. The Financial Commissioner and the Lieutenant Governor restored half the

properties as a token of mercy. Now he owns that half. In his mansion. Although this income of 30-40 rupees was enough for his upkeep, because it was only him and his wife—old age and weakness has overpowered him.

In such misery and wretchedness he would remember his old friends and cry. In this condition he wrote an elegy:

Tukdey hota hai jigar, jaan pe ban aati hai
Mustafa khan ki mulaqaat jo yaad aati hai
Kyon ne aazurda nikal jaye na saudai ho
Qatl is tarha se be jurm jo sahbai ho

The heart is getting torn into pieces, continuing to live difficult,
When I remember the meeting with Mustafa Khan.
Why should I not leave upset, and just wander about?
When Sahbai was murdered like this, without any guilt?

Imam Bakhsh Sahbai was hanged. Maulana Fazl Haq Khairabadi was sent to *Kalapani*[3] (Cellular Jail). Listen to what Ghalib has to say about the end of Ahmad Husain Maikash: 'Do you know or not about Ahmad Husain Maikash? He was strangulated, as if there was none with this name in the city.'

Numerous are the sons of Jahanabad, who died with its demise. The hanging board was installed in the middle of Chandni Chowk. This is the chowk where people would come in big numbers. In no time bargains worth thousands of rupees would be finalised. Now, blood was being shed everywhere. Outside the Dilli Gate, numerous honorable people who were arrested were sitting, awaiting their deaths. Among them was the father of Maulana Muhammad Husain Azad, editor of the *Dehli Urdu Akhbar*, Maulvi Muhammad Baqar. While the father was sentenced to death, the son disguised himself, took his teacher's *Diwan* [4] and went to

---

[3] *Kalapani* is how imprisonment in Cellular Jail on the Andaman Islands was popularly referred to.

[4] *Diwan* is the collection of poetry.

Lahore after wandering here and there. According to the author of the *City of Djinns,* '3000 Dilliwalas were arrested for rebellion and killed. Some were hanged, some others shot and some others were tied to the mouth of the cannons and blown.' The author writes that the English soldiers liked to see those being hanged to death writhe in agony. Thus, they would bribe the hangman to keep the convicts hanging for long.

In short whoever was captured was declared guilty and hanged. In the words of Ghalib, 'Everyone was being ordered as per whatever was being written. There is no law or rule. No precedence is considered, no argument accepted.' There were numerous people who fled for their lives and kept wandering throughout their lives.'

Humans were treated in this manner. Then the English turned to the lifeless objects. Jahanabad was destroyed. Pickaxes were put to work, streets ruined and lanes ravaged. Ghalib wrote to one of his friends:

> A strong animal combining the character of lion, elephant and monkey has been born. It goes about demolishing houses. It has shaken down to the ground the flower pots at the mansion of Faizullah Khan Bangash, which were popularly called *gumzi*. It destroyed everything. How strange a monkey! This transgression of limits! And within the city!

And the doomsday was not specific to the mansion of Faizullah Khan Bangash. The mansions, travellers' hostels and mosques; everything was ruined. Ghalib witnessed this and narrated it thus:

> Here the city is being demolished. Big, vast and renowned bazaars, Khas Bazaar, Urdu Bazaar and Khanam Bazaar, all towns in themselves, now they are invisible. The owners of the houses and the shops are unable to locate their homes and shops. Throughout the rainy season the sky did not pour down. Now with the deluge of the axe and pickaxe, the houses got demolished.
>
> The gate of the big Dariba market has been demolished. The remainder of the street of the Qabil Attaar has been smashed. The

Masjid of Kashmiri Katra became a patch of the earth. The road has doubly expanded.

From the Jama Masjid to the Raj Ghat, without exaggeration, it is a desolate desert. If the piles of bricks were to be removed there would be wilderness.

On that side of the garden of Mirza Gauhar there was a deep ditch. Now it has become level with the garden's courtyard. The gate of Raj Ghat has been closed. The turrets of the city-wall are always open. Everything else has been obliterated. For the Iron Gate, the land between Kalkatta Gate and Kabuli Gate has been flattened. Punjabi Katra, Dhobi Wada, Ramji Ganj, Katra of Saadat Khan, Haveli of Jarnail's wife, houses of Ramji Das Godam Wale, Garden of Sahab Ram and Haveli—none of them is traceable.

The Kashmiri Katra has fallen. Those high houses and two-sided big rooms are not there to be seen. The Masjid of Kashmiri Katra has become a patch of the earth.

The Imam Bada of Aagha Baqar is also the mourning house of God. It was such an old building—high, famous. Who will not be sad over its destruction!

To cut a long story short, the city has turned into a desert.

And the narration of the situation thereafter goes thus: 'The city is silent. The voice of pickaxe is not to be heard, no house is demolished through mines. There are no metalled road nor any *damdama*[5] being built. The city of Dilli is a graveyard city.'

Rather, say that now the city of Jahanabad is destroyed. In the words of Ghalib, it is a condemned city.

But two major signs of Jahanabad were still there: the Red Fort and the Jama Masjid. What to do with them? In the beginning, it was planned to demolish them. The author of the *City of Djinns* has reported a statement of an Englishman, Hugh Chichester:

> There are so many mosques in the city that are wonderfully beautiful. But I wish to obliterate them all from the pages of

[5] *Damdama* is a rough mud fortification or raised platform for military use (for troops or for mounting cannons, etc.).

> existence. The brutish scoundrels have desecrated our churches and cemeteries. So according to me we should not have any consideration for their stinking religion. Earlier the tradition was that shoes had to be taken off before stepping into their mosques. The same practice would be followed while presenting oneself before the Emperor. But now we do not care. And that old pig king, I went and saw him. He is a loathsome old man, and looks like a servant.

So these were the plans but the buildings built by Shahjahan proved too much for those who wished to demolish them. Listen to this description by Ghalib:

> Allah, Allah, mostly in the Fort and at some places in the city, such Shahjahani buildings were demolished that the pickaxes broke. But in the Fort, when the instruments did not work, the mines were dug and explosives were laid and the heavy buildings were blown up altogether.

In the beginning, the plan was to demolish the entire Fort and build a Victorian Fort in its place. It was also planned that the city-wall would be demolished. According to the original plan, the entire city was to be demolished and victory was to be celebrated by establishing a new city there. But the work which seemed easy in the passion of revenge was found to be quite difficult later. Regarding the city-wall, John Lawrence[6] said plainly that they did not have the amount of explosive required to demolish the seven-mile-long city-wall. Numerous buildings of the Fort were demolished and various beautiful portions were ravaged. But this, too, started appearing difficult. Ultimately, it was decided that instead of demolishing it, it was better that the army camped there. About the Jama Masjid, Lord Egerton proposed it be demolished.

---

[6] Lord John Lawrence was, at the time of mutiny, the Chief Commissioner of Jullunder Doab province. He was decorated by the East India Company and called 'saviour of India' for his role in containing the spread of the Mutiny and recapturing Delhi from the rebels. He was made the Viceroy of India in 1863.

Some of the officers added that a church should be built there after demolishing the Masjid. But no proposal about the city, the fort and the mosque could get consensus. Or you may say that 'Whom Allah keeps, nobody can harm'. Much damage was done to the Fort, but as a whole it was spared. Jama Masjid was fully safe. Yes, there were two more mosques, Masjid Fatehpuri and Zeenat al-Masaajid. As for Masjid Fatehpuri, Lala Chunamal who was a big banker of Dilli, purchased it. A bakery was started in the Zeenat-al-Masaajid.

20

Fate Consigns the One Blessed by the Wings of Huma[1] to Fly-whisking[2]

Gentlemen, a new flower has bloomed in the Red Fort. One of the very special sections of the Red Fort is the Diwan-e-Khas. It was here, in this marble building, where the peacock throne, the takht-i-taus was kept. Inside, above the arches, this couplet is inscribed in gold:

Agar firdaus bar ru-e-zamin ast
Hamin ast wa hamin ast wa hamin ast

If there is paradise on earth,
It is here, it is here, it is here!

As if Shahjahan had built paradise on land here. And today in this paradise of Shahjahan, the English are holding a court-martial of the heir to this paradise. The last Mughal, devoid of his crown and throne, is seen standing in the dock. The bill of

---

[1] In Persian folklore the shadow of Huma bird's wings is said to have powers of conferring kingship on anyone it flies over. This folklore was also popular among the Mughals.

[2] The word used in the original is *Magasrani*—job of whisking flies (*magas* in Persian). Mughal Kings used to practise ceremonial *Magasrani* with fans made of peacock feathers to holy relics in Jama Masjid.

indictment has been admitted by the court. Testimonies are being recorded and arguments being made. The old king, without his crown, sits as if he has nothing to do with the whole story. He is lost within himself; his eyes staring into nothingness, he dozes off in between. With a start he opens his eyes. From the ongoing exchange, he catches a line and refutes it passionately. This is wrong, fundamentally wrong. But again, he withdraws from the proceedings and when asked to argue, he excuses himself.

Ghulam Abbas's testimony is being recorded. This man is the king's lawyer. But he has to testify because he is also an eyewitness in a lot of matters. 'After some time', he continues to testify, 'both the infantry companies that were guarding the gates of the fort on guard and the rogue cavalry from Meerut came to the ground in front of the Durbar-e-Khas and started firing their guns, carbines and cannons in the air and created a ruckus.'

> The king, hearing the commotion, came out and standing on the threshold of the Diwan-i-Khas ordered his personal attendants to go and ask the people to stop firing and called the Indian officers to come ahead and explain their intention behind the protest. At this point the commotion abated. He was told that the soldiers had been asked to bite the cartridges and the intention behind such an instruction was to push both the Hindus as well as the Muslims away from their religions because cow-fat/tallow and pig-fat/lard was applied on the cartridges. Therefore they had killed the English and had now come to seek the patronage of the emperor.
>
> The King's response was: 'I have not called you. And whatever you have done is very wrong'. Hearing this hundred to two hundred of the soldiers, who had come from Meerut, started to climb the stairs and reached the (King's) room. On reaching the King, they told him that unless the lord, the King, is not with us, we are without a leader. And if the lord is with us we will be able to achieve our goal.
>
> Hearing this the king sat down on a chair. And every soldier and officer, with their heads bowed, went ahead and said to the King, 'Lord, put your hand over my head'. The King did just that

and everyone said whatever occurred to them and kept moving on....

Next morning in the fort, it was discovered that the cannons that were fired last night around ten or eleven o'clock were from Dilli's own armoury and fired in the honour of the King.

Question: When the king put his hand on the heads of the native officers and soldiers what was the intention? Did it imply that their request had been acquiesced to?

Answer: It was equivalent to accepting their duties and obligations. But I cannot say what intention the king had during that time.

Question: When did the rights of the King come to be known popularly in Dilli or when did it become popular that the king has assumed control/authority over the army?

Answer: I do not remember if any proper publicity of such nature was made. It is possible that it was done and I did not come to know about it. But the day the riot/violence took place his authority was established.

Question: Was this the reason behind the firing of cannons in his honour?

Answer: I do not know. What I heard was that the people in the armoury fired in honour of joining the royal authority.

Question: Do you know how many cannons' salute was given?

Answer: I think the cannons were fired for the usual royal salute.

Question: When did the King organise his first court with the common people?

Answer: From the day of the riot, the court was organised every day. The first instance on which the soldiers were given a chance to appear before the court should be considered as the first court.

It is the sixth day of the trial hearings. Hakim Ahsan Ullah Khan is standing in the witness dock of the court room.

Question: Are you acquainted with Muhammad Hassan Askari Waiz, resident of Delhi?

Answer: Yes, I do know him. He used to live near Dilli Gate and came to meet the King quite often.

Question: What time did he usually visit the King and when was the first time he appeared face to face before the King?

Answer: It was around four years ago that he met the king face to face for the first time. One of the King's daughters was his disciple. She had praised his austere ways so much that the King, in his days of sickness, hired him to pray for his health and provide him comfort. In two or three years his popularity increased considerably. The King's daughter used to live near Dilli Gate, close to Askari's house, and there was a rumour that she was his wife.

Question: Did this person, Hassan Askari, also cheat by claiming to have revelations; that he could foretell future events?

Answer: He used to interpret dreams and predict future events and he claimed to have revelations.

Question: Do you know if he ever forecast anything about the war that was going on between England and the King of Persia?

Answer: During the time England and the King of Persia were at war he did not say anything. Although around two years ago he took 400 rupees from the prisoner (king) and gave it to a man on the pretext that he was going to Mecca. But it came to be known later that the said person did not go for Hajj and instead went to the King of Iran. His name was Sheedi Qanbar; he was a native of Abyssinia and apparently came from there.

Question: Do you know why this person's plan to go to Mecca was revealed while his trip to the King of Persia was hidden?

Answer: I did not inquire about this. I was informed of this incident by the spy of the court named Jatu or Jatmal who said that Hassan Askari had sent that person to Iran instead of Mecca. And upon inquiring among the courtiers this news was confirmed.

Question: Did you ever hear what the meaning of sending the messenger was?

Answer: No. But I came to know from Quli Khan and Basant, two of the King's loyalists, that Hassan Askari gave Sheedi Qanbar some papers that night before sending him to Iran, and those papers had the royal seal on them.

Question: Were there regular discussions in the fort about the war between the English and the Iranians and did the King show any interest in them?

Answer: No, there were neither any special discussions on that topic nor any interest was expressed. It was through the Hindustani newspaper that came to the fort that the King and his people got news of how the war was progressing. And the King never showed remarkable interest in it.

Question: Did the Muslims of Delhi have any interest in the war? And was this war considered a religious war by them?

Answer: No, the Muslims of Dilli are Ahl-e-Sunnat Wa-al-Jamaat. And the Irani belong to the Imaiya. Therefore the former did not show much interest in the war.

Question: Did you hear that the King had sent along with the caravan going to Mecca a few people to Constantinople as well?

Answer: No, I don't know this.

Question: Was any message with a royal seal from the King of Iran found pasted (on the walls) in Jama Masjid or any other part of the city before the riot/violence?

Answer: Yes, a few months before the riot I had heard that an advertisement from the King of Iran was pasted (on the walls) in the Jama Masjid.

Question: Did you also hear why this note had appeared?

Answer: No. But I heard it being suggested that the note was written by the Shia.

Question: What was written on the paper?

Answer: I heard that it was an advisory to all the sects in the Muslim community to resolve mutual discord and to respond to the realities of the time; it was imperative that they united and fought under one flag.

Next, the news gatherer of the Lieutenant Governor of Agra, Jat Mal, was called to appear before the court and give his statement under oath.

Question: Do you know any person by the name of Hassan Askari?

Answer: Yes, I do know him. He used to regularly visit the fort and recite prayers for the King. He told me that God had blessed him with the miraculous power to interpret dreams. At that time the prisoner readily expressed his belief that Hassan Askari had all the powers that were attributed to him.

Question: Did you hear about any special dream?

Answer: Yes, when the Iranian army entered the city of Herat I had heard about a dream. Hassan Askari narrated one of his dreams to the King saying, 'I see a storm emerging from the west followed by heavy rains destroying the entire country.' He said that in the dream, during the storm, the King of Iran remain unperturbed and was sitting safely on his bed. Hassan Askari explained that it meant that the King of Iran would rout the English forces in Asia and reinstate the (Mughal) King on the throne. The sultanate/empire will again be back under his control. And the unbelievers, that is the English, would be killed.

Question: Do you know that this person, Hassan Askari, facilitated correspondence between the Shah of Iran and the prisoner?

Answer: Yes, I know that letters were sent from here. Around one and half, two years ago, a caravan was on its way to Mecca. Sheedi Qanbar, the leader of the African group, requested the permission to go for Hajj. Permission was granted and according to the prevalent custom, he was paid a year's salary in advance. It is said that the prisoner gave him a letter for God and asked him to hang it on the wall of the Ka'ba. After eight or nine days, I heard that Sheedi's visit for Hajj was a ruse and that he had gone to Persia, carrying a letter from the King of Dilli for the Shah of Iran.

Question: Did the king or his courtiers discuss the war between the English and the Iranians often?

Answer: Yes, inside the fort and out in the city it was discussed often.

Question: Was the war discussed in the context of religion and did the Muslims of the city have any kind of expectations that because of the war they would regain the power?

Answer: Yes, each person had such expectations/delusions. But the people who held knowledge of the matter found it difficult to believe that the King of Iran would ever be able to compete with the English.

Question: Were the people around you in the fort expecting the arrival of soldiers from Meerut?

Answer: Yes, they were awaited. On Sunday, letters were received stating that 84 soldiers were imprisoned and that riot/violence was imminent. Knowing all this, the gatekeepers of the fort did not keep the information secret and publicly professed their sympathies for them and said that the soldiers would reach Dilli after passing through Meerut.

Testimony of Hassan Askari

Pir Hassan Askari was then summoned to the court room and asked to give his statement under oath.

Question: It is being revealed in this court that you gave a letter to the King's servant, Sheedi Qanbar, and on his behalf sent him to Iran?

Answer: I have no knowledge of this matter.

Question: It has also been said in this court that you are a soothsayer. You interpreted dreams, spoke to God and claimed to be a miracle man?

Answer: With God as my witness, I state that I have never claimed anything like this.

Question: Did you narrate this dream of yours to the King in which a storm emerging from the west, or any other direction, was moving towards Hindustan and the flood ravaged all of the land. And because of this the King thrived and the English were destroyed?

Answer: God knows that I have neither had such a dream nor described it. But people of the fort often shared such dreams with me and I always explained them as superstition. And I don't believe in dreams.

Testimony of Mukund Lal, Secretary to the Emperor of Delhi

Mukund Lal answered various questions and said,

> On that day (11 May), it was announced that God was the emperor of the world and Bahadur Shah, the king of this country. And his (King's) order was above everything. The second day, 12 May, when the riders from Meerut and the soldiers of Dilli got together, the King while sitting on his throne ordered his minister, Mehboob Ali Khan, to organise a feast for the army the next day. Thus sweets were distributed among the army and officers were given some money as well. Before 1842, on special occasions the King would sit on his silver throne, placed in the Diwan-i-Khas, and give out rewards. But the agent Governor General had put an end to this ceremony and moved the throne under the alleyway

to the King's private room. On 12 May, the King had the throne brought out, sat on it and conducted the court.

These were the glimpses of the case, courtesy Mirza Hairat Dehlvi who translated the published English report in Urdu from beginning to the end. This case started on 27 January 1857 and, after 21 sessions, ended on 9 March 1857.

But the trial was just for show. Or, we can say that Shah Madar kills the one who is already dead. Amnesty was promised. And the promise was fulfilled. But this did not mean that the King would not be insulted and disgraced. The decision was as expected. The punishment was exile. A recommendation was made to send him to Kala Pani (Andaman and Nicobar) or wherever the British government deemed reasonable. Finally, it was decided that he would be sent to Rangoon (capital of present-day Myanmar).

On 7 October 1857, the captive King left the Red Fort. When he emerged from the fort he did not know where he was going. Among the people accompanying him and those who are worth a mention were Begum Zeenat Mahal and two princes, Jawan Bakht and Shah Abbas. This caravan after leaving Dilli reached Allahabad. From Allahabad to Kalkatta (Kolkata). On reaching Kalkatta, they paid their last tribute to the land of Hindustan and from there sailed on a ship to Rangoon.

21

Deserted City

'Deserted city. Neither a man nor mankind. But, a few artists have been allowed to settle there. They live. But they too, settled after their houses were destroyed. Even their remaining paintings were looted. That which remained, were readily bought by the British.'

This letter, Ghalib wrote to Munshi Shiv Narayan on 23 October 1858. It indicates that the city was still deserted even after more than one year had passed. The streets and the lanes were desolate. The people who had left the city had not returned. A considerable number of them had lost any hope of return and had moved on. Everyone had gone their own way. But a large number of people were still hopeful, waiting for the day when they would be able to return to their homes. It was, however, a long wait. Some built makeshift houses to gain shelter, but even this was unbearable to the British rulers. An order was passed for the existing houses to be demolished and a warning was issued that in future no such houses were to be constructed.

This was the condition when some of the artists were allowed to return to the city in October 1858. By November, the Hindus were also permitted to return. Muslims were not allowed still. However, the beginning of 1859 gave an inkling that perhaps Muslims too would be allowed to return. But how? In the words of Ghalib:

> And it is quite well-known that five thousand tickets have been printed. The Muslim who wanted to stay should give offerings as per his capacity. It is up to the ruler to estimate the amount. Give money and obtain (a) ticket. Even if your home gets destroyed (in the process of paying), you will at least get to live in the city. Until today this is the situation. Let us see when the auspicious moment for settling in the city will come. Those staying are expelled and those who were away are now coming to settle in the city. *Al mulkallaha, wal hukmallaha.* [1,2]

The report was accurate. Tickets were undoubtedly printed. They had this written on them: 'Tickets for settlement in Delhi city with the condition of paying the fine.' And what happened then:

'After making public announcements and getting the tickets printed Egerton Sahab Bahadur[3] went to Calcutta. The foolish Dilliwallahs who were lying outside were stunned. Now, only when he (Sahab) returns, then settlement or any new option will present itself.'

Listen to Ghalib about the new way that presented itself:

> The station house officer of Lahore Gate is sitting on the road on a thatch stool. Whoever escapes the eyes of the white and tries to enter, he detains him and sends in the custody. At the officer's he is flogged five times or a fine of two rupees per person is levied. He stays in detention for eight days. All the police stations have been instructed to check who is staying with tickets and who is without them.

General Burn informed Lawrence:

---

[1] *Al mulkallaha, wal hukmallaha* is literally, the country is that of Allah, all commands are from Allah.

[2] *Khutoot-e-Ghalib* (Letters of Ghalib) Volume I. Edited by Mahesh Prashad, Hindustani Academy, Allahabad, 1941. Excerpts from correspondence with Mir Mehdi Hussain 'Majrooh'.

[3] Phillip Henry Egerton was the magistrate and collector in Delhi from 1855 to 1859. He was on leave during the uprising of 1857 but returned to the city later in the year.

> 'I have calculated that per street ten people be allowed to enter.... The majority of those whom I allow to enter are Hindus and I take care to ensure that in every street there is one *bania*[4], one *punsaria*[5] and one *halwai*[6].... Until now fifty thousand people have been populated.... Among them Muslims are very few.[7]

However, in January 1852, after many appeals, Muslims were ultimately allowed to return, but with harsh restrictions; first prove your innocence, then pay the imposed penalty, and then only will you get the entry permit. There was no other option. The wretched bore all this humiliation. They paid fines. They got entry tickets after paying large amounts and walked towards their houses. They were amazed looking for the streets on which once their houses had stood; where were the lanes that were inhabited by their being and were used by them. Numerous lanes were destroyed beyond recognition. The remaining ones lay in an abysmal condition. Grass had grown all over the doors and walls:

Ug raha hai dar-o-deewar pe sabza Ghalib
Mein to jangal mein hoon aur ghar mein bahaar aai hai

Ghalib, at the door and walls of the house greenery is growing,
I am in the forest, and spring has arrived at home.

But it was still a matter of solace that some houses had existed even in such a state. Otherwise there were numerous houses that had been completely destroyed. No traces were found of such houses. Now that they are back the residents of the streets were amazed and anxious to find entire streets had disappeared. Where were the houses? Had the earth devoured them or had they been swallowed by the sky?

---

4 *Bania* is a trader or merchant caste group.

5 *Pansaria* is a grocer.

6 *Halwai* may be a cook and/or a seller of confectionery and savoury snacks.

7 See *Delhi between Two Empires, 1803-1931: Society, Government and Urban Growth* by Narayani Gupta, Oxford University Press, New Delhi, 2008.

Those who returned were in a strange condition. First they were expelled and humiliated, and now they were wandering around the city disgraced. Fortunate were the expelled ones who had died, or gone to some other place to take up residence. In returning, there was utter humiliation. First they were humiliated when trying to acquire tickets; when they had the tickets and entered the city, another type of humiliation awaited them. Well, some of them located their ruined houses and so they were safe from wandering here and there without a home, but there were other concerns:

'Well, we will stay in Dilli, but what is there to eat?'

That time was past when everything was cheap: wheat was one mun for a rupee, ghee was four ser for one rupee, and jaggery sugar was a ser for a taka. Now the price of wheat from a rupee for a mun had increased to one rupee for only 13 ser. Ghee was being sold at one and half ser for each rupee. The price of millet was 12 ser per one rupee; gram's price was 16 ser per one rupee and Urad dal was eight ser per one rupee.

Fortunate were those who despite going through the doomsday were able to use their insight and so had kept their saved wealth with some trustworthy person before going out of the city. There were, after all, some reliable personalities who did not move from their places. The greatest among them was Hakim Mahmood Khan who remained in Shareef Manzil despite the uproar and turmoil. But then he had another support. The guards of the Maharaja of Patiala were specially guarding his mansion and the area around it. When the neighbours left their homes, they entrusted Hakim Sahab with their savings. Hakim Sahab had set aside a room for this purpose. This room was stuffed with the bundles that those who were leaving had entrusted to his safekeeping. On their return, the miserable retrieved their bundles from among all these bundles and went to their homes.

But whether it was those who had shown prior insight or those who had not shown any, everyone somehow managed to make arrangements for daily provisions. When they settled a bit and looked around them they still felt anxious. Everything around was quite changed. So much had been lost. A large number of corners, hubs and haunts, that had been part of their lives, were no more. The most important among them were the Jama Masjid, its stairs and the chowk. It was all different. The gates of the mosque were closed to them. No Muslim could venture to the stairs of the Mosque. And the Chowk of Jama Masjid, which, according to Ghalib, was among the five places upon which the life of Dilli depended, was now extrinsic to their lives. It was as if there were a gaping hole in their social lives. It was as if their most precious object had been snatched away. First, there was the mental shock of the event. And now they were disappointed and anxious. There was a time when one could just leave home in a jiffy and go towards Chowk Jama Masjid. That was not possible anymore. What were they to do, where were they to go? The centre around which their lives revolved had vanished.

Slowly there was a motivation to snatch back their Qibla[8] from the others. Voices were raised for the return of the mosque and appeals were made to this effect. At first they fell on deaf ears. The British rulers did not pay any heed to them. But gradually their hearts melted. However, even this took around three years. It was only in 1862 that the Masjid was restored to the Muslim community. So, the Muslims stepped inside the Masjid again after five years. And Ghalib, who was pleased about this, informed Mir Mahdi Majrooh in a letter dated 16 December 1862:

> Those anxious to know the condition of Dilli, accept salaam.
>
> Jama Masjid has been opened. The kabab sellers installed their stalls at the stairs on the side of Chitli Qabar. Eggs, chickens and pigeons started to be sold. 10 people have been appointed managers. Mirza Ilahi Bakhsh, Maulvi Sadruddin, Tafaddul Hussain Khan —these three and seven others.

---

[8] *Qibla* literally means 'direction'. The Kaaba in Mecca is the qibla which Muslims across the world face while praying. Here *qibla* is used to denote a central location or a monument around which all social life is organised.

So, after five years the call for prayer was raised again from the Jama Masjid. Those who came to offer namaaz once again arranged themselves here in orderly files. A gust of life began blowing on the stairs of the Masjid. Some long-forgotten kabab sellers reached the stairs on the side of Chitli Qabar with their grills and started grilling kababs. Chicken and egg-sellers arrived, and started selling them. The sellers of avadavats and mynahs came with cages full of colourful avadavats and titmouse birds and sat on the stairs. And behold, it is the same market on the stairs that was seen before the doomsday of the year '57. Once again the crowd of tourists; again the water carrier clanking bowls to draw the attention of the thirsty and the thirsty asking him for water.

The same style and the same scene, though a little less populated. Yes, there was one more difference. Here and there some empty spaces could be seen. The businesses of the past had returned completely. But the storytellers who had left the stairs did not return. And yes, the traders in shields, swords and horses who once traded here; where are they now? None of them is seen. The horsemen and the swordsmen were defeated, but along with them the traders of horses and swords were also defeated. Although the scene on the stairs of the Jama Masjid and at Jama Masjid Chowk seemed as it had been previously, the blank spaces here and there were evident too. And they spoke volumes about how life would never be as it had been earlier.

Some previously unseen characters were also there. A strong muscular youth, handsome and well-mannered, was seen wandering around the stairs in a beggarly style even as he sang beautifully in a heartrending voice:

Na kisi ki aankh ka noor hoon, na kisi ke dil ka qaraar hun
Jo kisi ke kaam na aa sakey, mein wo ek must-e-ghubaar hun

I am neither the vision of anyone's eye, nor am I the solace of anyone's heart,
I am that handful of dust which can benefit no one.

Who can call this person a beggar? A little investigation disclosed that he was a robbed and beaten Mughal prince. Earlier he used to strut around in the Red Fort as a prince. Now, on the stairs of the Mosque built by his grandfather, he recites the couplets of his uncle like a faqir, and collects money to make ends meet.

Such was the conditions of the princes. And the princesses! Ghalib narrated their condition thus: 'If you were here and saw the Begums of the Fort. The face like the full moon but the garments dirty, the trouser edges in rags, the sandals torn off.' But now even that time has passed. With the passage of time, these moon-like faces mingled with the common people. Now, they could not be recognised. Perhaps by coincidence it might become known who they were. A woman gardener is going about selling flowers. Sometimes one of her gestures would reveal that she was not from a gardener's family. When probed it would be found that she was a flower of the ruined garden of the Red Fort. In the past, she was weighed against piles of flowers and now she lives by selling flowers. In some family a nanny would captivate all the members of the family with her etiquette; a bit of probing would cause a stream of tears to flow. She was a ruined princess. In the Fort she had been rocked in her cradle, now she rocks the children of others in cradles. A princess named Rabia Begum came out of the Fort and began living in the house of a cook called Husaini. Another princess named Fatema Sultan became a teacher in a Christian girls' school. These were the princes and princesses whom the government had account of. If they had made themselves known in the beginning, they would have been hanged. And if their identities were disclosed after the announcement of pardon, they were owed a pension: five rupees per month.

Those killed or expelled were safe from this humiliation. They did not remain themselves, only their stories remained which added to their honour. The story of stories was about the personality of Bahadur Shah Zafar. In the words of the women of Dilli, he was the *suhaag*[9] of Dilli. When he was expelled to Rangoon, Dilli's suhaag was wrecked. Now, according to these women, Dilli was a widow. Her husband was first expelled to Rangoon and then he left this world while in exile. Ghalib, in his letter to Mir Mahdi Majrooh dated 16 December 1862, gave him the news of the opening of the Jama Masjid of Dilli and with it he also informed him about a death. 'On 7 November/14 Jumadi-ul-Awwal, the current year, Friday, Abu-az-Zafar Sirajuddeen Bahadur Shah became free from the imprisonment of the English and the body. Verily we are for Allah, and to Him only will we return.'

Bahadur Shah Zafar left Dilli and settled in the hearts of Dilliwallahs. In appearance, he had gone to Rangoon, but in fact he was in Dilli still. Earlier, he lived in the Red Fort, and now he lived in the hearts of the people. His poetry would reach Dilli after traversing unknown and difficult paths, and would immediately spread like a fragrance. Ghalib, Momin, Zauq, all of them found it hard to stand in his comparison. Now, in the hearts of the Dilliwallahs, the poetry of Zafar would rule:

Na kisi ki aankh ka nor hoon, na kisi ke dil ka qarar hun
Jo kisi ke kaam na aa sakey, mein wo ek must-e-ghubaar hun

I am neither the vision of anyone's eye, nor am I the solace of anyone's heart,
I am that handful of dust which can benefit no one.

Kitna hai badnaseeb Zafar, dafn ke liye
Do gaz zameen bhi na mili ku-e-yaar mein

How unfortunate is Zafar, for burial
Did not find two yards earth, in the beloved land.

Ya to afsar mera shahaana banayaa hota
Ya mera taaz gadayaa na banayaa hota

---

[9] *Suhaag* usually refers to husband, it is culturally indicative of 'good fortune' of a woman in a patriarchal society because her husband is alive.

Either my reign should have been royal
Or my crown should not have been reduced to penury.

These words of the sovereign were the words of the nation. The poetry of Bahadurshah had the pride of place as people's poetry. It originated from a heart full of pain. It found its way into the pained hearts of the people and became part of the collective memory of the city.

So after bidding farewell to Bahadur Shah Zafar, all that was left of him was his poetry. Everything else was taken away. Neither the court remained, nor the courtiers. No armed women servants or beauticians, no Turk women, no watchmen, Mirdhe[10] or foot soldiers. No royal finery, no mobile throne. No honorary badges, nor the moving orchestra. Drums were no longer beaten. The elephant rides had ended. Bags of brocade are also no longer visible. The elephant has left. With it, horse has left too. It left in a very respectful and dignified way. When Bahadur Shah Zafar departed, his elephant Maula Baksh and his companion horse stopped eating and drinking. The mahout informed Saunders Sahab about the matter. Saunders Sahab took a basketful of exquisite and fragrant laddoos and kachauris and put it in front of Maula Baksh's stable. Maula Baksh wrapped its trunk around the basket and threw it away in anger. Saunders Sahab also got very angry. He declared that the elephant had turned rebellious. It will not live now in the fort. Take it to the market and auction it.

At the market the highest bidder was the one-eyed Bansi Pansari and he bought the royal ride for two hundred and fifty rupees. Then the mahout heaved a sigh of relief and addressed the elephant thus: Brother Maula Baksh, your and my destinies are now ill-fated. We are deprived of the royal patronage. Now we will serve the turmeric seller. Hearing this the elephant immediately fell to the ground and gave up his life.

---

[10] *Mirdhe* were Jat soldiers of the Mughal Army.

Zahir Dehlavi says that the companion horse also died the same day.

The death of Maula Baksh and his companion horse announced the end of the era of elephants and horses. Most of their riders had departed. Those left were tired of these rides. Hakim Mahmood Khan would earlier come out of Shareef Manzil riding grandly on a horse. Now he was seen riding in a phaeton. Before 1857 the only famous phaeton was that of Mufti Sadruddeen. Now, this means of transportation was seen at many places. As for riding elephants, the high gates of numerous mansions, those that were safe from the threat of demolition, had been constructed keeping in view the height and width of an elephant. But now these gates were deserted. Elephants were not to be seen there.

Anyway, these mansions were also in the last phase of their life. The people in these mansions could no longer afford to live in them. Many of them had already sold their mansions and many others were waiting to sell them.

22

Times Change, City Changes

1867 was beginning. Night camped still. In the Dilli air one could hear a strange noise. A train, belching smoke from its black engine and blowing its whistle, chugged into the building which was built especially for this vehicle. The railways had arrived in Dilli. The sound of the train's whistle seemed to be declaring the start of a new era to Dilli. After that the days and the evenings of the city kept changing and the air was filled with this new noise. Until now one could not know of any carrier entering or leaving Dilli. Their speed was also slow-slow. But this new carrier ran on machines with such thunderous speed that the very earth would shiver. It would announce its arrival from miles away; creating a din, it would arrive at the station with a rumbling of its wheels. When the plans of the railway line had been placed in front of Bahadur Shah Zafar, he had been right to worry that the train would hamper the peace of the city and had directed that the station be built away from the city. But now, after his departure, the original plan had been put in practice. The planners had built the railway station without any hindrance, right behind Chandni Chowk.

So now the time has come when the days of penury of devastated Dilli are about to get over. The arrival of the train has opened the doors of prosperity to the city. It is as if the trade in the city has grown wings. Hundred kinds of things are leaving, arriving. The traders are thriving. The riches of moneylenders know no bounds. Most of these are either Hindus or Jainis. Only an occasional one is Muslim. Above all there was Lala Chunamal, now that he was the richest man of Dilli. Anyway, this benefited the hard-up gentry among the Muslim community who were sitting ready to sell off their mansions. The mansion of Nawab Muzaffar Khan was bought by Pandit Jwala Nath. Hamid Ali Khan's mansion was bought by Hardhyan Singh and the mansion of the sons and grandsons of Shah Alam II was bought by Bishambar Nath. Exactly like this many of the nobility sold off their mansions somehow and then went to live in some small house in a far-off street. Later someone opened a provisions store. Someone set up a workshop. Someone took up the profession of tutoring. The state of a nawab's household has been described by Narayani Gupta thus: two members of this family had been executed by hanging in the middle of Chandni Chowk. In disrepute, they left their mansion in stealth and began living an obscure life in Gali Rodgiraan where people from lower classes lived. In the 1860s, a boy from this family began an apprenticeship in a blacksmith's shop. Another one began a workshop. A third one started doing filigree work. The two younger ones studied in school and received a diploma. One became a clerk in the municipality. The other got a job as an accountant.[1]

On the one hand this was the scenario. On the other hand, in the same city, the scenario was much the opposite because trade was going strong, and traders were frolicking in riches. Because of the traders and businessmen, business professionals from near and far—workers and artisans, in other words—all kinds of people were arriving in the city. Dilli which had been emptied in the years '57 or '58, was now looking crowded again. In 1847 the population of Dilli was 1,60,000. By 1857 it must have increased. But after the catastrophe of 1857 its population had reduced to 1,35,000.

---

[1] *Delhi between Two Empires, 1803-1931: Society, Government and Urban Growth* by Narayani Gupta, Oxford University Press, New Delhi, 2008.

But after 1857 the population increased rapidly. And by the time 1875 arrived the population was again nearing 1,60,000.

At the end, the centre of business stayed in Chandni Chowk. Thus this was the area which faced the population pressure. It was replete with Hindu and Jain traders. Actually, at the time of settling Jahanabad, Shahjahan had himself bestowed estates upon Hindu and Jain traders. Now as the times changed and their businesses acquired a new gleam, they further increased their riches by buying the mansions of the crushed and broke Muslim gentry and the nawabs.

When the population increased considerably in this area and businesses acquired a new shine, other kinds of activities also began here—social activities, literary activities, and most of all religious activities. To put it clearly, let us say that with the trading business, the business of religious propagation also began. This business flourished in this centre of trade. It probably began with Christian proselytising. An impressive church was built here around this time. In 1865, the Lord Bishop of Calcutta arrived here and laid the foundation stone of a church in the memory of those Christians who had been killed in the battle of the year 1857. It was decided to call it St Stephen's Church. By the time 1867 arrived, the church stood completed and it soon became a centre of Christian proselytisation. Only a few years had passed that the Jains also built a grand temple here. Soon the Arya Samajis also reached here with their propagative ambitions. The Muslims too were not to be left behind. Their religious centre had been here for very long. This centre was the Fatehpuri Mosque. If they were rather quiet until now it was because this mosque was in the possession of Lala Chunamal. Lala had bought it in 1860 for Rs 39,650. But now there was news that it was to be restored. Let it be restored and then see the religious propagation here resume with such vigour that it would leave the Jama Masjid far behind. The time for the restoration of this mosque had come. Lord Lytton was only waiting for the Durbar which was to be convened very soon.

Having conquered it, following 1857 the British Government abandoned this city. Their capital was Calcutta. But how long could they have remained sitting closed up in Calcutta by the seaside? They had pitched their victory flags in the middle of India in Dilli. Slowly it occurred to them to leave Calcutta and make Dilli their fort. So they began to pay attention to Dilli from a new perspective. This commenced with the *Qaisari* [2] Durbar.

Queen Victoria was until this time only the honorary queen. But now the great and vast country of India was a part of her empire. It was felt that there ought to be a title greater than 'queen' for her. After much thinking one title had the honour of being accepted. The title was *Qaisar-e-Hind.*[3] It was decided that on 1 January 1877, a spectacular durbar would be convened in Dilli, and this new title would be announced there.

Now there was much buzz about the Qaisari Durbar. The city had previously seen the grandeur of the Mughal Durbar. The Mughals were gone. The British had arrived. So now let us watch the grandeur of the British Durbar. Rajas, Maharajas, Chiefs and Nawabs had assembled for the Durbar from all over India. The Rajas arrived astride elephants. How grand were these elephants, standing in their orderly queues! Their howdahs were literally thrones of gold and silver. The era of the Company was over with the year 1857. Lord Lytton, the Viceroy now represented Her Excellency; Her Excellency who was now to become the Qaiser-e-Hind. The Imperial Command was proclaimed.

> By God's grace Her Excellency Victoria, the Queen of the Union and the Empress of India, through her Viceroy, bestows her Royal and Imperial Sanction upon all her chiefs, litterateurs, warriors, heads, nobles, and common subjects who are at present assembled in Dilli, and declares contented the people of Dilli from her attention and the people of India from her royal guardianship.

---

[2] *Qaisari* means Imperial (*Qaisar* is Arabic for Caesar).

[3] *Qaisar-e-Hind* means Empress of India.

The leaders who were present stood up after the imperial proclamation, appaluded and conveyed their congratulations. Maharaja Scindia stood up on behalf of all the Rajas, Nawabs and Chiefs and expressed his congratulations saying, 'Emperors, Kings and guardians of India congratulate you and pray that your reign and power may be eternal.'

So the Qaisari Durbar was now over. On this occasion the Fatehpuri Masjid was restored (to the Muslim community) so the Muslims were happy. No, but they were not really happy. The oppressors gave one thing but took away another. The announcement regarding the closure of Dilli College was also made on this occasion. It was said that the classes of the Dilli College had been merged with those of the Lahore College. Whoever wished to study could go there and take admission. What fine men had the Dilli College produced! Maulvi Zaka Ullah, Deputy Nazeer Ahmed. But who knows what occurred to the British government that they closed this gate to education.

After much trepidation the sound of the azaan could be heard from the Fatehpuri Masjid. The namaazis started arriving. Prayer queues began to be formed. *Ruku* [4] and sajda[5] began to be performed. With this religious propagation at the mosque also started gaining vigour. Jama Masjid was under the government's watch. The government used to put together its management committee. Furthermore, the Jama Masjid had its own traditions that did not let it leave the path of moderation. But the Fatehpuri Masjid had a different disposition. Here *Ahl-e-hadis*[6] were more

---

[4] *Ruku* is bending from the hip in prostration during namaaz.

[5] *Sajda* is prostration in a sitting position with the forehead on the ground during namaaz.

[6] *Ahl-e-Hadis* is a school of Islamic jurisprudence or their followers. The Ahl-e-hadis limit the sources of law to the Quran, Hadith, a systematic comparison of the Quran and Hadith, and consensus among the followers. They are considered the most orthodox of the various schools.

influential than the *Hanafi*.[7] It was under the influence of the *Punjabi Saudagaraan*.[8] So this mosque was not content with only ruku and sajda. It also had a deep interest in debates.

Lord Curzon started another matter. Lt Governor Sir Charles Rivaz slowly became convinced that the government should not involve itself with the management of Jama Masjid. That Muslims should themselves form the Management Committee. But Lord Curzon could not see how that was possible. The Jama Masjid was a national monument. The government could not abdicate its responsibility towards it. However, he drew a small serif in the matter that whenever any Europeans visited the Jama Masjid to sightsee they may certainly cover themselves before setting foot inside in honour of Muslim sentiment. The Muslim community of Dilli was upset that this kind of restriction was not made compulsory. The question whether the mosque could be entered while still wearing shoes took the shape of a conflict. So much so that on one occasion bricks were thrown at a group of British soldiers who entered the mosque wearing shoes.

So had the Muslims of Dilli become so daring that they could protest against the British like this? Yes. They had remained fearful for many years after 1857. But the times kept changing. And the impact of 1857 was being erased. It was now evident that the fear of the British which had bound the Muslims till now was slowly wearing off. This was also apparent in the way that the management committees of the Jama Masjid and Fatehpuri Masjid convened by the government began to be criticised roughly and harshly. Mirza Hairat Dehlavi was someone to be reckoned

---

[7] *Hanafi* is a school of Islamic jurisprudence or their followers. Their major characteristic is that they consider a wider variety of sources for deriving laws including the views of the companions of the prophet, religious scholars and considerations of public interest.

[8] *Punjabi Saudagaraan* is a community of Delhi Muslims who originally came from Punjab in the seventeenth century. *Saudagar* (pl. *Saudagaraan*) means merchant.

with. He began building up the offensive. He had the backing of the Punjabi Saudagaraan. He prepared a long scroll of allegations against the committee members.

Things did not pause at the matter of the mosques. In every matter Muslims could be seen raising their voice. Prior to this in any matter the poor people could not be heard at all. But after the Qaisari Durbar it seemed as if they also got a tongue. When the Urdu-Hindi dispute began, they made statements. In 1884, the Dilliwallahs supporting Urdu issued three statements in quick succession. One of the statements had mostly Hindu signatories. The second statement had more Muslim signatories. The third statement had 10,000 signatories which included people from outside Dilli.

The major newspapers also advocated the cause of Urdu over Hindi enthusiastically. In the 1860s, 12 newspapers were being published from Dilli. All the owners of the newspapers were loyal to the British government and stayed in touch with its officers. In the 1880s the number of newspapers had increased considerably but now these newspapers were being published by people who would roundly criticise the government.

The Jama Masjid Chowk was popular again. The revolt of '57 had destroyed the elites. The artisans, however, were not deprived of anything. In any case the idiom famous about the artisans of Dilli was that their 10 fingers were 10 lamps. All kinds of crafts had been transformed passing through these fingers. What to speak of crafts like filigree, sequin work and so on? They developed these crafts to the pinnacle of finesse. This niche was occupied more by women than men. And now many ruined princesses were also showing their skill at crafts. So the craftspersons, artisans and workshop owners worked all day. In the evening they had a bath, arranged their hair, placed a perfumed ball of cotton in the ear, wore a garland of jasmine in the neck and left for the Chowk. An entire market was arranged on the stairs. Dahi bada for the foodies, chaat with 12 condiments, haleem, kheer, phirni. Red

Avadavat, parrots, mynahs, pigeons for bird enthusiasts. And now an occasional Mughal progeny could also be seen in this business.

Time passes by so fast. Even though once it seemed that it would just not pass. For those who had been uprooted, it seemed to have just stopped. They could not get out of the situation '57 had put them in. But now it seemed that the year 1857 had been left far behind. In fact, the end of the century was approaching. The nineteenth century would soon be over. This century had been full of such important happenings. The British had set foot in Dilli in the beginning of this century. Their portentous entry had meant devastation for the city. That Dilli which was described as Jahanabad and which was a culture with its own standing was now gone. General Lake had conquered Dilli on 14 September 1803. He set foot in the Red Fort at some unfortunate moment and before one could realise, the camel was inside the tent and the Arab was outside it; indeed, within 55 years, the Mughal Sultanate had been brought to an end. The Mughal Emperor had saluted the Red Fort and left. Not only from Red Fort, but from Dilli, from India. The emperor had been taken away. And the rule of Her Excellency the Queen was now established. With this the Queen added a feather in her crown. Earlier she was the Queen of Britain. Now she was also the Empress of India. All this, a revolution, had taken place in the nineteenth century. And now the nineteenth century was coming to an end. But in passing on the baton, the old century seemed to have other plans as it took away with it the Queen of England and Empress of India. On the one hand, the nineteenth century ended and on the other, Queen Victoria passed away from this world exactly 21 days later, that is, on 21 January 1901.

23

Good Memories of Dilli College

As narrated in the previous chapter, with the beginning of the year 1867, the people of Dilli heard the train whistle in the city for the first time and understood that times had changed. But in the history of Dilli an occurrence even bigger than this had taken place 42 years earlier, in 1825, when the Dilli College was established. The seed for a new epoch had been sown in the soil. It was because of this college that the language that until yesterday was the language of poetry was now seen engaged in a dialogue with modern science. Madrasa Ghaziuddin, which was established in 1792, had now receded to the background. Consider it all but erased. In that building now English was popular and the new subjects of the West were being taught there. The Bengalis were already comfortable with this knowledge. Indeed, it was imparted to them first. Raja Ram Mohan Roy had led a powerful campaign in its favour. But for the people of Dilli this was a new instance and unacceptable. The language of the Christians and their way of teaching galvanised the elite. Deputy Nazeer Ahmed's father, Majid, severely criticised his son and said, 'My son, it is better to die than learn English.' But the son did not pay heed to the father. So many sons of Dilli rebelled against their fathers and joined Dilli College to learn the new language.

Have a look at the first crop of rebels. Syed Ahmed Khan[1] though did not study at that college. But have a look at the others. Mohammad Hussain Azad, Nazeer Ahmed, Maulvi Zakaullah, Maulvi Ziauddin, Master Ramchandar, Pyare Lal Ashoob and Master Nand Kishor. These rebels, after leaving the college, did things that shook up traditional Muslim society. Some elders too were fascinated by this knowledge. They joined the college as teachers. These were elders widely respected for their knowledge and intellect in Dilli, like Mufti Sadruddin Aazrah, Maulvi Imam Bakhsh Sehbai and Mamlook-ul-Ali Naanautavi.

The college had some excellent qualities because of which it heralded an intellectual movement. According to Maulvi Abdul Haq, three qualities in particular. One, 'this was the first institution where the confluence of East and West happened and under one roof, in one congregation, the knowledge and literature of East and West were taught together. This union provided a fillip to a change in thinking, enrichment of knowledge, and refinement of taste. This laid the foundations of a new culture, a new era and gave birth to a new faithful, enlightened and mature community of people and writers who have had significant bearings on our language and society.'

Two, the medium of instruction here was Urdu. All the Western disciplines were taught in Urdu.

Three, affiliated to it was one vernacular translation society. Around 125 works were translated and compiled under the supervision of the society. The translators were either the teachers of the College or their students. These translations and compilations 'covered material in disciplines spanning history, geography, principles of law, mathematics and its various branches, chemistry, mechanics, philosophy, medicine, surgery, botany, spirituality, economics, etc.'[2]

---

[1] Syed Ahmed Khan was an educationist and reformer widely perceived to have introduced modern Western education among the Muslims in colonial India.

[2] *Marhoom Dilli Kalij* (Deceased Delhi College) by Abdul Haq, Delhi, 1945.

The committee formed to research Dilli's historical heritage—consider it a blessing of the College—was called the Archeological Society. Some of its members were English officers. Most of them were pupils of the College. Its members boasted names such as Sir Syed Ahmed Khan, Maulvi Ziauddin and Master Ramchandar. Among the members, Sir Syed Ahmed Khan was the most active and after a lot of research and investigation he prepared a report and presented it before the Society. He then wrote a book titled, *Aasaar-us-Sanadeed* (The Remnants of Past), which came to be considered an authoritative work of research on Dilli's monuments and history, and was later translated to French by Garcin De Tassy.

During this time something else happened. The emergence of stone printing[3] led to the establishment of the Lithography Press. One press, then another, and a third. Many presses were established. Books began to be printed. Newspapers began to be published. Maulvi Mohammad Baaqar was a student at the Dilli College and later a teacher of Persian as well. He published the *Dehli Urdu Akhbar*.[4] This was the first newspaper in North India. In 1837 when it began to be published it was called *Akhbar-e-Dehli*. In 1840 it was renamed *Dehli Urdu Akhbar*. During the heady days of the battle for freedom it was renamed yet again: *Akhbar-ul-Zafar*.[5] After this neither the editor remained nor the paper as the English hanged Maulvi Mohammad Baaqar. His son Mohammad Hussain Azad left the city.

Some time in the 1880s,[6] Sir Syed Ahmed Khan's elder brother, Syed Mohammad Khan published a paper called *Syed-al-Akhbar*.[7]

---

[3] Lithography was widely adopted in India for publishing Persian and Urdu religious texts and periodicals.

[4] *Akhbar* commonly refers to newspapers in Urdu, Persian and Arabic. The word is the plural of khabar (news or information).

[5] *Akhbar-ul-Zafar* or the newspaper of (Emperor) Zafar.

[6] According to CM Naim, this was in 1841 (*Urdu Texts and Context: The Selected Essays of C.M. Naim,* Permanent Black, 2004).

[7] *Syed-al-Akhbar* or Syed's Newspaper.

Master Ramchandar, sitting in Dilli College, published a newspaper titled *Fawaid-ul-Naazreen* [8] in 1846. In 1946 he came up with *Muhibb-e-Hind*.[9] Dilli College itself published a scholarly journal called *Qiran-us-Sa'adain*[10] edited by its principal, Dr Aloys Sprenger[11] who was German. There was another teacher, a Frenchman, Boutros Sahab. Aloys Sprenger left the College after spending three or three and a half years there. After that Taylor Sahab became the principal.

The new knowledge created such an environment in Dilli that C.F. Andrews described it as Nishat-us-Saaniya.[12] But all of a sudden, like doomsday, 1857 arrived. Taylor and other European teachers and members of the management lost their lives. The College was shut down.

Then, some time in 1864 the College re-opened. But this was another time. The College's library had been destroyed and utterly ruined. The building of the Ghaziuddin Madarsa was still occupied by the police. The College ran out of a house in Gali Qasim Jaan. The big difference now was that the enthusiasm with which a lot of educational books had been translated to Urdu in the past had dissipated with time. The market for translation had gone cold. Now, Urdu itself had receded to the background. The emphasis now was entirely on English.

In spite of all this, the College was up and running and students were turning up in hordes. But one English educationist, for no apparent reason, bore a grudge against the College. Or, perhaps it was like this: where the people of Dilli were punished in so many

---

[8] *Fawaid-ul-Naazreen* means for the benefit of the reader.

[9] *Muhibb-e-Hind* or The Darling of India.

[10] *Qiran-e-Sa'adaian* is an Arabic astronomical term. It is also a metaphor for an auspicious occasion.

[11] His name is misspelt in many scholarly books as Springer. The author here inaccurately says he is German. Sprenger was actually Austrian.

[12] *Nishat-us-Saaniya* means glorious revival. C.F. Andrews actually called it the Delhi Renaissance.

ways, a punishment on the educational front was no surprise. This educationist's name was Dr Leitner.[13] A college of the same standards opened with an affiliation with the Punjab University in Dilli, and Leitner proposed that both colleges need not be funded. Why not merge the Dilli College with Lahore College? Since there was strong resistance to this proposal in Dilli, it was quickly scrapped. Lieutenant Governor McLeod assured the Dilli Society that its status would remain intact.

But Leitner was not going to concede defeat. In 1874, he again insisted on his proposal. This time the lieutenant governor was Egerton. He also refused to accede to the proposal. Here, Dilli College was making continuous progress. The results were also encouraging. But it was as if Leitner hated the College. Now, he along with a student, Hamid Ali Khan, hatched a conspiracy. According to Narayani Gupta's research, Hamid Ali, on behalf of Leitner, raised a tricky issue: the Aitmad-ud-Daula fund, from where the Dilli College received a grant, was established only for the benefit of Shia students. Why did Dilli College get a grant from there, they asked. It would be apt to place this fund under the supervision of Punjab University and scholarships given only to Shia students. Leitner Sahab added fuel to fire by asking where funds to run Dilli College would come from? It would be better to merge it with Lahore College.

Eventually, Leitner's conspiracy bore fruit. In February 1877, during the Dilli Darbar, the lieutenant governor announced that Dilli College would be merged with Lahore College. And Dilli College was shut down. *Inna Lillahi wa inna ilaihi raji'un*.[14]

And see, here Dilli College shuts down and there, in Aligarh, a son of Dilli lays the foundation for a new institution. And thus

---

[13] Dr Gottlieb Wilhelm Leitner. Wrongly referred to as English, he was actually Hungarian.

[14] Inna lillahi…: translated, means we surely belong to Allah and to Him we shall return. Quranic verse recited by Muslims upon experiencing loss, especially death.

opened the Muslim Anglo-Oriental College. In the days ahead, what of Dilli and what of Lahore, the educational destiny of Muslims came to be attached to this institution.

24

New Kajz New Capital

New century and a new king. The nineteenth century was a paean to Queen Victoria. When that century came to an end, the Queen too departed. Now it is the twentieth century. Gone is the era of the queen. Here starts the era of the king. Edward VII is now the King of England. He is also the Emperor of India. His coronation ceremony was held in Britain and now it will be held in India. It has been announced that at the beginning of 1903 the court will be adorned in Delhi for the coronation ceremony. The king will not be there, though. Instead his Viceroy Lord Curzon will make preparations for the Durbar. The King's brother, the Duke of Connaught, will grace the Durbar, along with his wife.

One British Durbar was held in the nineteenth century and the other at the beginning of the third year of the twentieth century. The first was called Qaisari Durbar and this one became famous as Curzon Durbar. Curzon Sahab, along with his wife, reached the court riding an elephant. Chiefs and the gentry had queued up on elephants to welcome them. When Curzon and his wife passed them the elephants raised their trunks to salute them. An amazing scene, elephants everywhere. With the destruction of the Mughal Durbar the elephants, too, had disappeared. It seemed as if the era of the elephants had ended with the death of Maula Bakhsh. But the Curzon Durbar brought elephants back to Delhi.

Rather, in Delhi, this Durbar was later known as the Durbar of the elephants. But this was the last spring of the elephants in this city. A new age had emerged and a new light had arrived. Besides, one more type of conveyance was to appear. This new conveyance would hit the elephants so hard that they would no longer be seen anywhere in court. By the time the next Durbar is convened, the motor car will dazzle everyone and the Durbar would be known as the Durbar of the motor cars. At this time though there were elephants everywhere. That was the pomp and show of Curzon's court. Through this Durbar Curzon Sahab attained such fame that a newspaper was started in his name. Mirza Hairat Dehlavi named his weekly gazette the Curzon Gazette. And yes, along with Curzon Sahab the name of his wife also became extremely popular in the city. When the official ball was organised Lady Curzon appeared in a dress that resembled the wings of a peacock; she danced as only she could. Akbar Allahabadi wrote:

Haal mein naachein Lady Curzon
Chhan chhan chhan chhan, chhan chhan chhan chhan

Dances in the hall, Lady Curzon
Chhan-Chhan Chhan-Chhan, Chhan-Chhan Chhan-Chhan.[1]

And what all did the Curzon Durbar bring with it—a few things arrived before the Durbar and a few after. One was electricity. The few chandeliers that were left in Jahanabad started glittering. Electricity had reached Dilli. Electricity came to Dilli in 1902. Close on its heels came the tram. The conservatives objected to both these things. They said electricity was a wasteful expense. What was the need for it? Dilli is not Kalkatta. Here the shops at Chandni Chowk closed at twilight. The light of the lanterns and lamps we light with kerosene oil is enough for our needs. A finicky person added, 'The tram passes by my street. But the time it takes to reach Chandni Chowk, I reach there before it on foot by walking briskly.'

[1] Onomatopoeic sound of an anklet. Rhymes with 'Curzon'.

One more vehicle with two wheels appeared in Dilli—the bicycle. But the greatest of all the rides was the motor car. Though it was spotted less often, but at least it had stepped into the city and by the next Durbar it would be a common sight. The next Durbar arrived soon. The reign of Edward VII was not long. He did not live a long life. His reign lasted only nine years and three and a half months. He died on 6 May 1910. At the time he was 67 years old.

George V succeeded Edward VII to the throne. He became the King of England and the Emperor of India. For Queen Victoria and Edward VII it had been enough that a court had been convened in their name in India. But George V decided to visit India himself and hold court there. He ascended the throne in May 1910 and the next year, he declared that a court would be convened in Dilli on 12 December 1911.

On 2 December 1911 George V disembarked at the coast of Mumbai. On 7 December he arrived in Dilli and on 12 December the Durbar was held in the city. With this court, the Union Jack was hoisted at the Red Fort for the first time. And with it, the tradition of paeans was renewed. Whether he had access to the court or not, Pundit Mohan Brijmohan Dattatreya wrote an ode as it was an old court tradition.

Aaj hai hind mein kya aish-o-masarrat ka amal
Muqaddam-ę-shah se naqsha gaya aalam ka badal
Qaisar-o-qaisra ba kaam rahein duniya mein
Qaafse qaaf tak unka rahey duniya mein amal
Georgepancham rahein ta hashr salaamatya rab
Khurram-o-shaad rahein raaj rahey unka atal

What opulence and happiness there is in India today
The picture of the world is altered by the king's arrival,
May the Emperor and Empress succeed in the world,
Let their actions remain in the world forever
O God, may George V be safe till the Hereafter,
May he be happy and content and may his kingdom remain firm.

At the Durbar, the decision about the destiny of Delhi, which had been postponed for long, was finally taken. The king announced that the capital of British India will be Dilli but he also announced that the present city would not be granted this privilege. For this, a new city would be settled right next to it. The very next day the foundation stone of the new city was laid which was to become famous as New Delhi.

But just then a bad omen presented itself. Although according to the Dilliwallahs a bad omen had already made itself known before the Durbar had been convened. The shamiyana erected especially to welcome the king caught fire. Dilliwallahs discussed this news vigorously. The women were especially worried, 'Virtuous sister, this is not a good omen. The British king has just arrived and an ill omen has already occurred.'

And now an even more ominous sign! When the foundation stone for New Delhi was laid, a procession was taken out. Viceroy Lord Hardinge rode on a grand elephant towards the Red Fort. But it so happened that when he passed by Chandni Chowk a grenade was lobbed at the *Laat*[2] Sahab's ride. Although Lord Hardinge was not destined to die yet, he was badly hurt and fell unconscious. He was spared death, however. The Viceroy was brought down off the elephant and taken to the Government House in a motor car. The *baraat*[3] entered the Red Fort without the bridegroom.

So, the old history was repeated. It had always happened that whenever a new ruler founded a new capital for his sultanate egged on by his royal pride, there would occur some inauspicious event. The same thing happened with the Viceroy. It was in accordance with the tradition of this land. What was so special about the British that this land would alter its traditions for them?

Anyway, now Delhi became the capital. At the same time it was divided into two. Another city had to be settled cheek by jowl

---

[2] *Laat* is a vernacular form of 'Lord'.

[3] *Baraat* is the marriage procession of the bridegroom's party.

with the old Dilli. This would be called New Delhi. This meant that Dilli now had to contend with its sautan. Now, Jahanabad would be called Old Delhi. The thing with Old Delhi was that it was undoubtedly old. Earlier histories and so many centuries of history were breathing in it. Now, with the passage of time, it took on a new colour. Chandeliers, candles, torches, lamps burning with mustard oil—this entire caravan of light was to depart. Some of the lights were extinguished, while some others were dimmed. There was a new light in the city. Electricity had spread its dazzling display. New lights; new conveyances. When the train entered Delhi's vicinity, its horn could be heard at Chandni Chowk. The network of tram tracks kept on expanding. Those in haste had bid adieu to the *tamtam* [4]; they now rode the two-wheeled ride called the bicycle. The greatest ride was the motor vehicle. This vehicle gained such popularity after the court of George V and ran at such a speed that it left the royal and majestic ride, the elephant and its golden and silver *Amari*,[5] far behind. The court of George V, for Dilliwallahs, was essentially the court of motor cars. Even those kings who rode elephants at this occasion would be seen riding in motor cars in the future. The elephant along with its howdah had disappeared. And it was not just the elephant that had disappeared. All the traditional conveyances including rath, litters and open palanquins could not compare with the motor car and were on the verge of extinction. The *ikka* [6] was defeated by the tonga. With the cavalry losing the battle, the superior status of horses had already diminished. Now the horse was attached to the tonga and ran over those roads where professional soldiers had been seen on horseback in the past.

The mansions which were civilisations in themselves were yielding to bungalows and masonry houses. And where were mansions left at all? During the doomsday of 1857, the grand

[4] *Tamtam* was a horse drawn cart.

[5] *Amari* was a canopied seat on the back of elephant.

[6] *Ikka* was a two-wheeled cart, pulled by a single horse.

mansions had been demolished by the order of the English. The land on which one mansion had stood before was adequate for settling an entire muhalla. The mansions that were safe from demolitions were sold by their inhabitants without care for profit or loss, to make arrangements for their future existence. The buyers thought differently. They demolished the mansions, and built bungalows and shops instead. And with the absence of the mansions the lounge halls also disappeared, and the chandeliers, the hookahs, the hookahs with long flexible pipes, the betel-boxes and spittoons went away with them. Only a few Diwan Khanas remaining in the city; one Diwan Khana was that of Nawab Faiz Ahmad Khan, one of Lala Sriram, one of Lala Paras Das Khazanchi and a Diwan Khana of the Shareefi family. Only in such Diwan Khanas could the chandeliers still be seen hanging from the ceilings and the handmade pictures of family elders on the walls; next to them some monograms, some epitaphs; on the floor durries were laid, chandni was spread over the durries and an Iranian carpet still laid in the middle. Upon them and along the wall, bolsters with flowery covers were laid. In the middle the hookahs with long flexible pipes, betel-boxes and spittoons were placed with care. On the threshold instead of a doormat there was deer-skin. On the door hung curtains of coarse red cotton. Outside either a palanquin or a phaeton still waited.

Elsewhere, these Diwan Khanas were replaced by bungalows and *kothis*. These had drawing rooms with sofas, chairs and tables; the chandni had disappeared, but the carpet was there. The hubbles and the long-necked hookahs were replaced with cigarettes. Outside in the porch a motor car waited. But so far the motor car was seen only in the porches of the English. One or one and a half years after the Durbar, Dr Ansari came to Delhi and bought a kothi in Daryaganj to live in and a motor car to ride. According to the research of Narayani Gupta, at that time only two Indians, Dr Ansari and Dr H C Sen, had motor cars.

The arrival of Dr Ansari in Delhi meant that allopathy, a new kind of medicine, had found its way into the abode of Unani medicine. And it had made such an emphatic entry because a doctor had been born in the house of Hakims. Hakim Nabeena was well-known. His brother Mukhtar Ahmad Ansari became a doctor and earned fame in his career. Now, in the city besides the dispensaries of the hakims there were also various hospitals; a couple of these were for women. Although, the Dilliwallahs still rushed to Hakim Ajmal or Hakim Nabeena for treatment, the patients also consulted the doctors now and could increasingly be seen going to hospitals too.

Who could have imagined that in the city where Unani medicine wielded such great influence, doctors too would be given importance? A time arrived when along with the popularity of the hakims, capable doctors too gained attention. This was an indicator of how much Dilli had changed and how much influence the new era had had on this traditional city.

But the chowk of Jama Masjid remained unchanged. It presented a familiar scene and it seemed almost the same. The water-carrier still distributed water, people rubbed shoulders with each other, visitors thronged the place, and fops and dandies crowded the area. What grace! What adornment! On the body was a long shirt of flowery chikan fabric and on the head a crossed cap with stars stitched into it; on the wrist would be garlands made up of various types of jasmine, in the ear a perfumed ball of cotton, and in the mouth the betel gilauri. They wandered around. Sometimes they were attracted to red titmouses and they could be seen bargaining over pigeons. Sometimes they rushed to the partridges and quails kept in cages. Kept in a line, away from the birds' cages, were all kinds of eatables. Chaat with 12 types of spices, chana jor garam, spicy dahi bada, saucers of firni, ice-creams, sharbat, and faluda. Foodies were everywhere. Hot kababs could be seen roasting on skewers. No sooner were they taken off the skewers than the foodies would gulp them down. Then they would stand licking their lips, calling for the water-carrier to quench their thirst with 'nectar'. Janaab water-carrier would uncork the mouth of the water-skin, and pour water into a glittering silver bowl. The foodies would gulp down the water and proceed to the next delicacy. Ahead is the hookah-carrier. One could see people take the pipe of hookah in their mouths and have some drags from it. Then they walked on till it was time for them to have a gilori from the betel-leaf vendor. Thereafter, they took a cotton ball soaked in khas perfume and stuffed it in the ear. When the aroma of khas wafted into the ear it subsumed the higher rises of the brain. And the song could be heard:

Woh chaley jhatak ke daaman mere dast-e-natawaan se

They left yanking the edge of their dress away from my feeble hand

These were the Karkhandari people. They have their style, their own language and their own accent. But this elder with a tall body, fair complexion, vast forehead and big, bulging eyes speaks chaste Urdu. But he lisps a little. People call him Mirza Chapati. His original name was Sahab Aalam Mirza Fakhruddin, the nephew of Bahadur Shah. From Mirza Fakhruddin he became Mirza Fakhr, and from Mirza Fakhr he became Mirza Chapati. He grew up in the Fort. The King had made him responsible for the distribution of chapatis at the tombs of *Aulia*[7] of Allah on their Urs. Those asking for bread would shout, 'Mirza, Chapati! Mirza, Chapati!' Then Chapati became his appellation. In the past he had led a luxurious life in the Red Fort and now he loafed about in Jama Masjid Chowk. But how was he saved? He just happened to have good luck. He escaped and rested only when he had reached Agra. When peace prevailed he returned to Dilli. Now the times had changed and the era of his princehood had come to an end. Now he was homeless. But all the leisurely pursuits of princehood remained

[7] *Aulia* (Arabic) is the plural of Wali, which variously means protector, custodian, or friend. In this context, it refers to saints who are thought to be close to God or considered a medium to access God.

unchanged—playing chess, flying kites, pigeon-flying and cock-fighting. He took much interest in cock-fighting. With pigeon-fighting emerged a new desire to fly parrots. As long as he had money, he spent lavishly to fulfil his desires and led a luxurious life. But when the money was scant, he used his passion for kite-flying to earn a livelihood. He opened a small shop and started selling kites which he would make himself. In the rainy season he would go to the Qutub with all his material; earlier he would just fly kites but now he began to make kites and sell them sitting in a corner.

He was the kind of poet who if encouraged a little would be happy to oblige. The famous courtesan of Dilli, Dooni Jan had her own dwelling. She used to be very well positioned in her youth and known to be elegant. But now she had aged. Mirza Sahab commented:

Ghistey ghistey ho gai itni malat
Chaar paise ki dooni reh gaee

Much grating has turned her to cardboard
Dooni's worth is now reduced to four paise

One of his friends recited an elegy:

Sar adad ka ho nahin sakta merey sir ka jawaab

The head of the enemy cannot be a reply equal to my head.

He looked at Mirza Chapati, who then added:

Shah ne Aabid se kaha badla na lena Shimr se
Sar adad ka ho nahin sakta merey sir ka jawaab

The king [8] said to Aabid[9] do not take revenge from Shimr[10]
The head of the enemy cannot be a reply to my head.

---

[8] Husain, in reference to the narrative of the Battle of Qarbala and the martyrdom of Husain.

[9] Zain-ul-Aabidin was Husain's son.

[10] Shimr was the killer of Husain.

This was Mirza Chapati. Now just have a look at this other person—bright colour, thin nose, body of moderate length, thin, white beard, wearing an angrakha, tight pyjama and a *dopalli* cap. Kept in front of him is an opium solution in a silver bowl. He will take a sip and then start telling stories. He is Mir Baqar Ali Dastaango (the storyteller). Iqbal had said that Daagh is the last poet of Jahanabad. Well, Ali may be considered the last storyteller of Jahanabad. Although the story of Jahanabad is over, his stories continue. And he is a fine story himself. There was a time when his stories were famous far and wide. Once he was invited to the court of Patiala. It was a tradition of the court that whoever attended it must wear a turban. When Mir Sahab came to know of this he exclaimed, 'someone who objects to my appearance can never value my art.' He said this and then began preparing to leave for Delhi. When the Maharaja was informed he exempted Mir Sahab from wearing the turban. Now, Mir Baqar Ali attended the court wearing a cap made of silver thread. He stayed there for a long period. When the Maharaja passed away, he returned to Delhi. Then for a long period he recited stories at Lala Chunamal's. When this patron also passed away he was without any patronage. Now, he can be seen telling stories sometimes in the Diwan Khana of Hakim Ajmal Khan and at the house of Nawab Faiz Ahmad Khan. As for the arrangements for telling stories—the chandni was spread. The audience would sit on the chandni. A small wooden cot would be placed for the storyteller; paan served and hookahs did the rounds. Mir Sahab asked for a bowl of water, took out a small silver box and a small bowl from his pocket. He then took out the opium tablet from the box and wrapped a piece of cotton around it, poured a little water into the bowl and dissolved the cotton-wrapped opium in it. He took a sip of the opium and then a gulp of tea, then began the storytelling.

But the times keep changing. Those fond of stories pass away with the passage of time. And now Mir Baqar Ali started cutting and selling betel nuts. If someone enquired, he replied that

Dilliwallahs had forgotten the proper way of chewing paan and he was trying to teach them to do it the right way. At the same time he wrote down short stories and he published them himself. Then he wandered the streets to sell them. When no one was left to invite him to tell stories he started holding gatherings at his own house. Anyone wishing to listen to the stories could join the gathering by paying one aanaa. He would start telling stories after the Isha prayer at nine o' clock and go on till eleven.

Salaa-e-aam hai yaaran-e-nuktadaan ke liye

A common invitation for anyone sagacious

These were the dregs of Old Dilli or Jahanabad. What fear could the English rulers have of the dregs? How could Mir Baqar Ali, the storyteller, and Mirza Chapati harm them? But it so happened that on the one hand, it was announced that Delhi would be made the capital and on the other the gifts of the new age started arriving in Delhi. The new lights and vehicles, the English had brought them voluntarily. But the insurgents and terrorists of Bengal reached here against the wishes of the English. One reason why the British made Delhi the capital was that it would rid them of the insurgents of Bengal. The power and strength of the Dilliwallahs was over with 1857. Now calm reigned here. But the calm didn't extend much beyond the stairs of Jama Masjid where the ordinary visiting tourists remained oblivious to the direction time was heading in. Just a little distance from here at Chandni Chowk, the scene had changed dramatically. It was not the Chandni Chowk of Jahanabad where a canal flowed in the middle, and on both sides stood trees of mango, rennet, banyan and moulsari under whose fragrant shadow litters, open palanquins, elephants with royal canopied seats and all kinds of rides ran sprightly. Now, the canal had dried up and the trees had been cut down. Now, the debaters of various religions had occupied this place. Their debates were raucous. Soon, another noise was added to this; the noise of political gatherings. By 1911, some more dimensions were added. While the rulers reached their capital later, the Bengali insurgents had arrived before them stealthily and sat firmly in their battlements. Muhammad Ali Jauhar too, arrived here with his *Comrade* [11] paraphernalia. Reaching here he began publishing an Urdu newspaper *Hamdard*. Dr Ansari had already arrived earlier. Not content with only being a doctor, he was determined to try his hand at politics. On the other hand Hakim Ajmal Khan wished to confine himself only to his clinic.

Some youths had gone to Aligarh in pursuit of modern education. In the city, Sir Syed Ahmad Khan had laid the foundation of modern education and opened a college for this purpose. The youth returned from there with a new consciousness and a new kind of cap. They went there wearing the *dopalli* cap and on their return they had on a high, red cap with tassels. The Dilliwallahs pointed at it and ridiculed it by calling it a *nechari* [12] cap. But soon it began to be called the Turki cap and it became part of Muslim identity. As if they were in a contest, the Hindus adopted the flat cap. Behold, now there were separate caps for the Muslims and the Hindus. This quibble was also that of a new age. In the days gone past in Dilli Hindus and Muslims had worn the same attire. The only difference was that the Hindu kept the buttons of his angrakha on the right side, and the Muslim on the left side. But, now the angrakha had disappeared entirely and had been replaced by the achkan. The footwear too had changed. The Saleem Shahi shoes had given way to shoes with laces. Now, the tradition of resting against the bolsters in the Diwan Khana was

---

[11] The newspaper, *Comrade*, was launched in Calcutta in 1911 and, after the change in the seat of government, shifted to Delhi the next year.

[12] *Nechari* refers to Naturalism or the philosophical position that all phenomena can be adequately explained through natural and materialist reasons. It entails a refusal to ascribe spiritual (super-'natural') reasons in explanations. It was often deployed as a pejorative term against rationalists and reformists like Sir Syed Ahmed Khan.

coming to an end. Therefore, the etiquette of taking shoes off before entering the Diwan Khana was also not being observed. The culture of the drawing room was that one entered with the shoes still on and sat on the sofa.

So, while an old scene still played out at the Jama Masjid Chowk, a new scene began emerging as well. Dilli was now the site of this mixture of old and new. But by laying the foundation of New Delhi, the English rulers had put the seal of Old Dilli over Jahanabad. And what delay was there in New Delhi making an appearance? The construction had started; the time of appearance of Delhi was near. Let Old Dilli sit with its history. The future is that of New Delhi. How long will it cling to its past? How much longer will the red titmouses, parrots, mynahs, partridges and pigeons be sold on the stairs of the Jama Masjid? Within half a century yet another doomsday would assault her. There is nothing new in this. The passage of time has been playing this game for ever.

Zafar ahwal aalam ka kabhi kuchh hai kabhi kuchh hai
Ke kya kya rang hein aur kya kyapeshtariyan the

Zafar, the condition of the world is sometimes this, sometimes that
What colours are there (at present), and what were there in the past?

25

The Last Rapture of Love

Jahanabad was the sunlight that disappeared following the sun. It had risen with the rise of the Mughal Sultanate and when the sultanate set, it too faded. However after the doomsday, as slowly life settled back into a pattern, it produced an illusion that perhaps the sun of Jahanabad had continued to shine, albeit feebly. But when Dilli was declared the capital in the 1911 Durbar, and the foundation of New Delhi was laid, this illusion too disappeared. Nevertheless, in the hustle and bustle of Jama Masjid Chowk and the pomp and show of the court, none could see what was happening to their city. Chacha Kababi continued making kabab as usual. Mirza Chapati went on making kites the way he always had, and starching kite-string. Chicken and eggs continued being sold in the same way, and the business of red titmouse and pigeons also continued. The splendour of the Chowk was not disturbed in the slightest degree. As for the social life and cultural atmosphere of the city, the changes that had to take place were already in effect. Old Dilli was transforming into New Delhi. However, even though the old scene was limited to just some corners of the city, it maintained its pomp and show. In the Diwan Khanas of Nawab Faiz Ahmad Khan, Lala Sriram, Lala Paras Das and the Shareefi family, the chandeliers were still glittering and the attitude of the gathering elders remained unaltered.

The dazzle of the Diwan Khana of the Shareefi Family was due to Hakim Ajmal Khan. Just see with the eyes of your imagination the buzurg who used to attend this gathering: the imam of Jama Masjid, Nawab Faiz Ahmad Khan, Nawab Saael Dehlavi, Nawab Taban Dehlavi.

What a remarkable buzurg was Nawab Saael Dehlavi. Shahid Ahmad Dehlavi, who had a chance to see him, said of him, 'Wheatish and clear complexion, round face, icy-white beard, spectacle with golden frame. On the head a wide, velvety cap with gold work; when seen more closely the inscription in gold embroidery, Saael Dehlavi, was clearly visible. Tight pyjama crumpled till the shin, feet encased in Saleem Shahi shoes, in one hand a stick with a silver handle, and in the right hand a six-inch long cigar.' He was the master of poetry of his time, son-in-law of Daagh. He considered his poetry the reward of being the son-in-law of Daagh and took pride in it.

Janab-e-Daagh ke damaad hein ham Dilli waaley hein

We are son-in-law of Mr Daagh, we are Dilliwaaley

He considered himself a successor of Daagh as a son-in-law as well as for his interest in ghazal. But in the city there sat another master of ghazal who had compiled an incalculable number of poems after Daagh's fashion. As per his own claim, he recited poetry like Daagh. And see, here the masters are pitched against one another. This produced a split into two parties. Some were lovers of Saael and the others the avid fans of Bekhud. When the duel intensified Saael Sahab stopped attending mushairas.

Poetry has its place but kite-flying has its own status. Saael Sahab composed many a ghazal and also made many kites. And he starched the kite-string as well. He was good at embroidery. It is said that when he cooked, he did it very well. As for his Nawab status he was a Nawab only in name. His father had been stripped of the status of Nawab during his lifetime. The English, suspecting that he was somehow a participant in the freedom struggle, snatched from him the Nawabi of Loharo and bestowed it on his uncle. In his last days, Saael Sahab would roam around in a rickshaw he had acquired. Unfortunately, once his rickshaw turned over and his hip bone broke in the accident. He would then weep and say, 'There was a time when I would catch the tail of the elephant when it came to my father's porch, and climb it. Now, I am destined to have a ride in a rickshaw which made me dependent upon others.'

Nawab Saael's older brother was Nawab Shujauddin Ahmad Khan Taban. He resembled his brother in complexion, stature and fashion. But there was a stark contrast in the temper of both the brothers. While Saael was tolerant, Taban was quick to get angry. Whenever even a slightly upsetting thing happened, he resorted to coining abuses of myriad kinds. Saael Sahab did not have the guts to reply. He was, anyway, the younger brother. He would just say, 'Bhaijaan, half of the abuse becomes true to me and the half to you.'

Sometimes, however, Saael Sahab would intentionally tease him and Taban Sahab would begin boiling over in anger. Once in the midst of an animated gathering, Hakim Ajmal Khan saw that Taban Sahab was silent. His heart was tickled and he signalled to Saael Sahab who did not fail to understand the signal. He turned to Taban Sahab and said, 'Bhai Sahab, I seek pardon for my rudeness, but our Ustad Daagh Sahab was matchless in expressing delicate thoughts and communicating emotions. He composed 50 couplets within an hour and with him ended the power over poetry.'

Daagh was Saael's teacher. So what if he was? But perhaps due to this Taban Sahab was jealous of Daagh. No sooner had he heard what his brother had uttered that he flew into a rage and said, 'What does Daagh know what a couplet is? Off-hand poetry is not a criterion of knowing poetry. If it is, then recite a *misra*[1] and I will add to it.'

Saael Sahab immediately read out a couplet:

---

[1] *Misra* is a single line of a couplet.

Shafaq ban ke charha hai charkh ke sar par lahu mera

My blood has taken the colour of evening twilight, and ascended the head of the sky.

Taban Sahab immediately added:

'Adu mera, na tu mera, na charkh e-fitna ju mera
Shafaq ban ke charha hai charkh ke sar par lahu mera

Neither enemy is mine, nor you, nor the mischievous sky,
My blood has taken the shape of evening twilight, and ascended the head of the sky.

Those present in the gathering were moved and spontaneously appreciated him. But by then Taban Sahab had become very angry and began abusing his brother, who after teasing him remained sitting with a lowered head.

The man who did not give any importance to Daagh, how could he give any significance to Maulana Shibli? But when Maulana Shibli came to Delhi and became a guest of Hakim Ajmal Khan, he expressed his wish to meet Taban Sahab. Hakim Sahab showed wisdom and did not go with him. Instead, he sent someone else with Shibli. Anyway, Taban Sahab met Shibli warmly and showed much humility to him. He also read out his ghazal upon Maulana Shibli's request. But Taban Sahab noticed as he was reciting the couplets, that the Maulana merely listened and sipped his tea, not appreciating even a single couplet. So, reading out a couplet he said, 'Hadrat, this couplet requires attention.' Maulana Shibli exclaimed mildly and praised the couplet. This infuriated Taban Sahab. He got angry and said, 'You lame Shibli! I wrote this couplet after three days of hard work and you understood this couplet within a minute? This is not *Sher-al-ajam*[2], this is a ghazal. Just try to compose such…' Then what he added to it were

[2] *Sher-al-ajam* is a book on the history of Persian poetry authored by Maulana Shibli Nomani.

positively abusive words. Poor Maulana Shibli found himself in a difficult position.

On the other hand, Ustad Bekhud was proud of his mastery. It did not matter if Ustad Saael was the son-in-law of Daagh, it was none but him (Bekhud) who was successor of Daagh. He composed ghazals, kept pigeons and went on hunting expeditions. He claimed to be a master in all three preoccupations. If he needed to exaggerate in order to prove his claims he would gladly brag. In the art of hunting, he presented a fantastic example. He narrated that once he had gone out to meet the Maharaja of Gwalior who was his admirer. Upon reaching Gwalior he thought that he had not informed Maharaja of his arrival. Just as he was pondering over this, he saw a flock of herons flying by. He asked Aminuddin, who had accompanied him, to give him his rifle and shot the herons. One of the herons fell at his feet and was tossing about. Another fell in the house where he was to stay. And the third one fell exactly before the Maharaja in the Raj Mahal. The host understood that it must be the work of Ustad Bekhud. When he reached his house he found the roasted herons served on the table. The Maharaja seeing the herons understood that Bekhud Sahab had arrived in Gwalior.

The next day Bekhud went out hunting with the Maharaja. The story in his words: 'When the lion appeared in front of us, the first to fire was the Maharaja. But he missed the target. The lion jumped furiously, and clung to the Maharaja's elephant. Then I fired and the lion collapsed dead on the ground.'

He was an expert hunter and a skilful pigeon-flyer. When he made the pigeons fly from his roof, his life was in the pigeons. In the meantime, if anyone visited him, he had to bear the chiding of the Ustad. Someone who was known to Bekhud Sahab came along with his son to meet him. Bekhud was on the roof and his kite was soaring in the sky. He did not like the disturbance and came down murmuring in annoyance. The visitor presented him with a basket of sweets and said, 'My son likes poetry. Take him as your disciple.'

Bekhud said, 'Son, read out any ghazal that you have composed.'

The son read out an unsuitable couplet. Bekhud was enraged, 'Get out of my house.' And he hollered at them so that the father and son had no option but to flee.

And Mirza Hairat Dehlavi, a naughty man, mischievous to the extreme! He had been no less a troublemaker earlier. But ever since he began publishing the *Curzon Gazette*, he became a catastrophe. If he wrote about someone he wrote only against him. And in opposition he crossed every limit. This became his way. Today, he is making fun of Hakim Ajmal Khan and tomorrow criticising Maulana Muhammad Ali Jauhar. And yes, he did not spare even the imam of the oppressed.[3] He denied the occurrence of Karbala. He argued that according to the narrations, the incident took place in summer, but just calculate and you will find that the month of Muharram in the year in which this incident is said to have occurred was in winter.

His stand was strongly objected to. And see, on the one hand he denied its occurrence, and on the other he recited the *zikr-e-shahadat*.[4] According to Mulla Wahidi, he narrated the martyrdom with such pain that the gathering would start weeping loudly.

However, he did meet his match once. Maulana Muhammad Ali Jauhar and Khwaja Hasan Nizami were once engaged in a fierce argument. Mirza Sahab meddled in the matter in support of Maulana Muhammad Ali. Whatever he wrote about Khwaja Sahab, he got a befitting reply very soon. He was sitting at his shop when an upset man came and started arguing with him. The man was so upset that he took off a shoe and hit Mirza Sahab in the face with it.

---

[3] Prophet Muhammad's grandson Husain who was martyred in a siege in Karbala.

[4] *Zikr-e-shahadat* are verses describing the events leading to the martyrdom of Husain.

So these were the seniors of Dilli. But among them Maulana Muhammad Ali Jauhar too carved a niche for himself. He had come to Delhi with the English newspaper *Comrade*. Here he also started publishing an Urdu newspaper *Hamdard*. As if one was not enough, now there were two. His newspapers changed the temperament of the city. He had entered the city shouting political slogans. No sooner did he step in the city than the Battle of Tarabulus[5] started. The Muslims of Delhi got furious and vented their anger over the Turki cap. In front of Masjid Fatehpuri there was a pile of Turki caps. By setting this pile on fire the Dilliwallahs vented their anger against Italy.[6] The Muslims of Delhi had accepted the cap after much hesitation; after all, in the beginning they had rejected it calling it a nechari cap. It was accepted only gradually. But before it could fully occupy people's heads the cap was pulled down and made to burn in the fire lit in protest. The fact was that the cap was imported from Italy. To vent their anger against Italy, people felt it was only right that an article being imported from there should be set on fire.

Nevertheless, this was not the first fire in Delhi. Before the Turki cap, the *Ummat-ul-Ummah* [7] written by Deputy Nazir Ahmad was piled up and set on fire. Deputy Nazir Ahmad was a practising Muslim and a translator of the Qur'an. But the public took his attempt to use proverbial language while writing about the holy mothers of the Ummah as a show of disrespect to them. They were furious and their anger abated only when they had set the book on fire. In fact, the destiny of the book was so. When it got published for the second time, it met with the same fate.

Exhibiting their anger on the occasion of the Tarabulus war was just the beginning. Thereafter, the temper of Dilliwallahs only got exacerbated. The World War began in 1914. The war had

---

[5] Italo-Turkish War 1911-12. (Tarabulus refers to the historic Tripoli region or Tripolitania).

[6] Italy demanded that the Ottoman Empire transfer control of the Libyan territory to them.

[7] *Ummat-ul-ummah* were the Mothers of the community of followers.

brought in its wake the causes of the destruction of the Ottoman Empire. With the Empire falling apart, Turkey reached the point of destruction. Indian Muslims could see that the Caliphate was in danger. At this stage, Muslims again became organised against the British. However, when the war had begun they had announced their support for Britain. This fight of the Muslims against the British created an atmosphere of unity between Hindus and Muslims. In Delhi, this was evident when in March 1917 a Medical Conference was held under the leadership of Hakim Ajmal Khan, and was chaired by Pandit Madan Mohan Malaviya. And on 24 March when the annual function of the Madrasa Tibbiya was arranged, it was chaired by Sir Sankaran Nair. Hakim Ajmal Khan emerged as the flag-bearer of Hindu-Muslim unity in the city. And when in 1918 the sessions of Muslim League and the Indian National Congress were held next to each other in Delhi, he had one foot in one session and the second in the other session. In both the gatherings the atmosphere was equally impassioned. In both places, demands were made to release those who had been taken into custody. Who were these detenus? Prominent among them were the Ali brothers.

In 1919 the Rowlatt Act was passed. It was seen as the black law by both Hindus and Muslims. Gandhiji announced that a strike would be held on 30 March. With this announcement there was a tempest throughout India. This announcement had results, perhaps even before time, in Delhi. Other cities were affected later. The date of the strike was first set as 30 March but it was postponed to 6 April. Delhi turned out to be an impatient city; the storm that engulfed other cities of India on 6 April spread across Delhi on 30 March itself. Markets were closed, shops remained shut, conveyances were missing—neither ikkas nor tongas, neither trams nor cars. Jama Masjid Chowk was deserted, Chandni Chowk was silent, Chawri was in a mess—no rich shoppers, no foppish flaneurs. Neither were the bowls being clanked, nor could one see the fragrant jasmine flowers. Marches were taken out, slogans shouted. The British management had been suspended. A Hakim and a Swami were ruling over the city. The words they uttered were like orders for both Hindus and Muslims. The Hakim was Ajmal Khan and the Swami was Shraddhanand. These days they were like one soul and two bodies. The Muslims of Delhi were so pleased with Swamiji that they took him to Jama Masjid and there Swamiji addressed the crowd of Muslims thronging the Shahjahani masjid as a popular leader.

The incident in Jallianwala Bagh took place in Amritsar around this time. And now here was a new doomsday. The Chief Commissioner of Dilli rightly apprehended that the news could cause havoc in Delhi. He called the trusted personalities of the city and sought their opinion. The gathering was held in the Town Hall. People came to know about it. They were already furious from within. Now, they came out of their houses. In no time there was a huge gathering of common people around the Town Hall. Someone spread the rumour that the leaders who had come here would be taken into custody. The gathering became mad with fury. They picketed the Town Hall. At this critical juncture, Hakim Ajmal Khan and Swami Shraddhanand came to the Chief Commissioner's aid. They came out and addressed the gathering till it was pacified.

The next day these two leaders marched on the streets. They spoke to the shopkeepers and pacified them. They persuaded them to return to work. Swami Shraddhanand went to the butchers and urged them to resume their work. The butchers obeyed him and resumed working; they slaughtered animals and sold meat.

And see, the strike has ended, the markets have opened and the business is running as usual. People have started selling and purchasing articles. But the ego of the rulers has been challenged. Their egotistical nature urged them on to make arrests and detentions. The police raided the markets leading to renewed tensions. The markets had not opened completely when they started closing down again. The public again gathered around the

Town Hall. The agitation was registered through protests. Now, the police showed strength and fired their guns. In the firing one person was killed and many others were injured.

The funeral procession of the deceased was well-attended. Fifty thousand people took turns to carry the bier of the friend.

This was the scene in Dilli. The poetry gatherings were now passe. It was the age of public meetings and processions. Slogans filled the air. The storm after the Jallianwala Bagh tragedy was yet to cool down when the issue of the Caliphate began to dominate the scene. This was such a powerful movement that many companions and elders got rejuvenated by it. And the status of the Ali brothers changed dramatically. Earlier, one referred to them as Janaab. It was only now that they became Maulana. Janaab Shaukat Ali was always well-dressed in 'suit and boot', with a shaven beard and a long moustache, he was tall, stout and heavy. He was also an experienced cricket player, and an officer in the department of opium. The Khilafat Movement changed him so much that he abandoned western attire, grew a beard and trimmed his moustache. Now he wore a loose kurta and trousers with wide legs, and a cap with the moon and stars. Such clothes looked tremendous on the heavy body. He began to be called the Man of the Caliphate and the Servant of Kaaba. Where is cricket now? He was now entirely devoted to the Khilafat Movement. Miyan Faizuddin of Lahore accompanied him as the herald of the Khilafat and travelled from city to city. He shouted high-pitched slogans and the Servant of Kaaba Maulana Shaukat Ali delivered thunderous speeches.

His brother Muhammad Ali, he too used to be Janaab Muhammad Ali, was fair-complexioned with shaved beard and tight moustaches, and wore a coat and slacks. When he entered politics and became a man of Khilafat, he too was transformed swiftly. He replaced his coat and slacks with kurta-pyjama and wore a cap with the moon and stars. Now he was a Maulana, fluent in speech and powerful at pen. A moment before, he was thundering and now he is weeping bitterly. He has become emotional!

And, Bi Amman, the mother of both the brothers. The Khilafat Movement accorded so much respect to the mother and the sons that a new kind of poetry was invented which you may call the folk-poetry of Khilafat.

Boli amma Muhammad Ali ki, jaan beta khilafat pe de do
Saath terey hai Shaukat Ali bhi, jaan beta khilafat pe de do
Boorhi amma ka kuchchh gham na karna, kalma padh kar khilafat par marna
Poorey iss imtehaan mein utarna, jaan beta khilafat pe de do
Hotey agar merey saat betey, karti sabko khilafat pe sadqey
Hein yahin deen-e-Ahmed ke raste, jaan beta khilafat pe de do
Hashr mein hashr barpa karoongi, pesh haq tum ko le kar chaloongi
Is hukumat pe daawey karoongi, jaan beta khilafat pe de do

Said the mother of Muhammad Ali, son, sacrifice yourself for the Khilafat,
With you is also Shaukat Ali, son, sacrifice yourself for the Khilafat,
Never mind about the old mother, read the Kalimah and die for the Khilafat,
Pass the test, son, sacrifice yourself for the Khilafat,
If I had seven sons, I would have sacrificed all of them for the Khilafat,
These are the ways of religion of Ahmad,[8] son, sacrifice yourself for the Khilafat,
On the day of judgement I will cause a tumult, I will go with you in front of the True,
I will claim this government, son, sacrifice yourself for the Khilafat.

The movement was at its peak. Khilafat committees had been formed in the provinces. A Khilafat Committee was formed in Dilli too. Hakim Ajmal Khan was the president of this committee. Under it an All India Khilafat Conference was held on 23 and 24 November 1919. Gandhiji and Swami Shraddhanand were invited to participate in it. They were told that the agenda included the issue of cow protection along with the protection of the Caliphate.

[8] Ahmad is another name of the Prophet Muhammad.

How large-hearted was Gandhiji's reply that 'if the issue of Khilafat is just, and according to me it is just, then the Hindus should stand with Muslims anyway. It is not right to bring the issue of cow in the middle.'

But Muslim leaders considered it necessary to let the issue of cow protection remain in the agenda. Thus along with the Caliphate, cow protection also became a part of the Khilafat movement. So much so that not to mention cow or goat, Bi Amman stopped cooking meat in her house. Hakim Ajmal Khan began explaining to Delhi Muslims that in consideration of Hindus they should stop eating beef. He suggested that they eat mutton instead, if they had to eat meat. Maulana Muhammad Ali came up with a different idea: let the mutton be as cheap as beef and then people will automatically stop eating beef. In fact, he added, beef is eaten because it is available cheaply.

Anyway, the movement had great influence in Delhi. According to Narayani Gupta, 250 cows were slaughtered in Delhi in 1919 while in 1920 only 29 cows were slaughtered.

On the other hand, Gandhiji proclaimed that Khilafat is the holy cow of Muslims and that we should contribute our best to preserve it. Swami Shraddhanand gave lectures in mosques. If he thundered a lecture in Jama Masjid, then in the same thundering voice he spoke in Masjid Fatehpuri. In view of the popularity of his speeches the government declared that mosques could be used only for offering prayers and speeches were banned there. So, once again, religious tolerance and large-heartedness which had always been a part of the culture of Jahanabad, returned to Dilli.

But it became clear later that this was just the boiling over of stale curry. Or it could be said to have been a promise too loosely made. It broke in just one jolt. The Civil Disobedience Movement led by Gandhiji started after the end of the Khilafat Movement. Civil disobedience had gained momentum when suddenly violence crept into it. The incident at Chauri-Chaura occurred. In this small village of Gorakhpur, the protestors became so furious that they set the police station on fire and burnt alive a number of policemen. This was in stark contrast to Gandhiji's philosophy of non-violence and he immediately announced the end of his movement.

The announcement turned everything topsy-turvy. The unity and accord was shattered. The Khilafat Conference was angry with the Indian National Congress; the Congress leaders were annoyed with one another; Hindus were annoyed with Muslims; and Muslims irritated with Hindus. The Khilafat leaders who till yesterday had supported Gandhiji, and had been ready to sacrifice themselves for Gandhiji's cause were not on speaking terms with Gandhiji anymore. It was just yesterday that they had had utmost faith in the Mahatma, but now they perceived a flaw in his intention.

The tension between Hindus and Muslims increased and led to riots. First, news came from Kohat that a riot had taken place, then from Multan. And how cruel the Kohat riot was that it created a rift between Maulana Shaukat Ali and Gandhiji. The two Ali brothers, Muhammad Ali and Shaukat Ali, had been unquestioning followers of Gandhiji. And now they were opposed to him.

Gandhiji observed a fast unto death for Hindu-Muslim unity. How much influence did it have? It did have a temporary influence. Gandhiji started the fast unto death at the house of Maulana Muhammad Ali Jauhar in Delhi. Maulana Muhammad Ali pleaded with him, 'Gandhiji, have mercy upon yourself and break the fast.' When Gandhiji remained determined, Maulana purchased a cow from the market and made it stand in front of him. Gandhiji gave a loving and affectionate look at the cow, but did not break his fast. It was only when the leaders of the Congress, along with the Ali brothers, Hakim Ajmal Khan and Dr Ansari took an oath that they would sacrifice their lives for Hindu-Muslim unity, that he broke the fast. But this atmosphere did not last very long. Just a few days later, the Kohat riots took place and it ultimately sowed the seed of differences between Gandhiji and the Ali brothers.

The Multan riots infuriated Pandit Madan Mohan Malaviya so much that he hurled abuse at Muslims and started the *Sangathan*[9] Movement. Along with it came the *Shuddhi*[10] Movement. Swami Shraddhanand associated himself with the movement. The romance of Swamiji with the Muslims of Delhi came to an end. The friendship of the Hakim and Swamiji too abated. Muslims retaliated sharply. In reply to Sangathan and Shuddhi they started, with the same aggression, the movements of *Tableegh*[11] and *Tanzeem*.[12]

Swamiji addressing Muslims in mosques, Bi Amman giving up cooking meat in her kitchen, Ali brothers becoming vegetarian, the honeymoon of Gandhiji with the Khilafat Movement, in no time it all became history. Now it was a different time. Bi Amman had started cooking meat in her kitchen again and Muhammad Ali and Shaukat Ali had repented becoming vegetarian and had started eating meat again. They would eat meat and criticise Gandhiji profusely. Swami Shraddhanand was now a shudhh[13] Hindu and a big preacher of Shuddhi. He was an enemy of the Muslims and Muslims were his foe. Maulana Zafar Ali Khan said:

Para hai sangathan se aur shuddhi se hamen pala,
Idhar is bhid ne kata hai, udha woh saanp dasta hai.

We have been facing Sangathan and Shuddhi,
Here this wasp has stung, and there that snake bites.

Tempers were high on both sides. There was a series of riots. How could Delhi be safe? The atmosphere was tense. Due to Hakim Ajmal Khan's efforts, Hindu and Muslim leaders gathered in Shareef Manzil. Many suggestions were presented to decrease

---

[9] *Sangathan* means organisation.

[10] *Shuddhi* is literally 'purification'; proselytisation.

[11] *Tableegh* is literally 'preaching'; proselytisation.

[12] *Tanzeem* means organisation.

[13] Shuddh means Pure.

tension and lectures were given. The result-nothing. In the middle of July 1924 there was a riot. Just before Eid al-Adha a greater riot took place. The efforts of peace-loving leaders went in vain. All the efforts of Hakim Ajmal Khan had been futile. Narayani Gupta writes:

'The efforts that Ajmal Khan made after 1924 were all in vain. The failure was a declaration of the end of an entire period. Now, the soul of Shahjahanabad was a flickering lamp whose light had dimmed.'

After the riots, the light had indeed dimmed. But now there was an explosion and the city faced a state of panic. The light that had dimmed was extinguished now. Now it dawned on people that the exhilarating exhibition of Hindu-Muslim unity that the city had seen in the last year and the speeches that Swamiji had given in the mosques and his motivation of Muslims were instances of how the lamp burns most brightly just before it dies out. The lamp had been snuffed out after its last flutter. Or in other words, the last nail in the coffin of Jahanabad had been hammered in. A gulf of hatred between Hindus and Muslims had already been created; now a blood line was also drawn there. This line was not going to be erased. It was soon to transform into a river of blood.

On the other hand, another lamp was being lit. New Delhi had been established beyond the Bara Khamba. The capital of the English seemed pleased with itself and well-populated. It was indeed a new city, shining brightly with new lights and electric bulbs. The new shops were aesthetically arranged with their grand corridors and interiors. With the spacious parks, wide streets, bright alleyways, and houses in the new style, the courtyards, balconies, chaubaras,[14] and high gates had all vanished. Now there were gates in the new style. You stepped in and first there would be grass lawns, and then a porch. These were not houses, they were *kothis*. When you went in you found no Diwan Khana. No chandnis, no

[14] *Chaubara* is a room on the upper storey usually with four doors or windows.

headrests and no bolsters. Neither were there hookahs nor spittoon, no saucers with gilauris. There was no decoration in the old style, no angrakha on the body, no turban or cap on the head and no Saleem Shahi shoes on the feet. The ceremony of taking off one's shoes outside the house had vanished. They wore the suit on their body, boots on their feet, and a hat on the head. They forthrightly entered the room and seated themselves on sofas and chairs. When outside, the motor was waiting in the porch. Gone was the age of elephants and horses. Along with it also went the litter and the open palanquin. And why should the *doli* remain?

Zamana aaya hai be hijabi ka aam didaar hoga

The time has arrived when shamelessness will be on public view

The conveyance of the *Memsahib*[15] is now the same as that of the Sahab.

This is the new capital. New is its culture. Jahanabad has become history. May the name of Allah remain.

---

[15] *Memsahib*, shortened from madam sahib, was used as a respectful term by the natives to refer to British women.

Bibliography

1.	Asarul Sanadeed	Sir Syed Ahmed Khan
2.	Waqiyat Daar-ul-hukoomat-e-Dehli	Bashiruddin Ahmed
3.	Seerul Manazir (translation)	Mirza Sangeen Beig
4.	Dastaan-e-Ghadar	Zaheer Dehlavi
5.	Charagh-e-Dehli	Mirza Hairat Dehlavi
6.	Bazm-e-Aakhir	Munshi Faizuddin
7.	Lal Qile Ki Ek Jhalak	Syed Nasir Nazeer Firaq Dehlavi
8.	Dilli Ka Akhiri Deedar	Syed Wazir Hasan Dehlavi
9.	Qila-e-Mualla ki Jhalkiyan	Arsh Taimori
10.	Dilli ki Chand Ajeeb Hastiyan	Ashraf Subuhi
11.	Mere Zamane ki Dilli	Mulla Wahidi
12.	Ujada Dayaar	Shahid Ahmad Dehlavi
13.	Bazm-e-khush Nafsan	Shahid Ahmad Dehlavi
14.	Chand Adabi Shakhsiyatein	Shahid Ahmad Dehlavi
15.	Aalam Mein Intekhaab: Dilli	Maheshwar Dayal
16.	Auraq-e-Mussawwir	Professor Khleeq Ahmed Nizami
17.	Marhoom Dilli Ki Ek Jhalak	Martaba Shamim Ahmed
18.	Dilliwalley	Martaba Doctor Salahuddin
19.	Zikr-e-Mir	Urdu Translation, Dr Nisaar Ahmed Farooqui
20.	Kulliyat-e-Mir	Kalb-e-Ali Khan Faaeq

21. Aab-e-Hayaat — Maulana Muhammad Hussain Azad
22. Khutut-e-Ghalib — Asad Ullah Khan Ghalib
23. Mazaamin-e-Farhat — Farhat Ullah Beig
24. Rusoom-e-Dehli — Syyed Ahmed Dehlavi
25. Bela mein Mela — Rashid-ul-Khairi
26. Sair-e-Dehli — Khwaja Hassan Nizami
27. Qadeem Lakhnau ki Aakhri Bahaar — Mirza Jaafar Hussain
28. Guzishta Lakhnau — Abdul Haleem Sharar
29. Ajmal Aazaam — Intizar Husain
30. Kulliyaat-e-Sauda — Mirza Rafi Sauda
31. Firhang Asfiya — Syed Ahmed Dehlavi

Magazines and Journals

32. Dilli College Magazine — Dilli number, Matbua 1959 Martaba: Sayyed Muzaffar Ali
33. Khayaal, Lahore — 1857 number Nasir Kaazmi Intizar Husain

English Books

34. Mahabharata — English Translation by Pratap Chand Roy
35. Medieval India — Stanley Lane Poole
36. City of Djinns — William Dalrymple
37. Zakaullah of Delhi — C F Andrews
38. Chronicle of the Mutiny — PJO Taylor
39. A Star Shall Fall — PJO Taylor
40. Cry for Freedom — Compiled by Salimuddin Qureshi
41. Bahadurshah Zafar — SM Burke and Salimuddin Qureshi
42. Delhi Between Two Empires, 1803-1931: Society, Government and Urban Growth — Narayani Gupta